EDUCATION IN EUROPE

This key text offers a detailed exploration of the wide range of theoretical approaches to theory, practice and research in Europe and how these can illuminate our understanding of contemporary education systems. Contributors working or living in countries across the continent offer their insights into different histories and contemporary problems, with each chapter exploring key themes and concepts to provoke critical thinking and discussion.

Key areas and debates examined include:

- Educational poverty
- Perspectives on democracy and citizenship
- Theorising education and educational research
- Epistemic injustice in the curriculum
- Educational provision and ethos

Drawing on these wide-ranging themes across a number of national contexts to provoke critical thinking and reflection, each chapter also includes discussion points and further reading.

This book is most suitable for students working towards their BA or MA in Education Studies or other education-related courses. It also offers a worthwhile resource for lectures and researchers engaged in the topic of international education.

Tom Feldges was an HE lecturer and researcher in both the UK and Germany. Retired from the Humboldt University of Berlin, he is now conducting research on embodiment in educational contexts while also lecturing at the Diploma FH in Germany. He has edited *Philosophy and Education* published in this series.

The Routledge Education Studies Series

Series Editor: Stephen Ward, Bath Spa University, UK

The Routledge Education Studies Series aims to support advanced level study on Education Studies and related degrees by offering in-depth introductions from which students can begin to extend their research and writing in years 2 and 3 of their course. Titles in the series cover a range of classic and up-and-coming topics, developing understanding of key issues through detailed discussion and consideration of conflicting ideas and supporting evidence. With an emphasis on developing critical thinking, allowing students to think for themselves and beyond their own experiences, the titles in the series offer historical, global and comparative perspectives on core issues in education.

Inclusive Education
Perspectives on Pedagogy, Policy and Practice
Edited by Zeta Brown

Gender, Education and Work
Inequalities and Intersectionality
Christine Eden

Contemporary Issues in Childhood
A Bio-ecological Approach
Zeta Brown and Stephen Ward

International and Comparative Education
Contemporary Issues and Debates
Brendan Bartram

Psychology and the Study of Education
Critical Perspectives on Developing Theories
Edited by Cathal O'Siochru

Philosophy and the Study of Education
New Perspectives on a Complex Relationship
Edited by Tom Feldges

Sociology for Education Studies
Connecting Theory, Settings and Everyday Experiences
Edited by Catherine A. Simon and Graham Downes

Understanding Education and Economics
Key Debates and Critical Perspectives
Edited by Jessie A. Bustillos Morales and Sandra Abegglen

Understanding Contemporary Issues in Higher Education
Contradictions, Complexities and Challenges
Edited by Brendan Bartram

Education in Europe
Contemporary Approaches across the Continent
Edited by Tom Feldges

Pedagogies for the Future
A Critical Reimagining of Education
Gary Beauchamp, Dylan Adams and Kevin Smith

For more information about this series, please visit: www.routledge.com/The-Routledge-Education-Studies-Series/book-series/RESS

EDUCATION IN EUROPE

Contemporary Approaches across the Continent

Edited by
Tom Feldges

LONDON AND NEW YORK

Cover image: © Getty Images

First published 2023
by Routledge
4 Park Square, Milton Park, Abingdon, Oxon, OX14 4RN

and by Routledge
605 Third Avenue, New York, NY 10158

Routledge is an imprint of the Taylor & Francis Group, an informa business

© 2023 selection and editorial matter, Tom Feldges; individual chapters, the contributors

The right of Tom Feldges to be identified as the author of the editorial material, and of the authors for their individual chapters, has been asserted in accordance with sections 77 and 78 of the Copyright, Designs and Patents Act 1988.

All rights reserved. No part of this book may be reprinted or reproduced or utilised in any form or by any electronic, mechanical, or other means, now known or hereafter invented, including photocopying and recording, or in any information storage or retrieval system, without permission in writing from the publishers.

Trademark notice: Product or corporate names may be trademarks or registered trademarks, and are used only for identification and explanation without intent to infringe.

British Library Cataloguing-in-Publication Data
A catalogue record for this book is available from the British Library

Library of Congress Cataloging-in-Publication Data
Names: Feldges, Tom, editor.
Title: Education in Europe : contemporary approaches across the continent / edited by Tom Feldges.
Description: First Edition. | New York : Routledge, 2023. | Series: The Routledge Education Studies Series | Includes bibliographical references and index. | Identifiers: LCCN 2022015738 (print) | LCCN 2022015739 (ebook) | ISBN 9781032121970 (Paperback) | ISBN 9781032121994 (Hardback) | ISBN 9781003223528 (eBook)
Subjects: LCSH: Education–Europe. | Education–Research. | Human geography–Europe.
Classification: LCC LA622 .E374 2023 (print) | LCC LA622 (ebook) | DDC 370.94–dc23/eng/20220713
LC record available at https://lccn.loc.gov/2022015738
LC ebook record available at https://lccn.loc.gov/2022015739

ISBN: 978-1-032-12199-4 (hbk)
ISBN: 978-1-032-12197-0 (pbk)
ISBN: 978-1-003-22352-8 (ebk)

DOI: 10.4324/9781003223528

Typeset in News Gothic
by KnowledgeWorks Global Ltd.

For Tessa P., a very special person whose kind warmth and generous support will always be remembered.

Contents

	List of contributors	ix
	Series editor's preface	xiii
	List of abbreviations	xv
1	Introduction: Ways to think about the concepts of 'Education' and 'Europe' TOM FELDGES	1

Preface to Section I: On the 'pains' of learning   11
TOM FELDGES

2	Crossing the border SONIA PIECZENKO	17
3	Language learning in France: De-territorialising language and culture JOSHUA N.W. GRAY	27
4	*Pädagogik* and (New) Education Studies: Striking up a conversation THOMAS ALTFELIX	37

Preface to Section II: Learning to become a 'whole' human being   51
TOM FELDGES

5	Perspectives on democracy, citizenship and value education in the Norwegian school JAMES MCGUIRK	57
6	Educational poverty as a challenge for the future: Concepts and criteria for combating non-material child deprivation in Italy DANIELE BRUZZONE AND SIMONA FINETTI	68
7	Everything, but a teacher: Notes from creative writing workshops within liminal space RONNY RITZE	83

8   Without hierarchy: A phenomenological contribution to the antiauthoritarian approach in pedagogy   93
    TATIANA SHCHYTTSOVA

Preface to Section III: How would we ever find out about 'learning'?   **103**
TOM FELDGES

9   Attention as the core of education: Collaborative learning from experiences in GP vocational training in the Netherlands   109
    MARIO VEEN AND MARIJE VAN BRAAK

10 Teaching with flow in the times of COVID-19   120
    DANAI TSELENTI AND ALEXANDROS TILLAS

11 Vignette research: An Austrian phenomenological approach to empirical research   130
    EVI AGOSTINI AND HANS KARL PETERLINI

12 Summing it all up: A concluding attempt   141
    TOM FELDGES

    Index   *151*

Contributors

Evi Agostini is an Assistant Professor at the Department of Teacher Education at the Centre for Teacher Education (ZLB) and the Faculty of Philosophy and Education at the University of Vienna. She lectures on learning theory and anthropology at different Universities in Austria and Italy and is concerned with teachers' and school leaders' professional learning in Austria, Germany and Switzerland. Evi was a visiting research fellow at the Hebrew University and Beit Berl College (Israel). She was nominated twice for the State Prize for Excellent Teaching at Austrian Universities by the Austrian Ministry of Education. Evi is a member of the German-speaking Innovative Learning Environment Network (ILE) and co-leader of the phenomenologically oriented International Vignette and Anecdote Research Network (VignA). Her main research interests are linked to (Phenomenological) Learning and Teaching Theories, Responsive Teacher Education and School Development, Aesthetic Education, Ethics and Epistemology.

Thomas Altfelix holds a doctorate in German Education Studies (*Erziehungswissenschaft*) and is currently a lecturer at the Europa-Universität Flensburg (EUF). He is the vice chairman of the Franz Fischer Society for Philosophy and Education Studies and co-editor of the society's yearbook. He lived in England for a number of years and is familiar with education policy and practice in the UK.

Marije van Braak is an educational scientist and a PhD candidate at the Department of General Practice Training at the Erasmus Medical Center, Rotterdam, the Netherlands. Her research interests include interactional approaches to teaching and learning in various educational contexts. Her PhD is on Learning from Experiences in the GP vocational training in the Netherlands.

Daniele Bruzzone, PhD, is Professor of Education, Università Cattolica del Sacro Cuore of Milan and Director of the research center on educational contexts, affects and relationships (C.A.R.E.) and Editor-in-chief of *Encyclopaideia. Journal of Phenomenology and Education* (https://encp.unibo.it). His research interests span meaning-oriented helping relationships, emotional skills in healthcare and social work and child and adolescent education. He has been an invited lecturer and keynote speaker in many international settings (Austria, Germany, Norway, Spain, Switzerland, Mexico, Argentina, Brazil, Colombia, Guatemala, Paraguay, Peru) and has published 6 books and over 100 papers in edited volumes or scientific journals.

Tom Feldges has studied psychology, sociology and philosophy. He obtained a PhD in phenomenological philosophy and worked for many years lecturing and researching in the UK and, before returning to Germany and the Humboldt University, Berlin. He has now retired, but has been a member of the executive board of the British Education Studies Association (BESA) and co-editor and reviewer for academic journals with an educational focus. Tom has authored a number of journal articles and chapters on educational issues. He has also edited another book in this series, which is the much-appreciated *Philosophy and the Study of Education*. His latest publication is a monograph about the interplay of Francisco Varela's neuro-phenomenology and Husserl's phenomenology, a book that gains importance by the rise of (often uncritical) neuroscientific approaches to teaching and a growing momentum of phenomenological approaches to education.

Simona Finetti, MA in Educational Design in Child and Youth Services, specialises in communications and interpersonal relationships and holds a master's degree in Counseling and Relational Training. She is a PhD candidate in Sciences of the Person and Education at Università Cattolica del Sacro Cuore, Milan.

Joshua N.W. Gray holds a PhD in Philosophy and is currently an English teacher and teacher trainer at the University of Bordeaux. He is also a PhD student in English language studies focussing on autonomy and intercultural competence. He is a member of the *Laboratoire Culture Education Sociétés* (LACES EA 7437) and has contributed to many intercultural telecollaboration projects in both secondary and tertiary education.

James McGuirk (PhD in Philosophy) is Professor of Philosophy at the Centre for Practical Knowledge in the Faculty of Teacher Education and Art. He is member of the Research Group: *The Theory of Practical Knowledge*. His latest appointment is 2018 Guest Professor School of Historical and Philosophical Inquiry, University of Queensland, Brisbane, Australia. His latest papers were on *Critical Thinking in Education: On the unavoidability of a value context*, *Suffering's Double Disclosure and the Normality of Experience* and *Leibliche (Lern-)Erfahrung qua Augmented Reality*.

Hans Karl Peterlini, Dr is Professor of General Pedagogy and Intercultural Education at the University of Klagenfurt (A), and Vice Dean of the Faculty of Cultural Sciences. He is the scientific head of the university course *Global Citizenship Education*, and holder of the UNESCO Chair *Global Citizenship Education – Culture of Diversity and Peace*. He is also the co-editor of the yearbook *Migration und Gesellschaft – Migration and Society* (transcript), and of the series *Erfahrungsorientierte Bildungsforschung* (Studienverlag and Beltz-Juventa). His research focuses on personal and social learning under the conditions of diversity, ethnicisation, migration and plurality.

Sonia Pieczenko studied Criminology and Health and Social Care and obtained an MA in the Philosophy of Psychiatry. She has worked for years in the education of future health- and social care professionals. Sonia has presented papers at international conferences and has written a number of journal articles and chapters in educationally relevant collections. She has taken part in educational research projects and her monograph on pseudo hallucinations has been translated into most major European languages. She has now retired from teaching and has left the UK, where she was born and raised.

Ronny Ritze is a social worker, course instructor and lecturer in creative and therapeutic writing. He studied journalism and creative writing before opening a bookstore. In 2014, he visited a juvenile detention centre for the first time and decided to initiate writing workshops in prisons. He then moved on to work in other institutions such as psychiatric specialist hospitals and educational support facilities followed. He is the author of various books that are critical of the German prison system.

Tatiana Shchyttsova (Dr habil. in Philosophy) is Professor at the Department of Social Sciences and academic director of the Center for Research of Intersubjectivity and Interpersonal Communication at the European Humanities University, Vilnius. She received a number of international fellowships and grants for research work at the Universities of Tübingen, Freiburg, Wuppertal in Gemany, Sheffield in the UK and at the St. Olaf College in Minnesota, USA. From 2007 to 2009 she was a research fellow at the Eugen Fink Archive (Freiburg, Germany) where she worked on the research project *Being-with-one-another and intergenerational experience* supported by the Alexander von Humboldt Foundation. She gave a number of guest lectures at the various European academic institutions, including the Institute for Human Sciences in Vienna, the University of Freiburg, the University of Helsinki, the European University at St. Petersburg and others. She is editor-in-chief of the journal for philosophy and cultural studies *Topos* and editor of the book series *Conditiohumana*. Her research interests are the phenomenology of intersubjectivity, in particular, the phenomenology of intergenerational and educational relations; philosophical anthropology; affect theory; existential/phenomenological psychotherapy; philosophical and ethical issues of biomedical technology.

Alexandros Tillas works primarily in the philosophy of psychology and cognitive science and has published on observational learning and education, concept learning, perception and selective attention, the relation between language and thinking and the neural underpinnings of endogenous thoughts, while he is currently working on emotion regulation and effective learning. Alexandros has also worked on social agency, communication and the role of emotion in thinking and learning. His PhD thesis (Bristol, UK) is a defence of concept empiricism against nativism and he situates his work in the scientifically informed tradition of philosophy. He has developed an interdisciplinary research project that investigates the nature of intuitions and the extent to which standing unconscious knowledge contributes to higher cognitive processes like reasoning and decision-making. Tillas is currently teaching Contemporary Philosophy at the Hellenic Open University and is a member of Byron Kaldis' Laboratory of Theoretical and Applied Philosophy, History and Sociology of Science and Technology at the National Technical University of Athens. He has taught, amongst other courses, Cognitive & Experimental Psychology (Panteion University Athens), Ancient Philosophy (Hellenic Open University), Epistemology, Wittgenstein, Empiricism (Aristotle University of Thessaloniki). He has previously held a postdoctoral position in a project focusing on 'Grounding Cognition' and on the Mathematical Modelling and Ontology of (representational) frames (in the human mind) project (both in Düsseldorf).

Danai Tselenti obtained a BA and a Master's degree from the Faculty of Political Science and Public Administration of the University of Athens. Since December 2015, she holds a PhD in Sociology, also from the University of Athens. Her current research focuses on new media and particularly contemporary offline and online reading communities (*Bookstagram, Instapoetry*, online book reviewing platforms), wherein she uses a broad range of qualitative methods in order to gain a deeper understanding of contemporary online audiences. Currently she is a postdoctoral researcher at the University of Porto and a research member at the National Technical University of Athens. Her research interests lie in the areas of new media studies, reading studies, sociology of reception, economic sociology, literary theories, cognitive theories of reading and educational theory.

Mario Veen, PhD, is an interdisciplinary educational researcher and philosopher at the Department of General Practice at the Erasmus University Medical Center, and action editor of Teaching and Learning in Medicine's series on Philosophy in Medical Education. He is interested in creating an interdisciplinary dialogue between the humanities. His interests include medical education, group interaction and discursive approaches to reflection and critical thinking.

Stephen Ward is Emeritus Professor of Education, Bath Spa University, formerly Dean of the School of Education and subject leader for Education Studies. A founder member of the British Education Studies Association, he has published on the primary curriculum, primary music teaching and Education Studies. His research interests are education policy and university knowledge.

Series editor's preface

Education Studies has become a popular and exciting undergraduate subject in some 50 universities in the UK. It began in the early 2000s, mainly in the post-1992 universities which had been centres of teacher training. Gaining academic credibility, the subject is now being taken up by post-1992 and Russell Group institutions. In 2004, Routledge published one of the first texts for undergraduates, *Education Studies: A Student's Guide*, now in its fourth edition (Simon and Ward, 2020). It comprises a series of chapters introducing key topics in Education Studies and has contributed to the development of the subject. Targeted at students and academic staff at levels 5, 6 and 7, the Routledge Education Studies Series offers a sequence of volumes which explore such topics in depth.

It is important to understand that Education Studies is not teacher training or teacher education (Crook, 2002). Although graduates in the subject may well go on to become teachers after a PGCE or school-based training, Education Studies should be regarded as a subject with a variety of career outcomes, or indeed, none: it can be taken as the academic and critical study of education in itself. At the same time, while the theoretical elements of teacher training are continually reduced in PGCE courses and school-based training, undergraduate Education Studies provides a critical analysis for future teachers who, in a rapidly changing world, need so much more than simply the training to deliver a government-defined school curriculum.

Education Studies is concerned with understanding how people develop and learn throughout their lives, the nature of knowledge and critical engagement with ways of knowing. It demands an intellectually rigorous analysis of educational processes and their cultural, social, political and historical contexts. In a time of rapid change across the planet, education is about how we both make and manage such change. Education Studies, therefore, includes perspectives on international education, economic relationships, globalisation, ecological issues and human rights. It deals with beliefs, values and principles in education and the way that they change over time.

Since its early developments at the beginning of the century, the subject has grown in academic strength, drawing explicitly on the disciplines of Psychology, Sociology, Philosophy, History and Economics. There has been a debate about the roles of the disciplines and whether Education Studies should be seen as a discipline in its own right. Chapter 4 in this book takes up this discussion and traces the links and divergence between the development of the 'New Education Studies' in Britain, and the longer history of *Pädagogik* in Germany. The subject has also broadened in scope to address the many social and political questions of globalisation, international education and perceptions of childhood. A glance through the list of book titles in the series on page ii reveals the ever-growing range of topics which Education Studies embraces.

The Quality Assurance Agency *Benchmark for Education Studies* states that courses should include 'consideration of the international and intercultural dimension of education' (QAA, 2017: 7). Growing up and being schooled in one nation and culture is the experience of most students and it is easy to take for granted the realities imposed by homeschooling. The study of international education gives students access to alternative realities, ideas and concepts: education doesn't just have to be like this!

One of the ways in which students gained knowledge and experience of alternatives in education was through the European Union's *Erasmus* Scheme which funded student and staff exchanges in universities. The withdrawal of the UK from the EU in 2021 reduced the ease of contact which universities had enjoyed with its closest national neighbours. This book is part of the attempt to sustain those relations with colleagues in Europe. It offers not just the practical alternatives in schooling, but the differing theoretical assumptions in pedagogy and research.

Even though the UK has left the European Union, English is still the dominant language in Europe. It should be noted that most of the contributors to this book are writing in English as a second or foreign language, and we should be grateful to them for expressing their ideas and experiences to an English-speaking readership.

Stephen Ward

References

Crook, D. (2002) Education studies and teacher education. *British Journal of Education Studies*, **50**(1), pp. 55–75.
QAA (2017) *Subject Benchmark Statement: Education Studies*. Gloucester: QAA.
Simon, C.A. and Ward, S. (Ed.) (2020) *Education Studies: A student's guide*. Abingdon: Routledge.

Books available to date in the series

Dylan Adams, Gary Beauchamp and Kevin Smith (Eds) (2022) *Pedagogies for the Future: A critical (re)imagining of education*. Abingdon: Routledge.
Brendan Bartram (Ed.) (2017) *International and Comparative Education: Contemporary issues and debates*. Abingdon: Routledge.
Zeta Brown (Ed.) (2016) *Inclusive Education: Perspectives on pedagogy, policy and practice*. Abingdon: Routledge.
Zeta Brown and Stephen Ward (Eds) (2018) *Contemporary Issues in Childhood: A bio-ecological approach*. Abingdon: Routledge.
Christine Eden (2017) *Gender, Education and Work: Inequalities and intersectionality*. Abingdon: Routledge.
Tom Feldges (Ed.) (2019) *Philosophy and the Study of Education: New perspectives on a complex relationship*. Abingdon: Routledge.
Nicholas Joseph (Ed.) (2022) *History of Education*. Abingdon: Routledge.
Jessie Bustillos Morales and Sandra Abegglen (Eds) (2020) *The Study of Education and Economics: Debates and critical theoretical perspectives*. Abingdon: Routledge.
Catherine A. Simon and Graham Downes (Eds) (2020) *Sociology for Education Studies*. Abingdon: Routledge.
Cathal Ó Siochrú (Ed.) (2018) *Psychology and the Study of Education: Critical perspectives on developing theories*. Abingdon: Routledge.

British Education Studies Association (BESA)

Many of the editors and contributors to the Education Studies book series are members of the British Education Studies Association. Formed in 2005, BESA is an academic association providing a network for tutors and students in Education Studies. It holds an annual conference with research papers from staff and students; there are bursaries for students on Education Studies programmes.

The website offers information and news about Education Studies and two journals: *Educationalfutures* and *Transformations*, a journal for student publications. Both are available without charge on the website: https://educationstudies.org.uk/

Abbreviations

AHS	Akademische Hochschule (Austria)
AROPE	At Risk of Poverty or Social Exclusion Index
BESA	British Education Studies Association (UK)
CARE	Research Centre on educational Contexts, Affects and Relationships (Italy)
CC	Core Curriculum (Norway)
CEFRL	Common European Framework of Reference for Languages
COVID-19	Coronavirus SARS CoV-2
CRC	Convention on the Rights of the Child
DGfE	Deutsche Gesellschaft für Erziehungswissenschaft
EU	European Union
FL learners	Foreign Language learners
FWF	Wissenschaftsfonds (Austria)
GP	General Practitioner
HDI	Human Development Index
IDELA	International Development and Early Learning Assessment
ILE	Innovative Learning Environment Network (Austria)
IPE	Educational Poverty Index
LACES EA 7437	Laboratoire Culturel Education Sociétés (France)
LfE	Learning from Experience
MPI	Multidimensional Poverty Index
NEET	Not (engaged) in Education, Employment or Training
NMS	Neue Mittelschule (Austria)
PGCE	Postgraduate Certificate in Education (UK)
PISA – OECD	Programme for International Student Assessment of the Organisation for Economic Cooperation and Development
QAA	Quality Assurance Agency for higher education (UK)
UDIR	Core Curriculum for Norwegian Schools
UK	United Kingdom
UN	United Nations
UNDP	United Nations Development Program
UNESCO	United Nations Educational, Scientific and Cultural Organization
UN SDG	United Nations Sustainable Development Goals
US	United States

USSR	Union of Socialist Soviet Republics
VignA	International Vignette and Anecdote Research Network
ZLB	Centre for Teacher Education (Austria)

1 Introduction

Ways to think about the concepts of 'Education' and 'Europe'

Tom Feldges

Europe as a more or less ideal concept regarding the western extent of the Asian landmass has a long history and has – despite its many critics – still an important role to play in our modern world. But Europe as the birthplace of Modernity and Enlightenment is also closely related to questions around education, schools and universities. The humanist self-assertion of the rational human being, controlling its own fate, is not conceivable without the availability of education for an ever-growing proportion of the population. Therefore, the pairing of Education and Europe certainly comes with the promise of an interesting read. However, before engaging with the topic of *Education in Europe*, it is important to have a clear focus; the topic is, by its very nature, incredibly vast and it is necessary to limit exaggerated expectations that could never be fulfilled in this introductory text. To achieve a narrowing focus, two important aspects need explicit mentioning. The first is the problem of geographical perspective, i.e. from *where* are we taking our view of Europe? The second is the extent of the project, i.e. what falls within the scope of the book and what does not? These are the two issues providing the guiding thread to lead us through the multifaceted, multi-layered and dense topics of education and Europe.

When reading the title *Education in Europe,* one could think of a book that attempts to offer a view from *outside* Europe, looking at what is going on *in* European education: something like a detached *view from nowhere.* For example, a reader from the United Kingdom (UK) could think: 'We left the European Union (EU), we have nothing to do with Europe anymore. So let's have a look across the borders (from outside) to see what is going on (in) there'. This perspective comes with two problems. One is the difficulty of a) defining Europe geographically and b) deciding whether a stretch of barely 21 miles of dividing water could ever settle the question of the UK's continental belonging. This is the question as to whether the mere cutting of the UK's political ties to the supranational entity of the EU could ever remove the UK from the shared cultural heritage of Europe and the close geographical proximity to its neighbours. This will be discussed in more detail below.

But there is a second problem. Europe is not only captured by real or assumed geographical borders. It is also often conceived as a space of ideas. Europe is about how people have lived and continue to live with each other based on common values and attitudes against a background of a shared cultural heritage. Our imagined observer from the UK could thus claim 'to have nothing to do with Europe anymore'. However, it would be impossible for this individual to escape the historical framework that has shaped her/his thoughts about education. For example: yes, girls attend school, yes, attendance is compulsory for all children and yes, female teachers can tell young male learners what to do. In that respect, it appears impossible for any UK-based educator to escape this

DOI: 10.4324/9781003223528-1

common European heritage while trying to assess objectively what is 'going on over there' and then to try to relate it back to the UK. Historical attempts to do this have applied a similar but inherently limited, *nation-centred* perspective. But, as it turns out, they were condemned to remain incomplete because the failure to take the situated-ness of one's own position into account and thereby failing to recognise the interconnectedness of the world. Bayly (2004) has addressed this problem very clearly by attempting to write a global history, tracing the influences upon the European emergence of Modernity in relation to the industrial revolution. This industrial revolution was often seen as a British initiative to set Modernity in motion. However, Bayly shows how Britain has always depended upon its neighbours in Europe in either an enabling or limiting manner and how Britain and Europe were dependent on global developments for good or bad. In this respect, it is not possible to cast that 'view from nowhere' as Nagel (1989) once famously called it. We, humans, are condemned always to look at everything we see from 'somewhere', and this god-like and seemingly *objective* 'nowhere' is simply unobtainable. However, even if we decide to ignore these problems by trying to take a view from the UK-internal educational landscape onto what these Europeans are doing, such an attempt would be doomed to fail. Within the UK, there are four different educational systems in England, Scotland, Wales and Northern Ireland, with their respective traditions. So even our UK observer would need to sit 'somewhere' and this 'somewhere' would not be the same everywhere in the UK, and neither would it constitute the overall UK educational reality. More could be said on this topic, but it should be clear by now that there is no neutral middle ground for *Us* to look at *Them*. It's an over-used aphorism, but we really are 'all in it together'!

Because of these difficulties, the approach in this book is different. While wanting to focus upon international education, the perspective is one that works explicitly on the notion of a shared cultural and educational past, present and future. This cultural framework means that the reader's own educational background invariably includes at least some elements of European origin: for example, the idea of general and compulsory schooling for every child or the invention of the European university by Wilhelm von Humboldt in 1810.

A second issue was mentioned above to gain the necessary focus and to guide our thoughts. There is the danger that the book's title might suggest that it offers a comprehensive overview of *all* the educationally relevant activities *all over* Europe. But such a far-reaching agenda could never be achieved in an introductory text such as this one. The book does not lay claim to providing such a complete overview on the multiple aspects of educational reality and theory, nor does it aim to cover each and every European country. Instead, authors from various countries in Europe were invited to report on interesting developments within the national context of the country in which they work and/or live. Chapters are intended to raise awareness of a variety of educational problems and educational theory to contextualise these problems and how various ways of trying to solve them are developed and theoretically justified. The reader is encouraged to engage intellectually with the authors' ideas while starting to think about their own practice in learning, research or teaching, and whether or how the proposed strategies or solutions could work in the reader's own day-to-day educational reality, wherever that happens to be. To assist the reader's cognitive engagement each chapter includes a series of questions and a brief list of recommended reading, making it something of a 'work-book' aiming to engage the reader. But that still leaves the question of what it is that is intended to spark the reader's interest and thinking. Having explained the limited scope of the book, it is now the time to turn towards education and Europe.

A nice little story of the Anglo-Irish philosopher Bishop Berkeley tells us that he was once called to attend an argument between two neighbours over their garden fence. It was hoped that Berkeley might be able to mediate and settle the dispute, but he soon declared that they would never settle because they were arguing from different 'premises'. In this play on words he used the term 'premises' to mirror the actual situation of the opposing parties standing on their respective patches of ground but also metaphorically to refer to the neighbours' incompatible ideas or theories upon which their respective arguments were built. The story is a good and quite frequently used reminder in philosophical seminars to first clarify the concepts upon which an argument is to be built. So, to understand the concepts of 'education' and 'Europe', such a clarification is the next step so that, when thinking with concepts, the premises of the argument will be clear to every participant in the discussion. After this conceptual clarification there is one more issue to be mentioned, a thread that became apparent when receiving the chapters from the contributors to this volume. There was a clear 'subject-centred' focus in most of the contributions, and this aspect needs a little more of an explanatory foundation. The remainder of this introduction will briefly outline the chapters that are to follow. The reader may decide in which order to read them, but the chapters are in a thematic sequence supporting an argument for the importance of the subject-centred claim that runs as the guiding thread through the content of the book.

Education

There are two main ways of trying to clarify a concept. One is to distinguish its essential features, the ones that make it *that* concept as opposed to any other one. Features that, if they were absent, would render any token as not belonging to this concept. So, to use a rather everyday example, if we were to define a vacuum cleaner as a device that sucks air to clean indoor surfaces, then any device that does not suck in the air for cleaning purposes could not fall under the concept of a vacuum cleaner as we defined it. This sort of definition by features is known as a definition by 'intension': defining the essential and necessary features of a concept. The other way is to endeavour to list the tokens that are captured by the concept, which is known as a definition by 'extension' (Honderich, 2005). It is probably best to have another example here as well: one could ask what a fruit is. A possible answer could be that these are soft tissue surroundings of biodegradable matter containing the plant's seeds. Hence, one could provide a definition by intension, specifying what the essential characteristics of all fruits are. But it is also possible to answer by providing a list of examples of fruit (tokens): apple, pear, apricot, grape, banana, pineapple and so on. One would thus capture the concept by examples that fall under the concept to provide the idea of what the concept is about. We leave it to the philosophers to dig deeper into these issues, but for our current purposes, we have two perspectives to assess what it is that we have in mind when discussing education.

If one – in the most general manner – states that education is supposed to capture all the wilful actions of an instructor (teacher) and the relevant institutions (schools and universities) that are directed towards a learner with the aim of bringing about the learner's acquisition of new practical or cognitive skills, one would have a good first definition by intension. The beauty of such a definition becomes clear when trying to distinguish 'education' from 'socialisation'. Quite opposite to the gains of wilful educational activity, socialisation gains are the results of a mostly tacit and informal working of culture that enables the socialised individual to function appropriately within a given society. Socialisation, then, seems to be a more basic concept than education, and although the borders might be blurred, a conceptual differentiation appears to be possible: i.e. wilfully and goal-directed – or not.

However, when it comes to the differences between education and indoctrination things get tricky. Here one faces the question of how much – if at all – education should be loaded with ideological learning. That is, should learners, along with the teaching of practical and/or cognitive skills, also be educated in a specific ideology such as communism or capitalism (Feldges, 2019)? The initial response to this question is probably a resounding NO! But if one, as outlined above, remains critical of the idea of a 'view from nowhere' then every position one could ever take would always and invariably be one that is soaked with the traces of a society's beliefs and underlying assumptions. In that respect it seems impossible to eradicate all societal bias from the pursuit of educational purity.

Of course, one could take a pragmatic view here, allowing learners to be taught how their society functions and then leave it to them to adopt such societal values individually. However, such a choice does necessitate a genuine reflection upon the appropriateness of these values for the reflecting individual (Benner, 2001). But by allowing for such a critical distance to emerge between the teaching contents and the learners' appropriation of these, one reaches another level. All of a sudden it is no longer about learning what is offered but experiencing a misfit between what one thought previously and what is encountered during one's education. This is a moment of crisis that, when skilfully brought about by an experienced instructor, can cause a reflective engagement in which the learner develops a new perspective upon the things, the world and him/herself in the process if the individual is willing/ready so to do. In Germany this form of educational practice is known as *Bildung*, i.e. the forming of a person. The first three chapters (see Chapters 2–4) will focus upon these issues, but for the moment we need to ask the question whether such an approach in which the learner does (or does not) do the actual work of sorting things individually within the seclusion of his/her mind can still count as education as defined earlier, or whether a sub-concept would be a good solution? Again, it is not necessary to discuss this any further here. But it should be clear by now that a careful clarification of the concepts used is of vital importance to an understanding of what one wishes to talk or write about. When one wishes to argue against the teaching of specific values, one would probably be well advised to distinguish the concepts of indoctrination and education clearly from each other in order to build a case against one (indoctrination) merging into the other (education).

Nevertheless, although the intensional definition leaves the educationalist with some work to do, the extensional definition is not necessarily easier. Is education supposed to be the exclusive effort of schools and universities with a focus on the curriculum, or can it have a wider focus? In Italy education entails aspects of social care that in the UK would probably be deemed to be the role of social services (see Chapter 6). In Germany, *Rehabilitationspädagogie* (i.e. education studies for medical, mental and even social rehabilitation purposes) is taught in the educational departments of the university sector, while in the UK it falls often into the Health and Social Care Faculty. The actual extension of what education means in various national contexts is wide and far-reaching and shows the potential ambiguity in the concept of education when not properly clarified.

Europe

On imagining the continental landmass of Australia, it is quite easy to link the concept of the continent of Australia to its geographical representation. What is not within the coastline of Australia does (mostly) not constitute a part of the continent of Australia. But things get more complicated when considering the western appendix of the Asian landmass, that stretch of land that we have come to refer to as Europa. There is no dividing ocean here that could help to keep the concept of a continental Europe separated and clearly distinguished from continental Asia. There is just one Eurasian landmass with an arbitrary border drawn to make it into two continents. So, one might ask, why separate what appears not to be separate at all? Or even with a slightly biting undertone: Have the Europeans living on that western appendix of the Eurasian landmass got above themselves by wanting to call their part of the Eurasian landmass a continent of their own?

Within the limited space of this introduction it is not possible to engage with the concept of Europa in any satisfactory depth. Therefore, a brief sketch crafted by a few broad strokes must suffice. The ancient history of Europe normally starts with the myth of the Greek god Zeus who is said to have abducted a beautiful Phoenician princess. Disguised as a bull, he took her on his back to escape from what is nowadays mostly Lebanon to reach Greece – Crete to be more precise – in order to seduce her there. The princess's name was *Europa* and, legend has it, since then the lands north of the Mediterranean were referred to as Europe. However, one has to be careful not to try to apply our current concept of Europe to ancient times when 'Europe' did not have the meaning it has today. The Greeks considered themselves 'the civilised people' while calling all who were not Greek simply 'barbarians' (Davies, 1996). The Greeks, with their reasoned attempts to understand their world and how humans ought to live, and the Romans, with their strictly codified laws and ordered society, are two of the pillars upon which the idea of Europe rests (Tarnas, 1991). But laws and philosophy are never enough to convince people, and so the Judeo-Christian view of an ordered world, overseen by one God, provided a third pillar and an overarching narrative. With the rise of the Christian faith and its spread across Europe, it became common to refer to the area covered by the adherents of this belief as 'the Christian Community' (Davies, 1996: 7). However, it would be unwarranted to assume that this Christian community, which covered most parts of what is now considered to be Europe, to be the same as the Europe of today. But it is reasonable to see the Christian practice of reflecting upon one's own conduct in relation to given rules and laws and to confess to any wrongdoing, along with the Greek attitude to cherishing the truth (i.e. *philosophia*), as a precursor of an emerging attitude that has gained importance ever since.

Despite the fact that throughout the ages many different peoples have reached the Americas, it was mainly the journey of Christopher Columbus in 1492 that marks a change. From then on the nations of the European continent started to systematically engage in colonising newly discovered territories to expand their sphere of influence and to exploit the riches of the East and West (Bayly, 2004). By that time Europe can be seen as defining itself against the 'Other', the non-European counterpart, perceived as primitive, inferior or even evil, as Said (1978) explains in his book on the European colonisation of the East. In 1517 a new protestant denomination was emerging in what is now Germany. Protestantism emphasised a direct relationship of the individual believer with God, a move that again required a developing reflective ability: individual deeds had to be individually justified before God via prayer. Max Weber (2002) saw this to be of crucial importance in the development of the entrepreneurial ethic and the emergence of capitalism that led to a massive and more or less exclusive economic growth on the European landmass. Of course, other nations of the world, such as India or China, had also developed impressive cultural achievements. But, as Landwehr (2021) argues, these, and other great civilisations, did not develop the critical, self-reflective attitude that characterises the European development and which constitutes at least one essential characteristic of Europe. Yes, it is uncontested that it must remain very difficult to capture Europe in terms of its geographical layout. Where does it end in the East? Does it end at the border with the Russian Federation, or at the river Don, or rather at the mountain range of the Urals (Davies, 1996); or is it even confined to the outer borders of the political entity of the European Union? Attempts to define Europe by a negative definition – by what it is not – are now mostly discarded because of an apparent colonial attitude. Furthermore, as explained above, it is always better to define something by intension than by providing a list of what it is or even of what it is not. Landwehr's notion of a critical and self-reflective attitude through which Europa and Europeans are constantly questioning itself/themselves makes it difficult to offer a clear concept of Europe. This is so because Europe's reflective search for Europe can never be fixed in time: it will always remain a developing project. As Landwehr (2021) explains, the concept of Europe can only be depicted by a continuous process of what he denotes by the neologism of '*Diskursivierung*', that is, by a continuous discourse about what Europe is and what it ought to be. So the definition of Europe must remain problematic. However, if this self-critical, reflective attitude is the core characteristic that shaped Europe, then anyone educated in the art of critically reflecting upon the world, on oneself and on one's relation to the world will not be able to step out of this way of thinking. Therefore, it seems impossible for anyone sufficiently educated to achieve a perspective upon any educational practice 'from nowhere'.

Subject-centred education?

As mentioned above, there is one more aspect that is in need to be briefly outlined in these opening lines about education in Europe. This is the problem of how to think, theorise, contextualise and – finally – research aspects of educational pursuit. Of course, it is possible to understand education as something that is imposed upon an otherwise mostly receptive learner. A learner who then, because of underlying psychological or neuro-psychological pre-determination, will react to a given set of presented 'educational stimuli' in a more or less predictable manner. That is a picture of education as the skilful application of rules to make use of the learner's underlying thought patterns to maximise learning success. Hence, a conception of the learner as an object shaped and formed exclusively by such outside forces and incentives imposed upon her/him by the skilled educationalist. Such a view, when taken to its extreme, neglects the alternative view: one in which the learner is to be understood as an independent social actor with an individual motive to learn or to refuse learning. Within this book about education in Europe it is possible to trace in almost all chapters the importance of this subjective influence to either engage with the educational offer or to decline engagement. This approach to theorising about the foundations and practice of education has a widespread and still growing basis in continental Europe, while it remains largely unnoticed in the UK (e.g., Pieczenko, 2019). In order to contribute to a hopefully increased application of this subject-centred approach (Holzkamp, 1995) the overall aim of this book is also to develop its readers' understanding that research and theory development along a subject-centred approach can be more than beneficial and rewarding, not only to the learner's learning success but also to the educational practitioner. However, arguing for such a paradigm change needs a more elaborated argument, one that cannot be provided at this point and in the limited space of an introduction. Therefore, this third issue will be developed throughout the book and in more depth in the final chapter (see Chapter 12) of the book.

What is to be expected next?

In order to offer a basis for the reader's orientation, a brief overview of the chapters is provided here. As noted above, they are ordered into three thematic sections that will support the overall argument for a subject-centred approach to education which is further developed in the final chapter.

Section I carries a provocative heading about 'the pains of learning'. But instead of taking issue with any kind of physical pain being inflicted on the learners it explores the discomfort they are likely to experience when having to give up previously held beliefs or assumed certainties, i.e. when education 'does something to them'.

In the second chapter Sonia Pieczenko uses her autobiographic experiences of moving from the UK to Germany. She introduces and discusses some of the theoretical foundations of German education, most prominently the concepts of *Bilding* and *Sprachenbildung*. Both concepts, originating in the German tradition of education, refer to a specific process that is to be accomplished by the learner if he/she is to fulfil his/her potential. It is a process that can be uncomfortable and indeed the relevant literature calls it a moment of crisis. By introducing and discussing these theoretical issues she points out how language and language use is an inherently culturally situated practice and how language carries the specific values of the wider linguistic community. She also discusses the problem of 'normativity', i.e. the question of the kind of justification the educational system and its practitioners are supposed to have when carrying out their task of educating the young.

The third chapter by Joshua Gray focuses upon the teaching of English to French students in France. It starts with a theory-focused discussion of a nation-centred view regarding culture and language, something inherited from (a nation-centred) history. As such a perspective is likely to evoke 'belonging' to some, it also creates the 'Other', i.e. the ones that are the binary opposite to those who rightfully belong. Nevertheless, as Gray argues, it is highly questionable whether such a traditional view could ever be suitable within a rapidly changing and increasingly global environment. Challenging these territorialised models of language and cultural education is one of the most demanding and exciting tasks that current educational efforts have to master, and not only in France. However, evoking a change in the learners' preconceptions about their own cultural identity will – at least for some – remain an uncomfortable, even painful, experience and need reflective engagement. Gray ends his chapter with some practical recommendations on how this can be achieved.

The fourth chapter by Thomas Altfelix considers German education studies (*Pädagogik*) and contrasts this critically the 'New Education Studies' as it is currently emerging in the UK. While Altfelix draws upon the differences in the respective philosophical-theoretical underpinning of both traditions, he develops an argument to the effect that German education studies are becoming more like UK Education Studies has been, while the UK's New Education Studies are strongly developing their theoretical grounding. Altfelix's text is very theoretical, but as the New Education Studies in the UK is aiming to enhance its own theoretical underpinning, the inclusion of such a demanding chapter in this collection is appropriate.

Section II takes its starting point with the apparent dichotomy in the fact that humans are both physical bodies and encultured beings. To become truly human necessitates a successful accomplishment of one's bodily development with initiation into a surrounding culture. However, this initiation is not complete by 'producing' a merely 'functioning' human being; it has to aim for someone capable of living a fulfilling life as a reasonable and responsible social actor sharing the values of the social context. Hence, one has to be prepared by education to become a 'whole' human being.

In the fifth chapter James McGuirk takes the issue of democracy, values and citizenship as his theme to discuss the Norwegian approach to the curriculum in preparing pupils to become competent citizens. McGuirk unpacks the tension inherent in each and every attempt to accomplish this sort of educational goal. Pupils are enabled to become autonomous social actors while binding them back to culturally embedded values that – by their very nature – limit individual autonomy. The second thread in his chapter is the ambition to move from merely aspirational values to everyday practice that is *lived* within schools.

The sixth chapter by Daniele Bruzzone and Simona Finetti discusses the issue of poverty and its impact upon a child's future chances within the Italian context. Quite contrary to a merely income- or consumption-orientated view of poverty, the Italian initiative they introduce focuses upon a wide range of markers that indicate 'educational poverty'. This concept is relatively independent of economic factors and is much more about a child's sense of not belonging or being left behind. By introducing and discussing this concept for an international audience in this chapter, Bruzzone and Finetti point towards future possibilities for the development of theory, research and practice.

In the seventh chapter Ronny Ritze reports about creative writing workshops in a German prison for young males. He points out the difficulties of these youngsters to relate to their bodies and their struggle to reflect upon themselves and their surroundings in an attempt to sort out their lives.

The eighth chapter by Tatiana Shchyttsova, who now lives and works in Lithuania, develops a link between authoritarian teaching practices in Belarus and the replication of authoritarian social structures in schools. Shchyttsova not only traces this specific tradition historically but also assesses the underlying patterns according to which these authoritarian attitudes and approaches survive. She suggests a change in perspective that makes it possible to allow a child to start 'searching for itself' with recourse to various phenomenological theories. Despite the fact that this is – once again – a taxing text, it was included in this collection because it demonstrates a continental attitude to educational theorising, not treating philosophy as a historical sequence to be learned and rehearsed but as an available toolset to gain a different view on problems and to be able to suggest otherwise unthinkable solutions.

Section III addresses the potential concern that often emerges around subject-centred approaches to education. That is the question of how to research an aspect of educational reality when not taking an almost scientific and detached view on the problem but rather by focusing upon the subject that lives through this educational reality. This section introduces three examples of educational research that aim to place a much greater emphasis upon those who experience education, be it as learners or as educationalists.

Chapter nine by Mario Veen and Marije van Braak introduces an aspect of the training of future medical general practitioners in the Netherlands. The focus of this approach is that learning is not always accomplished by an instructive transfer of skills or teaching contents. In the 'Learning from Experience' scheme it is rather the individual experience of individuals who have encountered difficult situations or who have shared these encounters by listening to and co-experiencing them in interactive discussion sessions. Interestingly enough, this chapter has also a second strand to it: the creation of value for all participants, facilitated by an open, unstructured form of education, i.e. a session that is not at all constrained by the demand to achieve the evidenced accomplishment of prescribed learning outcomes.

In the tenth chapter Alex Tillas and Danai Tselenti focus on a Greek project that aimed to research the effectiveness of online teaching during the COVID-19 pandemic and under lockdown conditions. Central to Tillas' and Tselenti's account is the notion of the 'flow' according to which the individual experiencing such a state is fulfilling tasks in an almost automated manner, no longer in need of constant cognitive monitoring and steering. By utilising their respondents' self-reports they were able to assess how much teachers and learners were able to reach such a state of flow and the implications of a crossover between a teacher's and the learner's 'flow experiences'. In that respect, Tillas and Tselenti demonstrate how subject-centred research could still utilise traditional research instruments.

In the eleventh chapter Evi Agostini and Hans Karl Peterlini introduce a novel Austrian approach to research learning in specific and multifaceted educational situations. This is done by the condensation of data into a concise description of school experiences of those who had undergone the relevant situation. In that respect, it is, they claim, possible to re-orientate the educational research focus away from an assessment of the results towards the actual process of learning. Within this approach learning is conceived of as the experience of a mismatch between one's expectations and a newly emerging individual sense that is generated for future use.

The concluding twelfth chapter aims to bind the previous three sections into one argument for a subject-centred approach to education within the wider phenomenological tradition. This argument will build upon the lived experience of a crisis as it was developed within the first section. Here the focus is on what an individual experiences when facing the crisis that the world or others fail to be/behave as expected, and how these experiences thus force individual change. A second step will focus upon the (educational) world as experienced by an individual learner (or teacher). The third step will assess the possibilities to establish these experiences and the world as experienced by the one within such situations in a sufficiently reliable and valid manner. The overall claim of this concluding chapter is that it is time to widen the focus of current (UK) educational research to pay heed to the true nature of humans as feeling, sentient beings with their own individual perspectives upon their surroundings.

After this brief overview of what is to be expected within the next chapters, one more word of caution is warranted. This book brings various chapters together to facilitate an overall argument for a change in the current research focus towards the individual. However, the book is also about celebrating the far-reaching variety of European education. Hence, it could be read by dismissing the overall argument and with a sole focus upon the wide selection of European educational practices. Nevertheless, in whatever way the reader decides to read and devote his/her attention, the book was written by authors from various countries all across Europe. They wrote from their own (national-) cultural situated-ness and they drew from literature of their own or of other national contexts. Some of these texts have not been – and probably never will be – translated into the English language. Nevertheless, regarding an academic text as unimportant merely on the ground that one cannot access them just because one has not gained the skill of mastering a second (or even third) language would be simply hubristic.

Recommended reading

Davies, N. (1996) *Europe – A History*. London: Harper Perennial.
Tarnas, R. (1991) *The Passion of the Western Mind*. New York: Random House Inc.

References

Bayly, C.A. (2004) *The Birth of the Modern World, 1780–1914. Global Connections and Comparisons.* Oxford: Blackwell Publishing Ltd.
Benner, D. (2001) Bildung und Demokratie. *Zeitschrift für Pädagogik* **43**. Beiheft, pp. 49–68.
Davies, N. (1996) *Europe – A History*. London: Harper Perennial.
Feldges, T. (2019) *Philosophy and the Study of Education – New perspectives on a complex relationship.* Abingdon: Routledge.
Holzkamp, K. (1995) *Lernen. Subjektwissenschaftliche Grundlegung.* Frankfurt a.M: Campus Verlag.
Honderich, T. (2005) *The Oxford Companion to Philosophy.* Oxford: Oxford University Press.
Landwehr, A. (2021) *Die unmögliche Definition Europas.* Hagen: FernUni.
Nagel, T. (1989) *The View from Nowhere.* Oxford: Oxford University Press.
Pieczenko, S. (2019) Educational Phenomenology – Is there a need and space for such a pursuit? In T. Feldges (Ed.) *Philosophy and the Study of Education – New perspectives on a complex relationship.* Abingdon: Routledge.
Said, E. (1978) *Orientalism.* London: Routledge and Kegan Paul.
Tarnas, R. (1991) *The Passion of the Western Mind.* New York: Random House Inc.
Weber, M. (2002) *The Protestant Ethic and the 'Spirit' of Capitalism.* London: Penguin.

Preface to Section I
On the 'pains' of learning

Tom Feldges

This first section contains three chapters with a provocative heading, stating its envisaged focus to be on 'the pains of learning'. As will be explained in this preface, it is less about pain in the normal way we refer to 'pain'; it is the idea of an uncomfortable crisis in learning. The introduction of an 'uncomfortable crisis' or even 'pain' as a means to bring about learning is something that probably sounds quite alien to most UK-based educators. This is remarkable as a similar concept known as 'transformative learning' exists in the Anglo-American literature (cf. Mezirow, 2018, Taylor and Cranton, 2012). However, as discussed in the following chapters (especially Chapters 2 and 4), while it is quite common practice in some European countries, in the UK teachers' conduct is said to be moving towards *edutainment*, i.e. educational entertainment (Kuh et al., 2008). And if education is, at least partially, about entertainment, then pain or discomfort can have no place in it. With this in mind the next three chapters have been put together. Chapter 2, from a German/UK perspective, suggests that 'pain' in this sense of the word can have educational benefits. Chapter 3 from France argues from a different position about the resistance of learners to engaging with what they perceive as a threat to their own self-concept. In this respect Chapter 3 almost begs the question as to whether one should give in and avoid individual pain being inflicted upon the learner and thereby avoid any harm to the learner's sense of self-concept. However, as explained in Chapter 2, a transfer of theory from one national or cultural context to another is not easily achieved. Although Chapter 4 from Germany argues that German *Pädagogik* and the UK's New Education Studies are becoming more alike, the question remains if and how the transfer of theory is ever possible.

However, before engaging with these chapters, it might be helpful to prepare for the element of pain that, as the title suggests, is essential to learning. Now, in general, titles should provide an indication of what is to be expected within the following text, but good titles also need a certain appeal or 'pull factor'. Titles have to evoke an interest for the prospective reader to actually engage with the text. It appears that the title has accomplished the pull factor in that you have read this far. Now it is up to the text to get you to continue reading. So what are these pains of learning? Normally, institutionalised learning in schools and universities is supposed to happen in a relaxed and enjoyable environment, free of stress and pain. For instance, Artelt et al. (cited in Ainley and Hidi, 2014: 205) explain:

> Education systems aim to enable students not just to acquire knowledge but also to be capable, confident and enthusiastic learners [...]. Beyond school, children and adults who have developed the ability and motivation to learn on their own initiative are well-placed to become lifelong learners.

Artlet et al. claim that the quality of learning and – even more – a learner's success in becoming a lifelong learner is the effect of motivation. They elaborate by explaining that

> ... the character of the experiences and the conditions that generate and support learning experiences are important issues for 21st-centrury educators.
>
> (*ibid*: 205)

Ainley and Hidi (2014: 216) go further by taking enjoyment and interest to be learning-relevant 'achievement emotions', i.e. as experiences that are essential to education. This is then a picture in which an individual's interest in learning is sparked off, or at least enhanced by, the enjoyable character of relevant experiences and by conditions that facilitate the emergence of such enjoyable experiences. However, less obvious is why such experiences should be more important for twenty-first-century educators and learners than they have ever been before. It can be assumed that both authors refer back to Stehr's (1994) characterisation of contemporary societies as 'knowledge-societies' where the demand for acquired knowledge and skills grew exponentially compared to previous centuries. Here is not the space to engage further with this attempt to create a specific sense of urgency for twenty-first-century educators. But what remains clear is that 'enjoyable' learning experiences are taken to be essential pre-cursors for a learner's motivation. Enjoyment is supposed to enhance motivation, and learners who enjoy school will be motivated to direct their voluntary attention to the sessions. Or, to put it differently, learners are likely to want to learn because they (mostly) appreciate being stimulated by the ideas offered to them within an amenable and interactive environment to become capable, confident and enthusiastic individuals.

But on second thought, there are qualitative concepts here (positive, enjoyable experiences, motivation, confidence, enthusiasm), qualities that are experienced by a single individual. This is not (yet) the place to explore this in any depth, but it is an important issue to be picked up again in Chapter 12 of the final section. For now it is important to be clear about the fact that experiencing certain aspects of school and learning provokes emotional responses that are the result of *unconscious* appraisal by the learner. Such appraisals rate situations as either desirable or to be avoided (Scherer, 1999). Joy or enjoyment constitute positive emotions, and humans seek to enhance their share of them. However, and as anyone will know, there are also unpleasant experiences that humans try to avoid. Disgust, sadness, anger, fear and shame are, for most people, experiences they think they could easily do without. These negative experiences do manifest themselves within education as well. One just has to think of the sadness occurring when having scored a mark in an assessment much worse than hoped or anticipated, the anger of being put on the spot when unprepared and unable to answer, the fear of not having lived up to one's own or others' expectations, as well as the shame when knowing that others witnessed one's embarrassing situations. These affective responses are familiar and frequent and they are all too often painful learning-related experiences. Probably now is the best time for a confession. In choosing the word 'pain' for the title, there was no intention to evoke any recollections of outdated – and thankfully outlawed – attempts to bring about positive changes to learning-related behaviour via corporeal punishments. The word 'pain' in this context tries to capture an array of negative experiences as they happen within education and that without the necessity that any physical harm is done. Pain in this context is thus more of the often overwhelming and negative feelings that befall the learner at times. When assessing institutionalised education in schools, colleges or universities, one invariably finds a mixture of positive and negative emotional states. All such states are integral parts of human life and an unavoidable part of educating as well as learning. However, when writing about the 'pains' of learning, one has to bear in mind that there is more to it than the mere practical pursuit of teaching (see Chapter 2). Beyond this it is equally possible to approach novel situations or problems with a hypothetical attitude, i.e. an attempt to rate what this specific sort of dynamic could do to challenge xenophobic or nationalist attitudes (see Chapter 3). Nevertheless, both ways of thinking about education have to be well founded on relevant theories. This is where one needs to begin to think about the possibility of picking and choosing from one (national) theory background to transfer what appears suitable to another (national) context (see Chapter 4).

Nevertheless, when focusing too much on motivation and enjoyment in learning there is a danger of neglecting the role and the importance of negative emotional states. We can fail to recognise that the individual experience of shame can make for a disposition to try harder next time, how the energy of anger can be turned (sublimated) into something positive, how sadness may spark off self-reflective episodes and a reflective engagement with the learning context. There is a danger of losing sight of the importance of all these combined emotional states in relation to learning and of the invariable dynamics in the overall experience of learning. Take the example of being put on the spot when not prepared or able to answer a question. It may evoke feelings of surprise, the surprise of being called up, along with a fear about the nature of the actual question being asked and of not being able to provide a suitable answer. Or the shame of failing to answer might be paired with anger about one's own inability to learn what was required but also directed about an unfair teacher or sniggering classmates. Finally, the example of a reluctant learner who doesn't want to learn a foreign language because it is perceived as part of the colonial take-over of one's own nation, i.e. an existential loss of identity (see Chapter 3). This cocktail of negative emotional episodes may, when carefully moderated by an experienced educator, result in a reflective assessment of why this event had happened and what could be done to avoid such occurrences in the future. Hence, the negative experiences could actually lead to an individual's striving to avoid more of this by the motivation to gain approval by complying with expectations and learning, or, even more, to alter one's sense of self. We would thus have not just the pairing of enjoyment and the motivation to have more of it but also the motivational striving to avoid negative experiences and to seek positive ones instead. On accepting such a view whereby negative experiences stand in a dynamic relation to motivation and positive experiences, a number of inferences could be drawn. But first, it is important to highlight one specific issue.

When speaking about emotional episodes – the emotions as they occur within the experiencing individual – these episodes are often conceived in the literature as an 'appraisal', i.e. as a kind of (pre-cognitive and pre-linguistic) judgement about situations or matters of fact, rather crudely divided into positive and negative (Scherer, 1999). But as these appraisals stand in a direct relation to a) the appraising individual and b) this individual's previous experiences, it is difficult to predict the emergence of a particular episode in specific situations simply because the experience of these appraisals is individual. One just has to think about an embarrassing moment, causing shame for one learner, while being the class-joker's reward and joy. In relation to the unpredictable nature of the educator's action, the input of the environment and the ensuing experiences, it is reasonable to speak of an, at least partial, breakdown of the causal link. The educator cannot know for sure what kind of reaction a certain situation may evoke, what kind of emotion will occur and how it will facilitate or hinder learning. Luhmann and Schorr (1979) refer to this causal uncertainty as a

'*Technologiedefizit*', i.e. a lack of precise and predictive technologies for successful teaching. Technology in this context does not refer to the availability of technological gadgets that are supposed to support teaching. Luhmann and Schorr rather use the term 'technology' in its basic sense as a (natural-) scientific approach uniting the Greek *techne*, in this case the art(istic skill) of educating with the *logos* (techno-logy) to give a reasoned, theory-guided application of general means to enhance teaching. Luhmann's and Schorr's point is that it must remain impossible to develop a reasonably precise technology of teaching because teaching always involves human beings who have their own individual reasons to act and may resist any predictions of their future behaviour. Given Luhmann's and Schorr's notion of the unpredictability of the results of educational action, it is now time to draw the inferences of the dynamic processes of emotive episodes as briefly described earlier.

1. The first point concerns the educator. If one were to accept that education is an art and not a science then it follows that carefully developed skills are needed for the educator to be able to skilfully create an environment in which the relevant dynamic processes are likely to emerge. It must be an environment where there is a constant need to moderate these processes in order to avoid hurt and to guide learners through processes in such a way that, through the skill and the caring attention of the educator, no lasting harm is done. It might be added here that the essential skill and experience, alongside a generally caring attitude of the educator, cannot be undercut by attempts to turn education into a science. A purely scientific and thus causal conception of human mental life via the utilisation of cognitive neuroscience, mind-brain-education or educational neuroscience (Mareschal *et al.*, 2013) can neither avoid the technology deficit nor replace the educator's skill and care. (For a detailed critique see Feldges *et al.*, 2017; Feldges, 2017).

   The second point of inference concerns the education system. Negative and sometimes even painful experiences are an unavoidable part of human existence. Therefore, it must equally be impossible to ban these experiences from the educational reality as it happens in the direct contact between the educational system's agents – educators – and learners. It is thus not possible simply to facilitate positive experiences while managing the negative experiences out. The dynamic is part of life and learning and, if educators are supposed to pay heed to this simple fact of life, educators have to be given the safe space to utilise this dynamic as well by the education system.

2. The previous point concerned the education system. Scholars from a variety of perspectives (see, for example, Luhmann, 2002 or Lyotard, 1984) have addressed the entirety of institutionalised education as a system. Education is seen to be a sub-system of an overall society, which itself is quite often also seen as a system. Some (Meyer and Scott, 1992) even go as far as to claim that it is impossible to disconnect the organisational structure of education from the overall structure of the social system. Any intended alteration of current educational practice would need to be in accordance with wider changes in a society's attitudes to education: what it is supposed to do and what it is expected to yield.

3. A final point in this limited list of possible inferences concerns the need for theory. If changes to the current conduct of educational practice are suggested, the one advocating change is always the one that needs to bring forward good reasons for the alteration of current practice and to lay out what advantages are to be expected. Hence, we need to consider education

as 'practice', but even more so the academic pursuit of studies into how education 'works'. This is the point of one of the following chapters (see Chapter 4) that focuses on a comparison between German Pädagogik and the recent emergence of New Education Studies in the UK. However, this needs supporting theories to contextualise specific aspects, clarify concepts and develop interdisciplinary links in order to be able to draw on neighbouring academic disciplines.

Hence, the comprehensive inclusion and utilisation of positive *and* negative experiences in educational practice would need changes on at least three levels: the practical, the institutional and the theoretical level of doing, researching and theorising about education.

Now the reader, having been hooked into reading this lengthy preface concerning the pains of learning, might ask what is the point of it. Well, the following chapters were briefly introduced at the end of Chapter 1, but now it will help to engage with a series of questions. These questions are not intended to be answered straight away or even after completing the reading of this section's chapters. They are more a set of thoughts to be parked in the back of your mind while reading. It is hoped that the questions will make you think differently about educational theory and practice.

- Is it possible to imagine educational practice that goes beyond the mere transition of skills and knowledge, and does it make sense to try to go beyond simply increasing the learner's ability to reproduce what was learnt for assessment purposes?
- Would it be possible, or desirable, to have a transformative impact upon the learner such that s/he is challenged to give up some former beliefs, including beliefs about him/herself? (See specifically Chapter 2 and 3 here.)
- Could such changes be achieved within an educational system that evidences its 'success' mainly by quantitative assessments of performance?
- What kind of justification would be available within the current (national) education policy to argue for such an intention? What kind of rationale would/could be sufficient not only to make attendance at school compulsory but also to justify the educator's intention to expose learners to painful (in the sense as 'pain' was defined here) experiences?
- To be more precise, and in the light of the dynamics of negative-positive experiences, would there be any long-term benefits that may outweigh the short-term pain?
- Would it be possible or desirable to transfer existing theories from different societies and graft them onto an already existing educational practice, or would such a transfer have to be more of a 'theory-appropriation' in which existing theories are partially utilised, adapted and further developed by the academic discipline of Education Studies?

References

Ainley, M., Hidi, S. (2014) Interest and Enjoyment. In R. Pekrun and L. Linnenbrink-Garcia (Eds) *International Handbook of Emotions in Education*. Abingdon: Routledge.

Feldges, T. (2017) Motivation and Experience versus Cognitive Psychological Explanation. *Humana Mente: Journal of Philosophical Studies*, **33**, pp. 1–18.

Feldges, T., Elton, J. and Pieczenko, S. (2017) The Art of Education or the Science of Education? *Educationalfutures*, **8**(1), pp. 50–67.

Kuh, G.D., Cruce, T.M., Shoup, R., Kinzie, J. and Gonyea, R.M. (2008). Unmasking the Effects of Student Engagement on First-Year College Grades and Persistence. *Journal of Higher Education*, 79(5), pp. 540–563.

Luhmann, N. (2002) *Das Erziehungssystem der Gesellschaft*. Frankfurt a.M: Suhrkamp.
Luhmann, N. and Schorr, K.E. (1979) *Reflexionsprobleme im Erziehungssystem*. Stuttgart: Suhrkamp.
Lyotard, J.F. (1984) *The Postmodern Condition: A report on knowledge*. Manchester: Manchester University Press.
Mareschal, D., Butterworth, B. and Tolmie, A. (2013) *Educational Neuroscience*. Chichester: Wiley Blackwell.
Meyer, J.W. and Scott, W.R. (1992) *Organisational Environments. Ritual and rationality*. London: Sage.
Mezirow, J. (2018) Transformative Learning Theory. In K. Illeris (Ed.) *Contemporary Theories of Learning*. Abingdon: Routledge, 114–127.
Scherer, K. (1999) Appraisal Theory. In T. Dalgleish and M. Power (Eds) *Handbook of Cognition and Emotion*. London: Wiley & Son.
Stehr, N. (1994) *Knowledge Societies*. New York: Sage.
Taylor, E.W. and Cranton, P. (2012) *The Handbook of Transformative Learning: Theory, research and practice*. San Francisco, CA: Jossey Bass.

2 Crossing the border

Sonia Pieczenko

Introduction

After retiring from years of lecturing in the UK's higher education sector I found myself in the classroom again. This time it was in Germany and this time I was a student. I had moved from the UK to Germany where it is necessary to gain a B1 qualification in the Common European Framework of Reference for Languages (CEFRL) to certify my ability to partake actively in German society. So there I sat as an immigrant amongst other immigrants who hoped to build a better future for themselves. Everyone was friendly and appeared eager to gain the necessary qualification as soon as possible. School began at eight in the morning and lasted until early afternoon, five days a week, attendance compulsory. On one particular occasion we had already sat at our tables and instruction had begun at eight o'clock sharp. Around ten minutes later the door opened and a young student slipped in silently, approaching his desk to sit down. The teacher let him reach the desk but interrupted him verbally while he tried to sit down. She told him in a friendly voice, but one that did not invite any response, that he should leave the classroom once again to have another attempt at entering late. This time first knocking on the door, then entering while bidding a good morning to everyone and briefly apologising for being late. The visibly embarrassed young man did just that, and everything was fine again. However, it left me with a strange feeling about the directness, almost bluntness of the teacher's instructions. I spoke with my German husband who found nothing unusual or blunt about the teacher's demand. Obviously, I had stumbled across a cultural difference in the way language was used.

This short scenario will serve as a basis for this chapter which introduces some aspects of German educational theorising. As a first step I will introduce and briefly discuss the peculiarly German educational concept of *Bildung*. *Bildung* requires the learner to experience uncomfortable moments of crisis as a mean to developing a reflecting attitude. However, if educational pursuit entails the inducement of uncomfortable crisis moments, then a convincing justification for inflicting such experiences is needed. This will be discussed in a second step by explaining the problem of 'normativity' and Kant's proposed solution to this problem. Nevertheless, even on accepting Kant's solution, the question remains as to whether his justification would be adequate to assess the above classroom scenario. I will, therefore, focus briefly upon Humboldt's notion of *Sprachenbildung* and Wittgenstein's discussion of language, language communities and the correct use of words. As the last step I will argue that educational practice has to be seen in the context of the cultural background of the society in which it unfolds. Nevertheless, with such immersion into German educational and philosophical discourses, it can be difficult to refer to literature in the English language as some of the concepts have not been prominent in British educational discourse.

The German concept of *Bildung*

Education happens within such highly complex social and environmental surroundings it is difficult to identify educational efforts empirically. Even more, humans develop individual motives and act wilfully upon such motives, rendering human action open and unpredictable. The system-theorist Niklas Luhmann (2002) speaks here of a *Technologiedefizit*: a lack of an established set of techniques for enabling predictable educational outcomes. The German academic discipline of Education Studies (*Erziehungswissenschaft* or *Pädagogik*) addresses this lack of established educational techniques and the general openness of human action by introducing some clearly defined foundational concepts (*Grundbegriffe*) around the main aspects of educational engagement (Krüger and Helsper, 2010). Hence, although Luhmann's technology deficit makes it difficult to causally connect actual practice with desired educational outcomes, it is at least possible to work with clearly classified and distinguishing concepts when formulating the desired achievements that – under ideal circumstances – pedagogical practice should yield. These concepts make it possible to distinguish wilful educational efforts from the tacit working of society known as 'socialisation', but also to separate the overarching concept of 'education' from the narrow sub-set of *Bildung* (see also Chapter 1). While, due to the technology deficit, in principle any intended educational results will still remain unpredictable, there is at least a clearly defined conceptual tool-set available that allows precise reference to the various methods and their underlying aims when engaging with learners.

The word '*Bildung*' can be literally translated into English as 'shaping' or 'forming', and, as an educational concept, means a 'forming' or a 'formative' effect on the learner. The concept has a long history in German discourse. From the eighteenth century onwards *Bildung* was used to determine the educational aims that go beyond the individual acquisition of learning contents and/or skills (Hörster, 2010). Although there is a continuing discussion about the current value of this old concept, German educationalists still discuss it as a means to reflect on the justification, the aims and the critique of educational practice (Koller, 2018), especially within an increasingly particularised and multi-cultural society as pointed out by Hörster (2010) (see also Chapter 4 in this volume.) However, an educational concept that proposes 'forming' (*bildende*) efforts implies a new role for the educator. The envisaged forming, according to Wilhelm von Humboldt (2010a), is intended to cater for a comprehensive unfolding of human developmental potential. Hence, this concept entails more than the mere transmission of content to be learned and skills to be accomplished by learners who simply absorb, learn and correctly display what they have learned when tested and assessed.

Humboldt's concept of *Bildung* is more about sparking off an individual trajectory that enables the learner to accomplish their individual potential. But this potential cannot develop within the hidden confines of an individual mind; *Bildung* necessitates the friction that ensues when a human being faces the resistance of the world outside him/herself (Humboldt, 2010a). Hence, developmental growth is an individual achievement that results from the successful mastering of the challenges to what one thought or felt before and which now requires a new or revised answer. To be clear, the process of *Bildung* requires more than merely encountering new facts: *Bildung* depends upon the actual work of engaging with these challenges and thereby altering one's experience of the world, of others, and of oneself. The obstacle of a resistant world is the stumbling block posed by the experience that things in one's environment turn out to be different from what one expected. This leads to a crisis moment that can serve as a basis for initiating the transformative process known as *Bildung* (Meyer-Drawe, 2012). There is a discussion around this crisis moment. Piaget (2001) held the view that this critical mismatch (disequilibrium) between expectation and actual experience could bear educational fruit via a cognitively mediated 'accommodation'. Even newer accounts of the concept see no problem in leaving the need for a cognitive mediation in place (Koller, 2018), despite the fact that such an account fails to explain why cognitive deliberations should (or could) evoke the uncomfortable experience of this crucial crisis moment that is of key-importance for *Bildung* to happen. Some psychologists do acknowledge that in order to capture the individual commitment to learn – Barnett (2007) called it 'a will to learn' – one has to take the individual and this individual's experiences as the seedbed for ensuing individual motivations into account (Holzkamp, 1995). This commitment to the experiential dimension of the learner is the main driver of the (educational-) phenomenological discourse that favours the view that the direct encounter of a crisis moment is one that needs to be experienced (Meyer-Drawe, 2012; Meyer-Drawe, 2019), one that causes emotions and feelings before it becomes available to cognitive processing (Pieczenko, 2019). However, and despite these continuous debates, it is uncontested that the importance of this crisis moment is the precursor to initiating the individual work that needs to be done to master and incorporate such crisis moments individually.

But if *Bildung* depends upon these crisis moments, then it is – at least partially – the task of the educator to guide learners towards appropriate challenges and to allow them to utilise these while supporting them during the process. The gain of this sometimes disturbing but always challenging process is, according to Humboldt (2010a), the facilitation of individual freedom: freedom to assess the facts of a situation and freedom to reach one's own reasoned judgements about them. But these judgements are always value-laden, i.e. judgements that always depend on social and individually held values. The resulting freedom is thus one that emanates from a specific, self-critical, reflective but not at all self-doubting (!) mode of engaging with one's world. Much more could be said about this complex concept, but what is important here is the realisation that if the individual experience of a crisis is key to the process of *Bildung*, then it follows invariably that:

a. the (negative) moment of a crisis cannot and should not be purged from educational practice, and
b. the individual experience of a crisis gains centre stage and should not be ignored by educational theorising.

Returning to the classroom scenario at the beginning of the chapter, the late-arriving learner encountered such a crisis moment. What he deemed as appropriate turned out not to fit the current context. In that respect the teacher's intervention could probably be seen as a 'forming' attempt. However, even if we agree that it is, there is still the question as to whether it was a skilful attempt. And this is a twofold question: one asking for an answer about the justification for inflicting such a negative experience upon a learner, the other regarding the appropriateness in the particular circumstances. The first question regarding the justification is known as the problem of 'normativity' and that will be the topic of the next subsection.

> **Questions for discussion**
>
> Have a look at the Standford Encyclopedia of Philosophy (https://plato.stanford.edu) and enter the word *Bildung* in the search engine. You can see how persistent a topic of German philosophy and the philosophy of education this concept was and still is. While following some of the entries you may want to start thinking about how useful you think the concept is to your own teaching practice. Could you see any obstacles to utilise it in your own teaching?

The problem of normativity

Already in 1916 Dewey (1942) proposed that educational practices should serve the self-maintenance of democratic societies by educating learners to be able to live in such a society as free agents (Feldges, 2019). As convincing as that might initially sound to most readers, it comes with an underlying problem: if education is supposed to cultivate freedom, how can it ever be warranted to impose such educational practices upon learners to cultivate freedom by actually *curbing* their freedom by exposing them to the stress of experiencing crisis moments? This surely is at best contradictory. The question *of how could it be justified to force learners to be educated to be free* does not play an important role in UK discourses about education. However, it is the source of rich and still ongoing discussions in Germany where it is known as the 'problem of normativity' (Meseth et al., 2019). It is a genuine philosophical problem concerning the underlying norms and values of education, and it aims to reveal a justificatory foundation for all educational efforts. One has to think of this as, on the one hand trying to rely upon empirical assessments of practice (UK) while, on the other hand, engaging with the underlying justification for this practice (Germany). It is possible to measure facts and social occurrences to gain an empirically founded picture about educational inequality. This can be done by assessing the extent of the problem, by determining which groups are most disadvantaged, or by trying to reveal attitudes, opinions and assumptions of the disadvantaged groups. However, although all such assessments carry a concern for disadvantaged learners, they nevertheless do not address the underlying question: the normative, the philosophical question of why? Why should one actually bother about the equality of chances? Why is it desirable for currently disadvantaged groups to have the chance to gain educational success? This is the important difference between *what is* in practice and *what ought to be* in practice (see, for example, Mecheril, 2010).

Emanuel Kant formulated this problem pointedly in his 1803 *Lectures on Pedagogy*. Here Kant (1978) works on the tension of, on the one hand, that learners have to submit to a legal compulsion of being educated while, on the other hand, learners are supposed to increase their ability to make use of their freedom. Kant (*ibid*: 451) explains:

> Thus compulsion is necessary! How do I cultivate freedom via compulsion? I have to get my pupil to tolerate a compulsion of his freedom while I have to guide him to make good use of his freedom. [...] In order to learn he must, from early years onwards, feel the unavoidable resistance of society, get accustomed to the difficulty to maintain himself, to disperse with and to gain in order to be independent. [*gendered personal pronoun in the original, my translation*]

Kant is thus very clear about the fact that pedagogical practice is not free from compulsion while also and invariably being tied to social rules and norms. But here some historical background will help in understanding Kant's solution to the problem of normativity, namely that compulsion is necessary. Kant was writing after the French revolution and his text exemplifies truly enlightened thought. The period of the Enlightenment saw the demise of the absolutist, hierarchically structured state with its limited opportunities and regulated obligations according to one's right of birth (Thoma, 2015). This is the background for Kant's vision of a free society as a space of, more or less, indefinite and limitless opportunities for reasonable free agents. But in order to be such a free agent, one has to be able to make independent decisions suitable for such an open environment and to reduce environmental contingency in order to cope successfully (Luhmann, 1984). Hence, it is no longer possible to simply follow the rules of a (no longer existing) static society. What is needed is an independent agent, ready to continuously encounter and reflect upon new and challenging situations. Someone who, based upon individual reasoning, is able to take a position and to pursue some options or to avoid others according to one's own judgements. Hence, a rational and free agent would need to have had the experience that emanates from encountering something that turns out to be different from what one previously thought, scrutinising it in the light of available evidence and reaching a reasoned judgement. This agent would need the practice of dealing with this general openness and the challenge it brings to the successful conduct of one's own life. What is needed is someone who is sufficiently trained in taking a stance and making a decision, someone who is able to adapt in a constantly changing world. One would need to be formed by *Bildung* to be prepared to stand up to or to even relish the challenges of plurality and contingency in an open society.

Kant's solution to justifying the imposed and uncomfortable experience of being challenged sees the pursuit of *Bildung* as a specific and transformative form of education. And Kant (*ibid*: 451) sees this as a pre-condition to preparing the learner '… to make good use of his freedom …'. But some aspects of education appear to have little to do with such an aim. One could thus be tempted to ask the question whether Kant's proposed solution to the problem of normativity could hold for less social – and thus freedom-centred – aspects of the curriculum as well. However, excluding some aspects of the curriculum as being of less importance when trying to support the forming of a learner to make good use of her/his freedom is based upon a wrong assumption. The ability to engage in a critical, rational and self-reflective manner of thinking is simply helpful in *all* areas of learning. Physics, for instance, does not immediately spring to mind when it comes to deciding how to enable learners to integrate themselves in a free society as free and rational agents. However, if one takes current research that points towards increasing, human-made warming of planet Earth's atmosphere as fake news, one's reasoning is not aligned with available and verified facts. Hence, such dismissive judgements about this issue would be unsubstantiated and most probably simply wrong. The ability to make good use of one's freedom is not limited to specific subject areas; it is a way of life that alters one's relation with the surrounding world and its challenges.

This very brief excursus cannot fully do justice to Kant's philosophy or the multifaceted problem of normativity. Nevertheless, it is still possible to the claim that:

1. Humboldt's concept of *Bildung*, as a specific form of education, has use-value for the learner educated in this way;
2. the uncomfortable challenges of *Bildung* can be justified with Kant's proposed solution that one has to accept the compulsion of education in order to become independent.

> **Questions for discussion**
>
> What are your thoughts about the difference between empirically accessing educational practice as opposed to a philosophical foundation to justify education? What are your thoughts about Kant's solution to the problem of normativity? Can it suffice to justify children being 'robbed of their childhood' by being confined to schools?

Returning to the young man turning up late and facing the teacher's injunction, it is safe to assume that he must have experienced a moment of crisis, that he must have felt ashamed, insecure, probably threatened, probably even afraid. Based on these feelings and experiences he was able to cognitively engage: should he comply or object to the demands of the teacher? In complying he overcame the crisis and he most certainly learned something about the importance of punctuality in a German context. Of course, one might say, this could have probably also been achieved by the teacher seeking a quiet word with him afterwards. But could it really?

At the end of this section we are left with Kant's proclaimed compulsion to endure embarrassing moments as part of an overall attempt to provide the learner with the ability to lead a self-determined life in an independent manner. However, having a general principle that could serve as a justification for action is one thing; another is the question whether this general principle could actually find application in a specific context. Hence, the question of whether a solution is appropriate, and this is the subject of the following section.

The concept of '*Sprachenbildung*'

When trying to discuss the appropriateness of exposing the learners to 'forming' (*bildende*) challenges, the discussion will unfold around Humboldt's concept of *Sprachenbildung*, i.e. the forming effects brought about by the learning of another language. The discussion will further use the classroom scenario introduced above: the social context of a group of learners trying to master a new language to prepare themselves for an independent – and hopefully successful – life in the country they have chosen as their new home. Hence, the specific ways in which such a society, Germany in this case, makes use of their spoken language gains importance. It is important to remember that relations between the individual and the environment are always mediated via language, whether the language is spoken, written or merely thought. This equally holds for attempts to induce the challenges associated with *Bildung*. Previously held opinions, convictions and attitudes are challenged, usually by skilful questioning. This is what Humboldt (2010b) had in mind when he stated that for humans there is no extra-linguistic locus: everything they do is always shrouded in a veil provided by language. But not every language is the same. And therefore Humboldt (2010b: 433) claims '… every language always entails a particular view of the world'.

The introductory scenario portrayed a specific manner in which the learner was made to rehearse the correct way of entering a classroom late. He was not asked if he 'would want to step outside and have another attempt', and the teacher did not even claim to be 'sorry'. Horribly rude! some readers may have thought, but in doing so they would have fallen for their own cultural situated-ness. Hence, they would have applied the British way of being polite and taken this – their own frame of cultural and linguistic reference – into the context of another culture and language. As I have learned by now, within a German context, the question whether 'one would want to …' is taken as just that, i.e. a question that requires an affirmative or negative response, depending upon the inclinations of the one questioned. The idea that such a question could have an assumed appealing or even commanding implication would be lost to most Germans, not being brought up to see through the subtlety of such a polite display. Much to our shared amusement my German husband often told me about his own embarrassment in relation to his linguistic mishaps and misunderstandings when he immersed himself into life and work in the UK. And indeed, there are a good number of crisis moments waiting for everyone who has learned the vocabulary and grammar but nevertheless stumbles into the traps provided by the simplest of everyday encounters. This felt embarrassment forces one to learn something more than vocabulary and grammar: it serves as a drive, a motivation to adjust one's way of speaking and using the language, which – on a technical level – one probably felt competent in. Humboldt (2010b: 434) recognised this clearly and explained: '… the learning of a foreign language is the acquisition of a new point of view'. Such a new point of view challenges the previously held view and, if not sufficiently acquired, will always contain the danger of humorous or even dangerous misunderstandings. The transformative element of *Bildung* is laid bare here: a crisis moment leads to the transformation of the way in which one relates to the surrounding world; one not only learns vocabulary and grammar but also a new way of assessing the world and her/himself within such a world. But how is it possible that learning the words and rules of a foreign language will still not suffice to master this learned language? What else could there be that governs the use of a language? Wittgenstein (1968), in his later *Philosophical Investigations*, assessed language and language usage. Wittgenstein (sec. 43) explains that the meaning of a word is mostly fixed by its correct usage within a language as spoken by the language community. Wittgenstein is thus suggesting that the correct use of a specific word is not only regulated by the language's grammar. The grammatical rules one learns at school are, for him, a mere 'surface grammar' (sec. 664). This formal set of rules regulates arranging the words in order to be understandable. But this has to be differentiated from what Wittgenstein calls 'depth grammar' that provides a far-reaching web of rules with a decisive matrix according to which it is possible to judge whether a certain word makes sense or not. Depth grammar provides the ability to reach a decision on the appropriateness when using, for example, the word *pussy* as opposed to *cat*, or *happy* as opposed to *gay* within their specific situational and temporal contexts (Feldges, 2013).

Questions for discussion

Our own cultural situated-ness is normally taken as a given; we apply it constantly and without even realising that we are doing so. Can you think of a couple of culturally founded baseline assumptions that guide your access to your surroundings as English, Welsh, Scottish or Northern Irish students – or as British students/educators – or even as European, Western students/educators? Can you engage in an attempt to imagine how some of your shared attitudes and customs may be experienced by people who do not share your cultural background?

While the choice of the wrong word from the pairs of examples mentioned here – and there are many more – could cause some laughter, there is a more important aspect. The laughter caused by the use of an incorrect word (i.e. we do not say it like this anymore!) reveals something deeper. The linguistic community of English-speaking Britons traditionally found sexual innuendo and double entendres quite funny. Although this sort of humour will hopefully lose ground as time goes on, the fact that it once was a quite popular form of British light entertainment (e.g. the 'Carry on ...' films) serves to highlight how a linguistic community charges words with meanings beyond their literal ones. Hence, the mere learning of the vocabulary will not suffice, there is more that needs to be accomplished and constantly updated. A linguistic community changes, and these changes are always and invariably engrained in the community's language. Another example is the equalising use of the second person singular pronoun 'you' in addressing people regardless of how well they are known to the speaker is another case. Germans, for instance, consider this as impolite or even rude and differentiate by using the more intimate '*Du*' for family and friends, while others are addressed formally as '*Sie*'. The British way of nevertheless making a similar distinction in addressing someone as '*you*' to then add a *Sir* or *Madam* to it is perceived as a stilted manner of speech by most Germans and, as my husband told me, one thing he never really understood.

However, both Humboldt and Wittgenstein have a point: learning another language indeed alters one's point of view, and the 'correct' use of words is regulated by more than vocabulary and surface grammar. Nevertheless, as much as a language transmits what is supposed to be polite, funny or how people speak to each other, they also convey cultural values in general, as for instance, the British emphasis on a specific form of politeness. But other cultures and linguistic communities differ from what is the standard in Britain. Germans speak more directly and do not veil their expectations; but that does not mean they are not polite; youngsters happily give up their seats on the bus for older passengers.

Nevertheless, and much closer to the opening scenario, Germans are fond of punctuality. According to the German state-funded broadcaster *Deutsche Welle*, the Germans are pathologically punctual and always on time (Zudeick, 2012). A good number of proverbs stress the importance of punctuality and young Germans are exposed to them – and with that to the language-conveyed importance of punctuality – from their nursery days onwards. Zudeick (2012) specifies this cultural phenomenon on the website by saying that:

> Nearly 85 per cent of Germans say they take their appointments seriously and expect others to do the same. In Germany, the rule of thumb is that it's better to be five minutes early than one minute late.

With the cultural expectation to be on time it is understandable that the linguistic community developed these punctuality-stressing proverbs to instil a sense of the need to be punctual, not only in the younger Germans but also in those who decide later in life to stay and live in this society.

Moving into such a different (German) background most certainly changes the frame of reference that governs the appropriateness of language use (Dirim and Mecheril, 2010). I had left the realm of one linguistic community (British and politeness-obsessed) and entered another one (German and punctuality-obsessed). Such a different linguistic frame includes traces of community values and customs, and it renders those previously held dear by the one who has 'crossed the border' to be less important or even outright wrong. In this respect the question as to whether the reaction of the teacher in the opening scenario was polite or not is one that immediately arose for me. The other learners in the group did not consider it to be of any concern, although they – of course – were not German, but probably because they were not British either? The same seems to apply to the question whether the teacher's concerns would not have been better raised in a private conversation with the late-arriving learner. If Germans are indeed pathologically punctual, then the forming (*bildende*) crisis moment of the negative experience of arriving late is one best encountered in the safe environment of a language class, and it is one all learners should be able to participate in. If the goal of a forming language education is to equip learners to '… get accustomed to the difficulty to maintain himself, to disperse with and to gain in order to be independent …' then, in order to learn, one has '… to feel the unavoidable resistance of society' (Kant, 1978: 451).

Conclusion

With reference to Humboldt's concept of the forming effects of language learning and Wittgenstein's considerations regarding the depth grammar in relation to different linguistic communities, it is now possible to assess the opening scenario once again. Although I still feel a bit uneasy about the way in which the young man was made to feel, I do now, having lived here in Germany for more than two years, appreciate the idea and intention behind the teacher's course of action. She wanted to pose a challenge to the learner's belief that arriving late and without apologising to the class and the teacher for being late was acceptable as long as it did not pose a major disruption for all. The intervention made it clear to all how important punctuality is in German everyday and work life. However, there is a second side to this chapter. Although the discussion might have been taken as an attempt to justify the teacher's behaviour, it was not my main aim. The chapter developed aspects of German educational theorising to critically discuss the practice or even the very foundation of educational practice. Hence, while serving as a background to assessing specific practices these theories also address the question of why education is necessary at all. And if, to stay with the example case of educating migrants, the goal of immigration policies goes beyond the shutting of the borders but rather recognises the humane and economic benefits of inward migration in general, then the question of *why* the state educates new arrivals is one that needs to come before the question of *how* to achieve this. While there is a massive discussion raging about this question in Germany (see, for example, Brinkmann and Sauer, 2016; Mecheril, 2010), education in the UK remains mostly bothered with the question of *how* to educate. I leave it to the reader to think about whether the 'how' question could ever be sufficiently answered when ignoring the underlying 'why' question.

Summary

In relation to an example case the following aspects of German educational theorising were discussed:

- The concept of *Bildung* as a subset of all educational efforts.
- The forming effects of *Bildung* cannot be shaped or predicted by an instructor; it is dependent upon the learner's own engagement with an experienced crisis.
- Leading learners towards the disturbing experience of these crisis moments need a justification.
- Kant proposed a solution to this problem of normativity by pointing to the fact that pupils need to be prepared to live an independent life in an open and contingent environment.

- Humboldt suggested that even the learning of a language entails crisis moments and so the learning of a language also entails the acquisition of a particular view of life.
- With these considerations, it is possible to turn back and question one's own tacit beliefs and customs and to question these critically.

Recommended reading

Baraldi, C. and Corsi, G. (2016) *Niklas Luhmann: Education as a social system*. Berlin: Springer.
Losonsky, M. (Ed.) (1999) *Humboldt: 'On Language': On the diversity of human language construction and its influence on the mental development of the human species*. Cambridge: Cambridge University Press.

References

Barnett R. (2007) *A Will to Learn – Being a student in an age of uncertainty*. Maidenhead: Open University Press.
Brinkmann H.U. and Sauer M. (2016) *Einwanderungsgesellschaft Deutschland – Entwicklung und Stand der Integration*. Wiesbaden: Springer.
Dewey J. (1942) *Democracy and Education*. New York: Macmillan.
Dirim I. and Mecheril P. (2010) Die Sprache(n) der Migrationsgesellschaft. In P. Mecheril (Ed.) *Migrationspädagogik*. Wiesbaden: Beltz Verlag.
Feldges T. (2013) *My Late Father's Pain*. Online. Available at: https://www.researchgate.net/publication/281639820_Is_it_possible_to_speak_about_pain (Accessed 27 July 2021).
Feldges T. (Ed.) (2019) *Philosophy and the Study of Education*. Abingdon: Routledge.
Holzkamp K. (1995) *Lernen – Subjektwissenschaftliche Grundlegung*. Frankfurt a.M: Campus.
Hörster R. (2010) Bildung. In H.H. Krüger and W. Helsper (Eds) *Einführung in Grundbegriffe und Grundfragen der Erziehungswissenschaft*. Opladen: Verlag Barbara Budrich.
Humboldt W.v. (2010a) *Gesamtausgabe, Werke I*. Darmstadt: WBG.
Humboldt W.v. (2010b) *Gesamtausgabe, Werke IV*. Darmstadt: WBG.
Kant E. (1978) *Werksausgabe – Band 12. Schriften zur Anthropologie, Geschichtsphilosophie, Politik und Pädagogik*. Frankfurt a.M: Suhrkamp.
Koller H.C. (2018) *Bildung anders Denken*. Stuttgart: W. Kohlhammer.
Krüger H.H. and Helsper W. (2010) *Einführung in Grundbegriffe und Grundfragen der Erziehungswissenschaft*. Opladen: Verlag Barbara Budrich.
Luhmann N. (1984) *Soziale Systeme – Grundriß einer allgemeinen Theorie*. Frankfurt a.M: Suhrkamp.
Luhmann N. (2002) *Das Erziehungssystem der Gesellschaft*. Frankfurt a.M: Suhrkamp.
Mecheril P. (2010) *Migrationspädagogik*. Wiesbaden: Beltz Verlag.
Meseth W., Casale R., Tervooren A. and Zirfas J. (2019) *Normativität in der Erziehungswissenschaft*. Wiesbaden: Springer.
Meyer-Drawe K. (2012) *Diskurse des Lernens*. München: Wilhelm Fink.
Meyer-Drawe K. (2019) Lernen als Erfahrung. In M. Brinkmann (Ed.) *Phänomenologische Erziehungswissenschaft von ihren Anfängen bis heute – Eine Anthologie*. Wiesbaden: Springer.
Piaget J. (2001) *The Language and Thought of the Child*. London: Routledge.
Pieczenko S. (2019) Educational Phenomenology: Is there a need and space for such a pursuit? In T. Feldges (Ed.) *Philosophy and the Study of Education*. Abingdon: Routledge.
Thoma H. (2015) *Handbuch Europäische Aufklärung – Begriffe, Konzepte, Wirkung*. Stuttgart: J.B. Metzler.
Wittgenstein L. (1968) *Philosophical Investigations*. London: Macmillan.
Zudeick P. (2012) *Germans and Punctuality*. Online. Available at: https://www.dw.com/en/germans-and-punctuality/a-16430264 (Accessed 2 August 2012).

3 Language learning in France
De-territorialising language and culture

Joshua N.W. Gray

Introduction

From 2nd August 2021, French citizens renewing their identity card received a card which features titles in both French and English. The vehemence with which this news was met on social media reveals how the English language is seen by some French nationals: words such as 'imperialism', 'submission' or even 'invasion' show it to be the language of an enemy, something to resist.

What then of language learning, and specifically, the teaching and learning of English as a second language? While in France language learning is now compulsory as early as primary school and continues through to the baccalaureate, both language and culture still appear to be considered as territorial entities. To this extent, language learning is not seen as enriching students' linguistic and cultural repertoires but as a form of learning about another country, different from their own. This difference, while it is presented in a positive light in national curricula, nevertheless corresponds to a form of 'othering' by which foreign nations are first and foremost defined by their *otherness*. This *otherness* is then either feared, as mentioned above, or admired.

Following the works of intercultural thinkers such as Kramsch and Zarate, this chapter aims to show that such a territorialised model of language learning no longer adequately accounts for the social reality learners face in a globalised and hyperconnected world.

Language and culture as territorial entities

In the past decades, the intrinsic link between language and culture has become well accepted in many countries by researchers, teachers and policymakers alike. Indeed, the French curricula from primary school through to the end of compulsory schooling all include references to the importance of cultural learning. The compulsory curriculum for high school students mentions that they should gain 'knowledge of the culture and history which the languages studied convey' so as to better understand 'the cultural anchorage of every language' (Ministry of Education, 2019 my translation].

However, this integration of culture often appears to view culture as both territorialised and reified. The third cycle curriculum (for pupils approximately 9–12 years old) explains that language learning must be anchored in the 'cultural realities of the countries whose language is being studied' (Ministry of Education, 2015: 38) [my translation]. The same document mentions 'ways of life, holidays and traditions', as well as 'historical and geographical notions' and 'people' 'from the culture of the area concerned' (*ibid:* 38).

DOI: 10.4324/9781003223528-4

This raises several questions, not least of which is how to understand the term 'cultural reality'. However, it is the link being established between culture, language and country which is of particular interest here. The idea of nations with a language, a territory and a culture, remains in popular opinion, as well as among language teachers.

> Hence, the propensity of foreign language teachers to view language as a national entity, native speakers as foreign nationals (for example, the French spoken in Quebec being seen as but a variant of the 'real' French spoken by the French-French in France), and culture also mainly in national terms.
> (Kramsch, et al., 1996: 100)

Thus, when culture is discussed in language teaching, it is often as the culture which is associated with the target language. 'Culture' in language teaching and learning is usually defined pragmatically as a/the culture associated with a language being learnt' (Byram, 2002: 193). When teaching a 'foreign' language, teachers and educational policies tend to consider that there is a one-to-one correspondence between a given language and the culture which is associated with it. The term 'foreign' is a natural product of this conception of culture.

> Whole edifices of curriculum, teaching practices, and policies for language teaching are constructed on the assumption that entire languages can be considered foreign, with pervasive repercussions in curriculum, program design, and pedagogy.
> (Lo Bianco, 2014: 312)

Thus, culture is studied in its basic form, as a set of characteristics, supposedly common to all speakers of the target language, and thus, to all members of the cultural community, itself constituted as intrinsically *other*.

As Zarate points out, textbooks and curricula often favour 'a simplified description of a foreign language and culture' as 'centred around belonging to a national entity' (Zarate 2008: 173) [my translation]. Furthermore, she explains that 'this simplification produces didactic compromises which lead, for example:

- Either to an enchanted vision of the country whose language is being taught, borrowing, for example, touristic valorisation techniques leading to the broadcasting of a reductive approach to social reality which lived experience can refute daily,
- Or to a generalising approach of national reality, listing a limited number of psychological, social and historical characteristics which describe the nation as a set of factual data which freeze the description and set it outside of time. (*ibid*: 173).

In fact, the latter vision discussed by Zarate leads naturally to the former. Indeed, the reduction of culture to a set of factual data cannot account for the lived experience of the individuals who constitute it, and can only lead to stereotypical views of culture, for better – as is the case in language classes – or for worse. Thus, language classrooms often rely on a conception of a culture as directly corresponding to a nation, its language, and its territory, be it one's own domestic culture or a foreign culture. This gives us 'an implicit view of a monolingual learner in a homogeneous society focused on a similar homogeneous society of native speakers' (Byram 2002: 43).

> **Question for discussion**
>
> Does the vision of language and culture as territorialised extend beyond education?

A concept of 'nation' inherited from history

This conception of culture corresponds to a specific period in history. The modern period saw European governments mount considerable efforts to unify their respective nations, forging the correspondence between a language, a culture and a territory. According to Kramsch, language teaching has remained deeply rooted in this modern period, as exemplified by the following features which many language teachers take for granted:

> the existence of nation-states, each with their national language and their national culture; the existence of standardized languages with their stable grammars and dictionaries that ensure the good usage of the language by well-educated citizens that FL learners are expected to emulate; the superiority of national languages over regional dialects and patois; the clear boundaries between native and foreign languages and among foreign languages so that one can clearly know whether someone is speaking French, German, or Chinese, standard Spanish or regional Spanish; the codified norms of correct language usage and proper language use that language learners have to abide by for fear of not being understood or not being accepted by native speakers.
>
> (Kramsch 2014: 297).

Today, according to Kramsch, this modern period is being called into question. 'Today, the modern and the late modern worlds coexist with increasing unease' (Kramsch, 2014: 297). A number of factors, which have been mentioned above, are posing a challenge to the Modern conception of culture. Indeed, globalisation, mass migration and global communication via the internet pose a challenge to this strict correspondence between culture, language and territory. National structures which are rarely questioned in our daily lives struggle to coexist with features linked to cultural exchange, moving populations and open borders.

But these structures are not natural structures: borders are drawn, language is standardised. This is the product of a deliberate effort, the results of which are often taken for granted. As Lo Bianco explains, nations are geopolitical spaces whose languages have often been diverse and varied. The construction of nations in today's sense requires cultural and linguistic harmonisation.

> A central part of the argument concerns the spatial distribution of languages, the result of centuries of effort by states, national and pre-national alike, to organize who speaks what where, conducted through overt and covert strategies of language planning.
>
> (Lo Bianco 2014: 312–313).

National languages are thus adopted by decree and standardised to create unity inside the nation and in clear opposition to foreign nations. Thus, the same process which created nations also created foreigners.

> The term foreign relativizes language and space, so that particular geopolitical spaces, constituted as national states, are dedicated exclusively or dominantly to standard forms of particular languages, and are differentiated from neighbouring or distant geopolitical spaces dedicated to different languages.
>
> (Lo Bianco 2014: 313)

Thus, the creation of the nation by linguistic and cultural harmonisation also created the foreign nation. The foreign is like the domestic, but *other*: another language, another culture, another territory. According to Liddicoat and Taylor-Leech, this linguistic harmonisation was born during the sixteenth century but gained momentum in the eighteenth and nineteenth centuries. They quote Geeraerts to explain its two principal motivations.

> The ideology that a single unified nation-state required a single language gained particular impetus with the French Revolution, during which the argument for the necessity of a single language for the state made based on two main perspectives (Geeraerts, 2003): one pragmatic – promoting effective communication and access to state institutions and political functions – and one symbolic – creating and reinforcing a single, unified identity.
>
> (Liddicoat and Taylor-Leech 2015: 2)

This vision of culture as associated with a language and a territory is often discussed in so-called comparative intercultural studies. Comparative models identify characteristics of a culture and compare them to those of another, seeking similitudes and differences (Coffey 2013: 268).

> Such research tends to characterize cultural groups, typically nations, on a limited set of dimensions pertaining to values, self-construals and so on, such as individualism/collectivism (Hofstede 2001) or independence/interdependence (Markus and Kitiyama 1991).
>
> (Noels *et al.*, 2012: 60)

These researchers are careful not to 'essentialise' these characteristics. 'Because they are tendencies, this frame of reference varies among members of a cultural group and may shift within any individual depending upon the context' (*ibid*: 60). However, once a given characteristic has been identified as typical, all behaviour which goes against this typicity is characterised as an exception. To this extent, these models are sometimes called 'neo-essentialist'. Though exceptions are admitted, cultures are still considered as unified and homogeneous and thus warrant comparison. 'Inherent in comparative models of culture types is the naturalised assumption that cultures are in a relation of relative congruence or divergence' (Coffey, 2013: 268).

The creation of otherness

This conception of national unity is present not only in research and in politics but also, and more or less openly, in education policy. Education is a key tool in successfully implementing national unity, but this is done at the expense of diversity and heterogeneity, which are perceived as problematic for this vision of national culture. '[…] education has often been understood as working to reduce diversity in order to promote something that is seen as preferable (better communication, national identity, etc.)' (Liddicoat et al., 2014: 272).

Given that in many countries, including France, national governments are, to a greater or lesser degree, responsible for education, this vision can be all the more present in educational policy. When an education system is built by a state or a nation, its goal is often to construct a shared vision of identity, which can seem at odds with the 'discovery of alterity borne by foreign languages' (Zarate 2008: 174) [my translation].

> A nation-centred approach can culminate in the representation of a homogeneous national identity based on the principle of 'living together', united by the cult of the ancestors, a territory which resists, or doesn't resist, invasions, endogamous filiation, the rejection of religious, regional, ethnic, or linguistic minorities, in favour of a group, sometime itself a minority, but dominant.
>
> (ibid: 174)

Thus, once a restrictive vision of culture is adopted, culture can serve to exclude minorities and close the country upon itself, rather than opening it to *otherness*, either inside or outside its borders. This above-mentioned vision, which Zarate calls 'nation-centred', is opposed to a national vision 'which integrates in national memory, by democratic consensus, the memories of minority groups, the ruptures in national history, the contribution of diasporas to the national community' (ibid: 174).

When considering national culture as unified, homogeneous, and immutable, stereotypes emerge as they are themselves immutable and attributable to sections of the population in their entirety. 'The images that emerge from stereotypes are often stable and decontextualized' (Moore, 2003: 16). The *other* is thus reduced to a set of stereotypes, the most fundamental of which is his/her *otherness* itself. Considering the *other as other* first and foremost, that is, reducing the *other* to his/her very *otherness*, is what is called 'othering'.

> Othering consists of 'objectification of another person or group' or 'creating the other', which puts aside and ignores the complexity and subjectivity of the individual (Abdallah-Pretceille, 2003). In intercultural research, culturalism and essentialism, among other things, have tended towards Othering by imposing cultural elements as explanations for people's behaviours, encounters, opinions ...
>
> (Dervin, 2012: 187).

This process of othering is inevitable to a degree, as the other is indeed *other*. However, the concepts of 'identity' and 'alterity' which are forged when national culture is considered in a reductive manner as a unified and homogeneous identity, are not the only ways of accounting for identity and alterity. In a world defined by mass migration and worldwide communication, such binary conceptions cannot account for the reality of sociocultural relations.

When it comes to language, more specifically, Kramsch, following Bommaert et al., elaborates on three such binary oppositions which we have inherited from the modern period. As we shall see, traces of all three can be found in French curricula.

Firstly, order and disorder underpin the idea of correct and incorrect usage and of standardised national culture as being preferable to local dialects or regional accents. In the case of France, the notion of correct usage remains a central aspect of language learning, with the standard assessment guidelines for the General and Technological Baccalaureate granting a quarter of the total number of points to the 'correctness' of both written and oral language. (Ministry of Education, 2020: 2–3).

Secondly, purity and impurity mean codeswitching, or translanguaging, are to be avoided and make bilingualism a double monolingualism, a mastery of two languages in their pure form. Here too, French curricula encourage teachers and students to 'communicate and interact as much as possible in their foreign language', with references to codeswitching and translanguaging noticeably absent (Ministry of Education, 2019: 2).

Third and finally, normality and abnormality present monolingual natives (preferably from a dominant social class) as the norm, and learners are to aim to emulate them (Kramsch 2014: 298). On this point, there has been a shift in French curricula which now recommend a 'more realistic' assessment of students' pronunciation than a native speaker model (Ministry of Education, 2019: 4). However, presenting this as more realistic tends to show that the ideal remains unchanged.

Thus, *otherness* is created by defining what is normal, pure and correct and establishing those who do not conform as 'other', and this model pervades foreign language education. Such a model, however, faces a growing number of challenges and can no longer account for the social reality of a globalised and hyperconnected world.

Challenges to territorialised models

Indeed, all three of the binary oppositions mentioned above are being challenged by globalisation and the advent of online communication. 'In particular, with so much communication happening now online, global technologies compel us to review our notions of cultural authenticity' (Kramsch 2014: 299). Indeed, while 'standard' language is still in use, 'non-standard' language is now also allowed to spread via the internet. While the norms of 'standard' language use are still abided by online in areas such as academia, high-end journalism, and political speech, other uses of languages such as online chats, marketing pitches, blogs and emails are characterised by 'pragmatic unpredictability, semiotic uncertainty, and a commodification of language that inject additional layers of meaning into the supposedly stable signifiers of the dictionary and the predictable norms of conventional genres' (*ibid*: 301).

To this extent, whether in language learning or cultural learning, learners are no longer only confronted by 'standards'. This is not to say that such 'standards' should be abandoned and replaced by other forms, but approaches should at least be varied so as to show learners the heterogeneity of language and culture as rooted in lived experience.

> The purpose is not to abandon all standard pedagogic norms of language use as the goal of instruction. It is, rather, to strive to make our students into multilingual individuals, sensitive to linguistic, cultural, and above all, semiotic diversity, and willing to engage with difference, that is, to grapple with differences in social, cultural, political, and religious worldviews.
>
> (*ibid*: 305)

Given this complexity and diversity of language and culture, the concept of 'nation' can only function as one level of description and in its desire for homogeneity, cannot account for the multiple layers that interact within what it supposes to be a linguistic or cultural sphere.

> Belonging to a cultural community can also be expressed through gender roles, local identity, ways of thinking determined by social class, generational identity. All these criteria tend to offer a much more complex description of identity than those traditionally used, such as 'il est espagnol', 'she is English' or those related to the employment status, such as 'he is an engineer', 'elle est secrétaire'. Identity appears more as a kaleidoscope with which each individual plays, hiding some facets in some circumstances, revealing others according to his/her social interests.
>
> (Zarate, 1995: 24)

Thus, the concept of nation, while it may usefully describe some cultural phenomena, must be understood as one of many levels of description, not enshrined as the overarching definition to which all studies of culture must conform.

This cultural and linguistic diversity has been accelerated by globalisation and the increase in human migration. 'More people are on the move today crossing cultural boundaries and national borders than ever before in the history of humankind' (Sorrells 2012: 372). With these massive movements of populations come movements of ideas, customs, and languages, to the extent that multiculturalism and multilingualism have also been accelerated.

> This vast population mobility has converted most countries of the world into plural societies, so that the experience of community-level multiculturalism and multilingualism is now itself universalized.
>
> (Lo Bianco 2014: 314)

Thus, societies which had long been engaged in efforts to homogenise and unify at a national level now find themselves confronted by linguistic and cultural diversity from within. Almost thirty years ago, Byram was already writing that this would bring change, not only to the way people view the *other*, but also to people's conception of their own identity.

> Young people in schools today will live in quite different political circumstances in the next few decades and will, I suspect, have quite different perceptions of themselves and their identities.
>
> (Byram, 1992: 10)

Since cultures are no longer closed national cultures, individuals no longer have to consider themselves as belonging to fixed and impermeable cultures but can exist at the intersection of what were once distinct cultural spheres. 'Furthermore, recent demographic mixing has shown the model of discrete cultures to be inadequate' (Coffey, 2013: 268). The very concept of cultural spheres as separate entities is being replaced by a view in which individuals carry cultures with them, share them and modify them by their words and actions.

> Culture has become deterritorialized, crystallized in the forms of memories, identifications, and projections that people carry in their heads. It is passed on in the form of stories, images, and films, multimodal creations, and multilingual speech productions that problematize the one language = one culture equation and that foster hybridity, *mestizaje*, and the shape-shifting avatars of the internet.
>
> (Kramsch and Michiko, 2012: 212)

> **Question for discussion**
> What educational policies could help promote a shift in teachers' and students' mindsets?

Individual positioning and third spaces

To this extent, understanding the cultural positioning of an individual is crucial. Since the national level of description does not account for the reality of cultural diversity, an intercultural speaker (Byram, 2008) will understand the importance of asking to whom he/she is talking.

> Pupils should learn to establish how representative an item of information is, that is to say, linking information with its origin, estimating the quality of the sample. Is the informant in a dominant position? How marginal or prevailing is his opinion or practice?
>
> (Zarate, 1995: 24).

Thus, the presupposition of homogeneity must be replaced by an awareness that an individual position in a society is never neutral, nor is his/her position in relation to an intercultural interlocutor. Communication will always take place at the meeting point of individual desires, presuppositions and interests, some of which will be linked to cultural specificities, others to individual personalities, etc. It is this meeting point at the intersection of the personal and cultural histories of interlocutors which Bhabha (1994) refers to as a 'third space' in which meanings interact and are negotiated.

Learning a language, in this context, can either mean imposing one's own cultural bias on the language being learnt or letting the other's cultural bias impose itself as the norm; or else it can mean attempting to position oneself in this third space, this contact zone, hoping to enrich one's vision both of the target culture and one's own, but furthermore, to enrich both cultures themselves by becoming engaged in both. 'I would like to suggest that language teachers focus less on seemingly fixed, stable cultural entities and identities on both sides of national borders, and more on the shifting and emerging third place of the language learners themselves' (Kramsch, 1995: 90). Learning a language should not mean embracing all aspects of the culture traditionally associated with it, nor should it mean imposing one's own cultural vision, simply translating existing meanings into another language.

> Americans need to learn other people's languages, but whose meanings? In our rush to counteract English-only mindsets, let us not inadvertently replicate its colonising practices by essentialising foreign languages and cultures and, in the process, inadvertently reproduce dominant Anglo-American meanings. The role of the language teacher should be to diversify meanings, point to the meanings not chosen, and bring to light other possible meanings that have been forgotten by history or covered up by politics.
>
> (Kramsch, 2006: 103)

By showing language learners that the target culture(s) are not homogeneous but diverse and in movement, the language teacher incites them to become involved in this third space and to call into question the notion of a unique and objective culture. Learners can then create and share their own meanings by participating in an intercultural exchange rather than positioning themselves as belonging to a predefined and immutable culture. In this sense, for language learners, taking part in intercultural communication and becoming involved in this third space means repositioning themselves, redefining their role, not as mere learners of cultural meanings which precede them and must be accepted as they are, but as participants in a culture which they are both discovering and helping to forge.

> **Question for discussion**
> What role can educating for citizenship play in de-territorialising culture?

Coming full circle: Conclusion and practical recommendations

This chapter began by showing how language learning in France remained anchored in a territorialised conception of culture. The idea that languages somehow intrinsically correspond to countries and cultures pervades French curricula. In the above discussion it has been shown that such territorialisation forges *otherness* by defining what is normal and abnormal, correct and incorrect, and excluding the latter. De-territorialising language, therefore, would allow for language and cultural learning to better conform to the globalised and hyperconnected world in which we live. The use of 'authentic documents', which is already recommended by French curricula, could be expanded and diversified so as to include non-native speakers as well as native speakers, and among native speakers shift towards a more inclusive palette of accents including those which are marginalised.

The use of English as a *lingua franca* which has attracted interest in the past years is also a way to make students realise that the English language is not tied to the United States and the United Kingdom alone. Communication between, for example, French and Italian students using English, is not only an interesting way to place students in authentic communicative settings but also corresponds to how much English is spoken today as the second or third language of both interlocutors.

To this extent, learning another language can shift from being seen as a threat to the French language and culture towards a way of enriching individuals within this culture by broadening their linguistic and cultural repertoires to better suit their expressive needs in globalised world.

Summary points

- This chapter has shown how the French approach to language learning remains anchored in a territorialised vision of language and culture and, as such, approaches cultural learning in a simplistic and reified manner.
- An intercultural approach can help escape this vision by viewing culture as heterogeneous and constantly shifting, thus allowing the cultural practices of migrant and marginalised populations to be integrated into the target cultures.
- The positioning of the learner as an individual intercultural speaker is also crucial, as it establishes him/her as the bearer of cultural meanings which can encounter other such meanings in an intercultural third space, thus allowing him/her to become involved in cultural practices rather than learning stereotypical cultural 'facts' in the form of encyclopaedic learning.
- Finally, the cultural positioning of an individual learner in relation to 'foreign' cultures will also allow him/her to reflect on his/her own culture, rethinking the relation between language, culture and territory in order to constitute a more inclusive conception of what it means to belong to a culture.

Recommended reading

Derivry, M. and Potolia, A. (Eds) (2022) *Virtual Intercultural Exchanges in Education*. Abingdon: Routledge.
Jackson, J. (Ed.) (2012) *The Routledge Handbook of Language and Intercultural Communication*. Abingdon: Routledge.
Kramsch, C. (2009) *The Multilingual Subject*. Oxford: Oxford University Press.
Liddicoat, A.J. and Scarino, A. (2013) *Intercultural Language Teaching and Learning*. Oxford: Wiley-Blackwell.

References

Bhabha, H.K. (1994) *The Location of Culture*. London: Routledge.
Byram, M. (1992) Foreign Language Learning for European Citizenship. *The Language Learning Journal*. **6**(1), pp. 10–12.
Byram, M. (2002) Foreign Language Education as Political and Moral Education: An essay. *The Language Learning Journal*. **26**(1), pp. 43–47.
Byram, M. (2008) *From Foreign Language Education to Education for Intercultural Citizenship*. Clevedon: Multilingual Matters.
Coffey, S. (2013) Strangerhood and Intercultural Subjectivity. *Language and Intercultural Communication*. **13**(3), pp. 266–282.
Dervin, F. (2012) Cultural Identity, Representation and Othering. In J. Jackson (Ed.) *The Routledge Handbook of Language and Intercultural Communication*. Abingdon: Routledge.
Kramsch, C. (1995) The Cultural Component of Language Teaching. *Language, Culture and Curriculum*. **8**(2), pp. 83–92.
Kramsch, C. (2006) The Traffic in Meaning. *Asia Pacific Journal of Education*. **26**(1), pp. 99–104.
Kramsch, C. (2014) Teaching Foreign Languages in an Era of Globalization: Introduction. *The Modern Language Journal*. **98**(1), DOI: 10.1111/j.1540-4781.2014.12057.x
Kramsch, C., Cain, A. and Murphy-Lejeune, E. (1996) Why Should Language Teachers Teach Culture? *Language, Culture and Curriculum*. **9**(1), pp. 99–107.
Kramsch, C. and Michiko, U. (2012) Intercultural Contact, Hybridity, and Third Space. In J. Jackson (Ed.) *The Routledge Handbook of Language and Intercultural Communication*. Abingdon: Routledge.
Liddicoat, A.J., Heugh, K., Curnow, T.J. and Scarino, A. (2014) Educational Responses to Multilingualism: An introduction. *International Journal of Multilingualism*. **11**(3), pp. 269–272.
Liddicoat, A.J. and Taylor-Leech, K. (2015) Multilingual Education: The role of language ideologies and attitudes. *Current Issues in Language Planning*. **16**(1–2), pp. 1–7.
Lo Bianco, J. (2014) Domesticating the Foreign: Globalization's effects on the place/s of languages. *The Modern Language Journal*. **98**(1), DOI: 10.1111/j.1540-4781.2014.12063.x.
Ministry of Education (2015) BO spécial du 26 Novembre 2015: programmes d'enseignement de l'école élémentaire et du collège. DOI: https://www.education.gouv.fr/au-bo-special-du-26-novembre-2015-programmes-d-enseignement-de-l-ecole-elementaire-et-du-college-3737.
Ministry of Education (2019) Annexe 2 Programme de langues vivantes de première et terminale générales et technologiques, enseignements commun et optionnel. *BO spécial* n° 1 du 22 janvier 2019, DOI: https://eduscol.education.fr/1726/programmes-et-ressources-en-langues-vivantes-voie-gt
Ministry of Education (2020) Annexe – Grille pour l'évaluation de la compréhension de l'oral ou de l'écrit. *BO spécial* n° 6 du 31 juillet 2020, DOI: https://www.education.gouv.fr/bo/20/Special7/MENE2019474A.htm.
Moore, D. (2003) *Les Représentations des Langues es de leur Apprentissage*. Paris: Dider.
Noels, K.A., Yashima, T. and Zhang, R. (2012) Language, Identity and Intercultural Communication. In J. Jackson (Ed.) *The Routledge Handbook of Language and Intercultural Communication*. Abingdon: Routledge.
Sorrells, K. (2012) Intercultural Training in the Global Context. In J. Jackson (Ed.) *The Routledge Handbook of Language and Intercultural Communication*. Abingdon: Routledge.
Zarate, G. (1995) Cultural Awareness and the Classification of Documents for the Description of Foreign Culture. *The Language Learning Journal*. **11**(1), pp. 24–25.
Zarate, G. (2008) Introduction: Appartenances et lien social. In G. Zarate, D. Lévy and C. Kramsch (Eds) *Précis du Plurilinguisme et du Pluriculturalisme*. Paris: Édition des Archives Contemporaines.

4 *Pädagogik* and (New) Education Studies
Striking up a conversation

Thomas Altfelix

It would surely be better for Pädagogik to concentrate as much as possible on its own concepts and cultivate an autonomous way of thinking, thus becoming the centre of an area of research, no longer running the risk of being ruled as a distant, conquered province by a foreign power.

(Johann Friedrich Herbart, 1806 – founding father of
German Education Studies, [my translation])

Introduction

This chapter outlines the basis for a dialogue between the Anglophone discourse of (New) Education Studies in the UK and its Germanophone counterpart of *Pädagogik*. So far, few attempts have been made to align these two traditions on a theoretical level. One recent example is a comparative approach by the Dutch philosopher of education Gert Biesta (Biesta, 2011). Juxtaposing these two academic traditions, Biesta argues that in Anglophone *Education Studies*, educational theory is seen through the lens of the academic disciplines deemed relevant to education and hence treated merely as an 'applied field of study' (Biesta *et al.*, 2013: 3). However, in the Germanophone context of *Pädagogik*, Biesta claims that the study of education is afforded the status of an 'academic discipline in its own right' (Biesta, 2011: 176). The concept of education in itself thus becomes the subject of study, not merely the object of ancillary disciplines, as purportedly the case in Anglophone discourse. By drawing attention to this difference, Biesta reasserts a claim initially made by the Finish Educationalist Michael Uljens (2002).

However, a closer analysis suggests that the underlying assumptions of this comparison are over-simplified and no longer hold true. It will be shown that the lines of development of both traditions have become, in fact, chiasmic, i.e. more of a cross-over than a divergence. While German *Pädagogik* appears to be suffering from the progressive loss (in the standing) of a General Theory of Education as its academic raison d'être, there is growing support within Anglophone *New Education Studies* for the idea that 'knowledge, skills and values' may be 'considered as they relate to Education Studies […] existing as a subject in its own right and not through other disciplines' (Burton and Bartlett, 2006: 390).

This chapter will therefore trace some key markers in this cross-over and stress the importance of conceptualising education as a discipline-defining concept *qua* subject of study by underscoring the current need for both discourses to enter into closer dialogue.

DOI: 10.4324/9781003223528-5

A (very!) brief outline of the history of *Pädagogik*

In its 250-year-old history as a university discipline, German Education Studies, or *Pädagogik*, has come full circle in its role as an ancillary to other subjects. Originally a quasi-subdiscipline of Theology, Philosophy and then Psychology, it finally reached a state of (at least nominal) autonomy with its inception as a humanities subject or *Geisteswissenschaft* at the beginning of the twentieth century. However, in the period following the Second World War leading up to the 1960s, *Pädagogik* once again experienced a paradigm shift ending with its far-reaching transformation into a social science or *Sozialwissenschaft* (Casale, 2016). To mark this change, the subject was commonly referred to as *Erziehungswissenschaft* (science of education). This development placed German Education Studies at the centre of a broader paradigm shift from a humanities approach hitherto pursued by university disciplines dealing with the interpretation of human society ('arts') to a social science perspective based on empirical research. Crucially, this change of identity reverted *Pädagogik*'s status back to an ancillary – this time mainly to Psychology and Sociology.

Nevertheless, in the course of its varied university history, *Pädagogik* had managed to establish and sustain a subdiscipline specifically dedicated to systematic research on a General Theory of Education (*Allgemeine Pädagogik*). Although *Allgemeine Pädagogik* originated from the humanities tradition, it followed a strategy of including competing approaches and methodologies (both philosophical and empirical) from different university subjects in the attempt to provide the broadest possible perspective on educational theory (hence: 'general'). Thus, German Education Studies would always retain – at least in part – its role as 'keeper' of the German concept of education (*Bildung, Erziehung*), bringing together relevant discourses from different periods and subject areas and converting them into an assembly of 'educationalised' themes and topics (Fuhr, 1999).

This role would remain unchanged until the demise of *Allgemeine Pädagogik* in Germanophone higher education at the turn of the millennium (Weiß, 2013). Since then, the concept of education appears to have lost its 'curator' and consequently its discipline-founding status. Remnants of the former subdiscipline of *Allgemeine Pädagogik* have survived as degree programme modules within different university courses (e.g. in teacher training programmes or *Schulpädagogik*). Although maintaining a broad adherence to the multidisciplinary legacy of a humanities-oriented *Pädagogik*, these modular remnants have reduced the meaning and importance of educational theory to studying rudimentary aspects of educational phenomena at foundation course level.

Retracing developments from an autobiographical perspective

I first came into contact with German Education Studies (*Pädagogik*) at the turn of the millennium. Having decided to join this discourse as a cultural studies lecturer and doctoral student, I was privileged to find a supervisor who introduced me to *Pädagogik* as an autonomous discipline and field of study. He held a chair in 'General Theory of Education' (*Allgemeine Pädagogik*) focussing on Systematic Educational Theory, Anthropology of Education and the Theory of *Bildung* (Altfelix, 2009). The scope of this field of expertise identified him as a representative of that fast-dissolving subdisciplinary strand concerned with foundational research on the concept of education. In this capacity, he drew my attention to the fact that general theorists of education now found themselves at the tail end of a long-standing epistemological conflict between two principal schools of thought: While one school continued to hold that *Pädagogik* was still a member discipline of the humanities (*Geisteswissenschaft*), the

Pädagogik and (New) Education Studies 39

other school defined it as a social science (*Sozialwissenschaft*). To me, this dispute bore a strong resemblance to the Anglophone debate on the existence of 'two cultures' in academia, the humanities and the sciences, initiated in the late 1950s by the physicist and novelist C.P. Snow (1959). My supervisor would introduce me to the German Education Studies version of this debate as follows.

Adherents of the humanities view would argue that, as an arts subject based on a systematic and historical approach to all aspects of education, German Education Studies had already achieved the status of an autonomous discipline, allowing for the multidisciplinary inclusion of different subjects and their methods. Although now commonly labelled a 'science' (*Erziehungswissenschaft*), this inclusive university subject should not (and could not!) be subsumed under the empiricist (neo-positivist and critical-rationalist) ideal of a 'unified science', according to which humanities were to be treated as social sciences which in turn were to adopt or at least approximate the methodology of the natural sciences. (Whether this notion can be said to have grown into what is now called 'human sciences' – *Humanwissenschaften* – currently remains unclear in view of conflicting definitions of this new conglomeration of disciplines.) To the humanist, the German term *Wissenschaft* had a broader and older meaning than that subscribed to by advocates of the unified science theory which is also inherent in the English concept of 'science' (Standish, 1995).

However, proponents of the social science view would argue that German Education Studies had long evolved into a field of applied psychological and sociological research, largely sustained by an empirical (qualitative and/or quantitative) methodology common to other sciences (and not the arts). To the social scientist, working with a presuppositional (multidisciplinary) concept called *education* was metaphysical and therefore unscientific. Instead, education could only be defined as a propositional term to be operationalised according to its relevance to a particular research assignment within the context of a (unified) human science as a whole.

Accompanying and supporting my supervisor's research and work at the university soon made me realise that the social science view predominated in educational discourse and would continue to do so for some time. Strategic funding policy considerations and the frustration of pragmatics with the perceived ineffectiveness of a humanities approach to educational matters – set against the apparent success of empirical research – would ensure this. Although the epistemological debate on the nature of German Education Studies would survive into the twenty-first century under proxy or surrogate headings such as 'Philosophy of Education versus Education Research' (*Bildungsphilosophie* versus *Bildungsforschung*, Pongratz et al., 2006), in reality, this juxtaposition (which in itself runs counter to the inclusive intentions of the humanities approach) is symptomatic of a now purely symbolic contest in the politics of knowledge production, since the former discourse continues to be marginal(ised), while the latter has long taken centre stage.

Implications of the paradigm shift

The paradigm shift in German Education Studies from *Geisteswissenschaft* (humanities) to *Sozialwissenschaft* (social sciences) is more than a mere change in epistemological approach and methodology. It is a fundamental reorganisation in the terminology and language of the subject, redefining the way educational processes and their purpose are understood. The following example may demonstrate this point. The German language offers the choice of two concepts to describe a pedagogue's ability to encourage their students to perform a task: *Begeisterungsfähigkeit* (the ability to enthuse and inspire) and *Motivationsfähigkeit* (the ability to motivate).

Reference to *Begeisterung* implies activating and encouraging the kind of desire to participate that originates from within the students themselves. It recognises and respects that processes of human will (*Geist*) possess an integrity and individuality that are partially inaccessible to external influence and observation, making them difficult to ascertain empirically. This interpretation of an educational interaction is *humanities speak* or the language of *Pädagogik*.

Use of the term *motivation* may appear to signify a similar process of pedagogical encouragement. However, in this case, there is an emphasis on the application of specific external measures by the pedagogue to ensure the type of observable participation compliant with the principle of causality (motivate = literally inciting discernible intellectual and physical 'movement'). The term is borrowed from psychology and (potentially) employed as a means to operationalise assessable patterns of behaviour. This is therefore *social science speak* or the language of *Erziehungswissenschaft*.

Closer scrutiny of the apparent synonyms shows that each concept follows entirely different definitions, procedures and value systems in their assumptions about the meaning and nature of educational processes. In the words of the late German educationalist Hansjörg Neubert:

> [...] the language games of Educational Studies have become poorer! In our pedagogical tradition, the educator's 'ability to enthuse' [*Begeisterungsfähigkeit*] was once an important issue and it was considered an indispensable pedagogical virtue. Today, we speak of the 'ability to motivate' [*Motivationsfähigkeit*], thus reducing a thoroughly expressive ability that is deeply rooted in biography to a meagre skill in psychological strategy. But the ability to enthuse means more. It means commitment, buoyancy, enthusiasm, captivation, vibrancy, persuasiveness, dedication – and not least getting involved and embracing the world with optimism [my translation]
>
> (Neubert, 2010).

The example demonstrates that the language of *Pädagogik* is somewhat more complex than that of 'psychologised' *Erziehungswissenschaft*. It pays careful attention to the concepts that describe the diversity of interhuman relationships in education. And it therefore requires something the Philosopher of Education Robin Barrow once called 'conceptual finesse':

> A person with conceptual finesse [...] has this tendency towards fine discrimination in relation to such perennial objects of human interest as politics, morality, interpersonal relations, love, parenthood, art and education or, simply, the stuff of daily life as distinct from the stuff of a developed academic discipline. [...] it is also partly to do with methodology or, more accurately, a lack of a narrow, finely-honed methodology. [...] what is characteristic of such developed disciplines as science, mathematics, and even sociology is that they are largely defined in terms of looking for a particular kind of explanation of a particular narrow set of events in a particular way.
>
> (Barrow, 1987: 4, 10)

However, being rooted in the stuff of daily life means that *Pädagogik* has shown a strong dependence on the culture-specificity of the German language which so far has prevented the subject from presenting its achievements effectually beyond the scope of its national boundaries, for instance in Anglophone discourse (Friesen, 2014: xvi). It remains unique in worldwide academia, so much so that the German educationalist Jürgen Oelkers speaks of the 'strange case of German *Geisteswissenschaftliche Pädagogik*', claiming that it is a 'uniquely German [subject] [...] that has no correspondent internationally and also cannot be seen as *avant garde* – something that other countries had neglected to consider. [...] it has never been exportable to any larger degree' (Oelkers, 2006: 191).

This assessment is reminiscent of the issue of *untranslatability* that the British philosopher Barry C. Smith once raised in his discussion of German Idealist Philosophy. Smith makes reference to '[a]spects of style that are primarily characteristic of a poetic and demagogic use of language, aspects such as the emotive power believed to be inherent in the writings of this philosophy [my translation]' (Smith, 1992: 129f.). Something similar may be said of *Pädagogik* which evolved from German Idealism. Indeed, the problem of (culturo-linguistic) particularism has been a decisive factor in the transformation of German Education Studies into a modern social science. The paradigm shift has enabled it to move towards greater connectivity with the technical vocabulary of international discourses on (psychology and sociology of) education. However, insofar as *Pädagogik* always strove for an autonomous theory of education, replacing it substantially with *Erziehungswissenschaft* also meant abandoning the project of describing, analysing and interpreting educational matters using an already existing discourse on educational theory and thereby finding and cultivating an educational methodology *sui generis*.

Now, if we are to assume that the notion of conceptualising education in an educational way is not inherently German (!), then the all-important question remains: What might Anglophone discourse tell us about the possibilities of accessing the concept of education in this manner from an alternative culturo-linguistic perspective? Has Anglophone discourse (we will concentrate very briefly on the British case) maintained an affinity to what we have termed the *social science view*, or has it found its own way of addressing the issue of an autonomous educational theory of education?

Questions for discussion

Can you make out two cultures (humanities and social sciences) in Anglophone Education Studies?

Is conceptual finesse an essential tool for describing, analysing and interpreting educational processes? What do you think?

Biesta's assertion

The Dutch Philosopher of Education Gert Biesta is one of the few educationalists who have addressed the issue of difference between Germanophone and Anglophone Education Studies on the level of general theory. His main assertion is based on the following observation:

> What is *virtually absent* in [...] the *Anglo-American construction* of the field is the idea of education as an *academic discipline in its own right*. In this regard this construction differs significantly from the way in which the study of education has developed in Continental Europe, particularly in the *German-speaking world*. Here the study of education has developed more explicitly as *a separate academic discipline with its own forms and traditions of theorising*. [my emphasis]
> (Biesta, 2011: 175f.)

How does Biesta elaborate on this point? Table 4.1, adapted from Biesta, presents an ostensive overview of his line of argument.

Table 4.1 Differences Education Studies – Pädagogik

	Education studies	Pädagogik
Original and primary focus	School/formal education	*Menschwerdung* = process of becoming human
Status of 'education' as central notion	object of study → requiring intellectual resources from the outside	subject of study → look[ing] at education in [...] an educational way
Methodological perspective	theory question in education	education question in theory

Sources: Biesta (2011: 188f.; 2014: 35; Biesta *et al.*, 2013: 3,7).

Initially, I was very convinced by this assessment. It helped to pinpoint and explain some difficulties I had encountered in relating both discourses. Most evidently, it provided a plausible reason for my experience of a mentality barrier in explaining this relation in my own research: Biesta's comparison alludes to a fundamental – albeit rather stereotypical – epistemological difference between both traditions, a distinction roughly drawn along the lines of Anglo-Saxon empiricism and inductionism versus Germanic idealism and deductionism (Böhm, 2006: 104). Thinking in these traditions means following one logic or the other. They appear to be mutually exclusive. In identifying this link, I felt reminded of Johan Galtung's well-known anecdote on 'four intellectual styles' in international research: saxonic, teutonic, gallic and nipponic. Galtung, a Norwegian sociologist and mathematician, once famously remarked in a comparative study on nation-specific intellectual communities:

> Let me try to summarize what I have said by putting down in the shortest possible form the typical question put in the four intellectual styles when somebody is faced with a proposition:
>
> - saxonic style: how do you operationalize it? (US version)
>   how do you document it? (UK version)
> - teutonic style: wie können Sie das zurückführen – ableiten?
>   (how can you trace this back – deduce it from basic principles?)
> - gallic style: peut-on dire cela en bon français?
>   (is it possible to say this in French?)
> - nipponic style: donatano monka desuka?
>   (who is your master?)
>
> (Galtung, 1981: 838)

Has Biesta simply come across another case of deduction versus documentation? A good indicator in support of this claim would be a brief comparison of some terminological equivalents from both discourses. While German textbooks on educational theory refer to foundational concepts (*Grundbegriffe*) (Koller, 2010), English sources speak of key concepts (Trotman *et al.*, 2017; Winch and Gingell, 2008). Foundational implies a peculiar metaphysical depth and scope which the English rendition appears to replace with a far more pragmatic and flexible notion (key). Correspondingly, the main German concepts themselves, i.e. *Bildung* and *Erziehung*, appear to be more difficult to pin down than the English concept of education.

Bildung is notoriously difficult to define, with a semantic range well beyond that of education (see also Chapters 1 and 2 of this book). Its meaning can reach from a so-called *Pathosformel* (Ribolits, 2011) – an emotionally charged concept, deeply entrenched in the romantic-idealist notion of holism, implying the search for a lost unity in an attempt to reverse our personal and social sense of estrangement in the world and society (Buck, 1984) – to practical aspects such as formal learning (*Schulbildung*), informal learning (*Allgemeinbildung*) and various soft skills (*Kompetenzen*). Its untranslatability has led to its inclusion in the English language as a highly specialised German-specific loan word (Friesen, 2014: xvi)!

Erziehung, which in English is normally rendered quite unphilosophically as child-rearing or 'upbringing' (Friesen, 2014: 20), also carries a heavy baggage of philosophical presuppositions in its German context. They emanate from '[o]ne of the greatest problems of education [*Erziehung*]' that the German Idealist philosopher Immanuel Kant (1904: 131) already identified in 1803 in his famous 'lecture notes on pedagogy': 'How do I cultivate freedom under the conditions of force?' If a child experiences its relationship to an adult as heteronomous (or subject to external forces), how might it ever know, when and how it has actually achieved autonomy? The paradoxical implications revealed in this (rhetorical) question continue to reverberate in every informed discussion about intergenerational relationships in Germanophone discourse.

Didaktik, defined as the principles of teaching, is commonly translated into English as 'curriculum studies' (Hopmann and Riquarts, 1995). While the German concept centres on grounding aspects such as 'why teach what?' … 'in pursuit of which goal?' … 'based on which guideline or recommended procedure?' … 'using what type of theory-generated judgement?', the English concept adopts a far more pragmatic approach by asking 'what how?' … 'in fulfilment of which task?' … 'following which planned action?' … 'applying which mindset with what kind of intuition?' (*ibid*: 24).

Finally, as Biesta himself points out, the aim of *Pädagogik* is '*Menschwerdung*' (Biesta, 2011: 189) which may translate as: developing our full potential as human beings and assisting others in this development. Pat Petrie *et al*. remind us that, in the continental understanding, *Pädagogik* 'can relate to the overall support of children's development. […] [I]t is 'education' in the broadest sense of that word' functioning as 'a foundational concept that informs many sorts of services, providing a distinctive approach to practice, training and policy' and involving 'work with the whole child: body, mind, feelings, spirit and creativity' (Petrie *et al*., 2009: 3). This notion therefore implies a degree of performativity and participation in dealing with this subject that far exceeds any academic dimensions implied in studying education theoretically and vocationally. It entails personal involvement to the extent that '[p]arents are sometimes referred to as the first pedagogues' (*ibid*: 9). Here, the boundaries between knowing (theory and its professional application) and being (ethos of personifying this knowledge) are transcended by qualities many would describe as authenticity, calling or simply a responsiveness to existential demands – i.e. *the stuff of daily life* in the words of Robin Barrow (1987).

Questions for discussion

If the term *foundational concept* suggests deducing educational processes from grounding principles, while the term *key concept* alludes to a more pragmatic approach to confirming certain educational phenomena by describing and documenting them, how would you put this difference into practice? Consider some central notions and think about how you would formulate a brief encyclopaedic entry in an introductory companion to Education Studies.

Do you think that a more profound engagement with educational phenomena (ethos of personifying knowledge) proves that these phenomena must be 'lived'?

Critiquing Biesta's assertion

In the previous section, I argued in support of Biesta's description of German Education Studies. Biesta is right insofar as he equates this subject with the humanities tradition of *Geisteswissenschaftliche Pädagogik* (Biesta, 2011). However, I also made it clear that this school of thought has been superseded in the main by the social science view. Consequently, we must critically qualify Biesta's assertion by stating that he seems too optimistic about current German Education Studies' capabilities of treating education as its subject of study. In view of his bi-paradigmatic assertion, we must also critique his assessment of Anglo-American Education Studies, since it does not take sufficient account of recent developments in Anglophone discourse and the inception of 'New' Education Studies (Bartlett and Burton, 2010). Here, Biesta seems too pessimistic about its current capabilities of overcoming its practice of treating education only as an object of study. Instead of following divergent paths, both discourses have in fact unbeknown to each other converged and crossed over! What indications are there of this crossing over, of this chiasm?

The German domain of theory formation, *Allgemeine Pädagogik*, has gone from being the backbone of its discipline to providing students with introductory courses on foundational concepts. This decline in the quality of theory is particularly evident in a historical overview of major works carrying the title of '*Allgemeine Pädagogik*' (Table 4.2). Here, we may identify a clear caesura around the turn of the millennium in the understanding of educational theory. A long tradition in metaphysical groundwork has given way to the current strategy of providing a practical overview:

In this regard, the late German General Theorist of Education Klaus Prange critiqued the latest book by Margit Stein on this subject (Stein, 2009) in the following manner:

> From a textbook with the title *Allgemeine Pädagogik* you would want to expect that it either deals with what is covered in the subject bearing this title or that it presents and establishes a new concept of a General Theory of Education. The author has presented nothing of the sort. Instead, she offers what you might call an overview of the issues und findings that we currently encounter in the popular understanding of education. [my translation]'
>
> (Prange, 2009: 449)

This status-reduction of theoretical groundwork is also evident in the recommendations by the German Society for Education Studies (*Deutsche Gesellschaft für Erziehungswissenschaft, DGfE*) for a Bachelor's core curriculum. Although these proposals translate into an extensive new modular unit called Foundations of Education Studies (*Grundlagen der Erziehungswissenschaft*), this construction contains no integral notion of a general theory of education (Kraft, 2012). Instead, it is subdivided into four sections: 1) Foundational Concepts of Education Studies and Its Neighbour Disciplines; 2) History and Theory of Education; 3) Epistemological Approaches in Education Studies and 4) Qualitative and Quantitative Research Methods in Education Studies (DGfE, 2007). Rather than structuring degree courses from the integral perspective of different theories of education in accordance with a particular train of thought – a so-called *pädagogischer Grundgedanke(-ngang)* – such modular units only help to consolidate and legitimise the centrifugal tendencies that have turned *Pädagogik* into a nondescript propaedeutic receptacle. Deduction has been replaced by description, preparing students for adopting the applied social science view during the specialisation stages of their study. Unfortunately, the recommendations for a Master's core curriculum for

Table 4.2 Development of German Literature Regarding *Pädagogik*

	Johann F. Herbart (1776–1841) →	Wilhelm Flitner (1889–1990) →	Dietrich Benner (1941–) →	Alfred Treml (1944–2014) →	Margit Stein (currently working as a Professor of Education)
Author →					
Title	'*Allgemeine Pädagogik*'	'*Allgemeine Pädagogik*'	'*Allgemeine Pädagogik*'	'*Allgemeine Pädagogik*'	'*Allgemeine Pädagogik*'
Date of publication	1806	1950	1987	2000	2009
Approach	Transcen-dentalism	Hermeneu-tics	Praxeology	Evolutionary Epistemo-logy	Introductory Companion
Aim	Establishing a system of deduction for foundational concepts of education	Identifying education in a foundational train of thought	Formulating foundational principles of educational practice	Developing categories for observing processes of education	Introducing key concepts and methods of German Education Studies

Allgemeine Pädagogik – which actually show potential for a profounder specialisation in general theory of education (DGfE, 2009: 151–162) – are somewhat impeded in their implementation because the structure of preceding Bachelor's courses is not conducive to such a progression. The logic of modularisation combines the market economy principle of course content commodification with a degree of predetermination in teaching and learning objectives that prevents lecturers and students from exploring the contingencies of more complex discussions and reflections typical of the humanities approach to education (Binder, 2006; Kokemohr, 2005). In other words, discussions about education cannot be led in an educational manner. Yet, this is a prerequisite for a successful Master's degree in General Theory of Education!

In fact, the consequences of implementing these Bachelor's course recommendations reach further still. The new curriculum is designed to evolve *Pädagogik* as a former discipline in its own right even beyond its status as an applied interdisciplinary social science of *Erziehungswissenschaft* into a transdisciplinary field, now often called *Bildungswissenschaften*. The plural form indicates the definitive rejection of a disciplinary epicentre, implying that different disciplines have their own versions of education studies (Kiper, 2009)! The replacement of *Erziehung* with *Bildung* not only signals a strategic move towards a *passe-partout* diversification (*Bildung* having become a very extensive catch-all term) but also towards greater entwinement with vocationalism: What *Bildung* may now mean is no longer the result of informed academic discussion but is determined primarily by pervasive economic requirements and professional innovation (Faulstich, 2004; Liebau, 2002).

In this evolution, German Education Studies has now reached a level of pragmatism that British Education Studies appears to have moved away from. Although, in many ways, the 2019 Quality Assurance Agency's benchmark report for Education Studies in the UK (QAA, 2019) is very comparable to the proposed core curriculum of the DGfE, there are clear references to a reorientation away from vocationalism towards an academic search for a disciplinary centre. The report states categorically: 'Education studies has evolved from its origins in teacher education to a subject in its own right' (QAA, 2019: 1). Crucially, this change underscores the growing autonomy of British Education Studies. While some still consider it 'a *subject* defined by its curriculum content and drawing selectively upon the methods of the contributory disciplines of psychology, sociology, philosophy, history and economics' (level 1), others choose to describe it as 'a *discipline* with its own academic community, its own distinctive discourse and methods of enquiry' (*ibid*: 2) (level 2).

Although these positions appear to represent two conflicting viewpoints, they have in fact led to a third possibility (level 3) which arguably does most justice to the peculiarity and uniqueness of the performative qualities of education: If education does not appear to have an epistemological substance of the kind that other foundational concepts have for their respective disciplines, such as life (*bios*) for biology, society (*socius*) for sociology or the mind (*psyche*) for psychology (Altfelix, 2014), if it has no 'solid body of knowledge' necessary for a 'disciplinary identity' (Palaiologou, 2010: 274) (cp. level 1), then it must draw on other (parent or neighbour) disciplines and act as 'a focus or meeting point for synthesis and synergy' (*ibid*.) (cp. level 2). Furthermore, however, it may also strive to do so in an educational manner in itself and thus (re-)gain its own disciplinary autonomy (cp. level 3)!

All three levels of understanding are currently theorised in Anglophone discourse. Germanophone discourse, on the other hand, has discarded the option of systematically moving from the second to the third level by dismantling its subdiscipline of *Allgemeine Pädagogik* and retreating in good part to the first level.

A three-tiered model as a basis for an Anglo-German dialogue

In this final section, I would like to propose a simple three-tiered model to illustrate the development of British Education Studies (see below) and locate the point of cross-over between the two national traditions. Moreover, I want to propose that it is on the third level that both discourses can enter into a fruitful discussion, since this level represents the best opportunity of finding a common disciplinary understanding. It addresses the performative quality of education which lies beyond the potentially conflicting issues of incommensurable nation-specificity (Keiner and Schriewer, 2000) and the concomitant danger of agreeing to differ prematurely.

Level 1 = Contrast medium: 'Education' is rendered visible by other disciplines so that social science questions are asked about education. Typically, Education Studies involves extracting educationally relevant content and methods from disciplines such as history, philosophy, psychology and sociology. This level is 'based on the view that Education as an academic study cannot be a discipline in its own right because it does not have its own characteristic modes of enquiry, or its own ways of reasoning; its reasoning necessarily draws upon one or another of these four disciplines' (Standish, 2007: 160).

Level 2 = Cocktail (Eclecticism): 'Education' reconstitutes discourses of other disciplines so that education questions are asked about the social science of education. Here, 'Education Studies facilitates a meta-analysis of theories from the [parent, T.A.] disciplines and the formulation of new relationships through them' (Bartlett and Burton, 2010: 392).

Level 3 = Self-eventuation: 'Education' is treated as an autonomous mode of analysis and research, turning other domains into something educational so that education questions are asked in an educational way. This involves developing the type of degree course programme that 'is not just about education but is educational in itself' since it 'fall[s] to Education Studies to include within its own field of study exactly what *educational* means here?' (Tubbs and Grimes, 2001: 6). As Patrick Ainley has defined the performative nature resulting from this task: '[I]n comparison with other subjects of study, Education Studies enjoys the advantage of combining the object of study – education – with reflection upon the process of study so that what students study is also what they do (study studying)' (Ainley, 2009: 5).

This is the level that German discourse has fallen behind – the level of understanding education's unique quality of being a discipline that comprises a reflective and active self-involvement (of students and teachers) within the context of an event called *education*. As the Austrian Philosopher of Education Franz Fischer once said: 'As soon as we enquire into the meaning of *Bildung* and get involved in the process of searching for answers, we are precisely fulfilling its purpose' [my translation] (Fischer, 1975: 13). In other words, to educate is always to be educated; to talk about education is in itself an educational event; teaching always involves the teaching of teaching, etc. This principle must guide content and methodology of any future Education Studies.

Returning to Biesta on a very conciliatory and affirmative note: When he speaks of the 'need [for] a pedagogy of the *event*', it is this third level that he envisages. And in order to reach and maintain it, 'we should refrain from trying to totalise communication through our theoretical understanding of it' and 'risk those theories themselves by bringing them into communication' (Biesta, 2013: 139f.) – performatively!

> **Questions for discussion**
>
> Can you identify aspects from all three levels of Education Studies in your own student experience?
>
> In your opinion, is the performative quality of 'education' something that Education Studies can build on in order to (re-)establish its disciplinary autonomy?

Conclusion – Entering into dialogue

Pädagogik once embarked on a project of establishing an autonomous discipline of Education Studies. This endeavour was largely abandoned with its conversion into an ancillary to other social sciences. British Education Studies set out as an ancillary and now appears to be searching for disciplinary autonomy. Interestingly, this suggests that there is a transnational rationale in the humanities approach to developing general theories of education. Insofar as the search for this goal in Anglophone discourse has led to a performative dimension of educationalising the study of education (level 3), British Education Studies appears to be picking up the discussion where *Pädagogik* left off. This point of contact represents an important opportunity for striking up a mutually beneficial conversation. There is a real danger that both national discourses will behave like 'ships that pass in the night', in the words of the poet W.H. Longfellow. This is not least because these discourses 'have emerged in conjunction with national cultures of schooling and education', establishing their own 'historical canon' that has been developed continually ever since the mid-nineteenth century within each respective national frame of reference 'without ever disengaging from their fixation on it' [my translation] (Oelkers, 2006: 174). The aim of this chapter is to assist in overcoming this fixation (largely supported by locating educational discourse on levels 1 and 2) and to help promote closer cooperation in matters of educational theory (by exploring level 3).

Summary points

- Relating (German) *Pädagogik* to (British) New Education Studies
- Education Studies as a humanities subject and as social science
- General Theory of Education (*Allgemeine Pädagogik*)
- Education as performative concept

Recommended reading

Friesen, N. (2020) 'Education as a Geisteswissenschaft': An introduction to human science pedagogy, *Journal of Curriculum Studies*, **52**(3), pp. 307–322.

Palaiologou, I. (2010) The Death of a Discipline or the Birth of a Transdiscipline: Subverting questions of disciplinarity within Education Studies undergraduate courses, *Educational Studies*, **36**(3), pp. 269–282.

References

Ainley, P. (2009) What Education Studies Is and What It Might Be, *Educationalfutures*, **2**(1), pp. 3–13.

Altfelix, T. (2009) Nachruf auf Christoph Lüth, *Erziehungswissenschaft*, **20**(39), pp. 227–229.

Altfelix, T. (2014) Educational Situation: Some preliminary remarks on a basic concept of Education Studies, *Franz Fischer Jahrbuch*, **19**, pp. 42–69.

Barrow, R. (1987) Conceptual Finesse, *Paideusis*, **I**(1), pp. 3–12.

Bartlett, S. and Burton, D. (2010) *Introduction to Education Studies*. London: Sage.

Biesta, G. (2011) Disciplines and Theory in the Academic Study of Education: A comparative analysis of the Anglo-American and Continental construction of the field, *Pedagogy, Culture & Society*, **19**(2), pp. 175–192.

Biesta, G. (2014) Remembering Forgotten Connections: Klaus Mollenhauer's opening to theorising education differently, *Phenomenology & Practice*, **8**(2), pp. 34–38.

Biesta, G., Allan, J. and Edwards, R. (2013) Introduction. In G. Biesta, J. Allan and R. Edwards (Eds) *Making a Difference in Theory: The theory question in education and the education question in theory*. London: Routledge.

Binder, U. (2006) Modularisierung. In A. Dzierzbicka, A. Schirlbauer and Alfred (Eds) *Pädagogisches Glossar der Gegenwart*. Wien: Löcker.

Böhm, W. (2006) Europäisches und nordamerikanisches Denken über Erziehung. In J. Ruhloff and J. Bellmann (Eds) *Perspektiven Allgemeiner Pädagogik. Dietrich Benner zum 65. Geburtstag*. Weinheim/Basel: Beltz.

Buck, G. (1984) *Rückwege aus der Entfremdung: Studien zur Entwicklung der deutschen humanistischen Bildungsphilosophie*. Paderborn: Schoeningh.

Burton, D. and Bartlett, S. (2006) The Evolution of Education Studies in Higher Education in England, *The Curriculum Journal*, **17**(4), pp. 383–396.

Casale, R. (2016) Der Untergang des Geistes, der Aufstieg der Evidenz. Wissensgeschichtliche Überlegungen zur Vergangenheit und Zukunft der Erziehungswissenschaft. In S. Blömeke, M. Caruso, S. Reh, U. Salascheck and J. Stiller (Eds) *Traditionen und Zukünfte. Beiträge zum 24. Kongress der Deutschen Gesellschaft für Erziehungswissenschaft (DGfE)*. Opladen: Budrich.

DGfE (2007) *Kerncurriculum für konsekutive Bachelor/Master-Studiengänge im Hauptfach Erziehungswissenschaft mit der Studienrichtung Pädagogik der frühen Kindheit*. (Vorläufige Version; endgültige Publikation im November 2007), pp. 1–6. Online. Available at: https://www.dgfe.de/fileadmin/OrdnerRedakteure/Stellungnahmen/2007_KC_PdfK_konsek.pdf (Accessed 25 August 2021).

DGfE (2009) Kerncurriculum für konsekutive Master-Studiengänge im Hauptfach Erziehungswissenschaft mit der Studienrichtung Allgemeine Pädagogik, *Erziehungswissenschaft*, **20**(39), pp. 154–157.

Faulstich, P. (2004) Hauptfach Bildungswissenschaft, *Erziehungswissenschaft*, **15**(28), pp. 55–62.

Fischer, F. (1975) *Darstellung der Bildungskategorien im System der Wissenschaften [1956–1960]*. Kastellaun: Henn.

Friesen, N. (2014) Mollenhauer and Forgotten Connections: An intellectual/biographical sketch, *Phenomenology & Practice*, **8**(2), pp. 20–25.

Fuhr, T. (1999) Was ist Allgemeine Pädagogik? Begriff, Leistungen, Defizite, *Pädagogische Rundschau*, **53**(1), pp. 59–82.

Galtung, J. (1981) Structure, Culture, and Intellectual Style: An essay comparing saxonic, teutonic, gallic and nipponic approaches, *Social Science Information*, **20**(6), pp. 817–856.

Hopmann, S. and Riquarts, K. (1995) Didaktik und/oder Curriculum, *Zeitschrift für Pädagogik, Beiheft*, **33**, pp. 9–34.

Kant, E. (1904) *Lecture Notes on Pedagogy*. Edited by E.F. Buchner. London: Lippincott. (First published 1803.)

Keiner, E. and Schriewer, J. (2000) Erneuerung aus dem Geist der eigenen Tradition? Über Kontinuität und Wandel nationaler Denkstile in der Erziehungswissenschaft, *Schweizerische Zeitschrift für Bildungswissenschaften*, **22**(1), pp. 27–50.

Kiper, H. (2009) Bildungswissenschaften – Begriff – Profile – Perspektiven, *PÄD-Forum: Unterrichten erziehen*, **37/28**(3), pp. 127–131.

Kokemohr, R. (2005) Internationalisierung der Universität, Standardisierung des Wissens und die Idee der Bildung. In A. Liesner and O. Sanders (Eds) *Bildung der Universität. Beiträge zum Reformdiskurs*. Bielefeld: Transcript.

Koller, C. (2010) *Grundbegriffe, Theorien und Methoden der Erziehungswissenschaft. Eine Einführung*. Stuttgart: Kohlhammer.

Kraft, V. (2012): Wozu noch Allgemeine Pädagogik? *Zeitschrift für Pädagogik*, **58**(3), pp. 285–301.

Liebau, E. (2002) Bildungswissenschaft. Zur Weiterentwicklung der Disziplin, *Vierteljahrsschrift für wissenschaftliche Pädagogik*, **78**(3), pp. 293–299.

Neubert, H. (2010) *Erziehen und Lehren. Was muss ich wissen, was muss ich können, was soll ich tun?* Talk given at the Symposion 2010: Erziehung – gemeinsames Anliegen von Lehrpersonen und Eltern, held at the Pädagogische Hochschule Vorarlberg on the 19th March 2010. Available at: hneubert@zedat.fu-berlin.de (Accessed 20 March 2018).

Oelkers, J. (2006) The Strange Case of German 'Geisteswissenschaftliche Pädagogik'. In R. Hofstetter and B. Schneuwly (Eds) *Passion, Fusion, Tension. New education and educational sciences; end 19th–middle 20th century*. Bern: Peter Lang.

Petrie, P. Body, J., Cameron, C., McQuail, S., Simon, A. and Wigfall, V. (2009) *Pedagogy – a holistic, personal approach to work with children and young people, across services, Thomas Coram Research Unit, Institute of Education*. University of London, Briefing Paper. Available at: http://eprints.ioe.ac.uk/58/1/may_18_09_Ped_BRIEFING__PAPER_JB_PP_.pdf (Accessed 25 August 2021).

Pongratz, L., Wimmer, M. and Nieke, W. (2006) (Eds) *Bildungsphilosophie und Bildungsforschung*. Bielefeld: Janus.

Prange, K. (2009) Margit Stein: Allgemeine Pädagogik. München: Ernst Reinhardt Verlag 2009. 170 S. [Rezension], *Zeitschrift für Pädagogik*, **56**(3), pp. 449–451.

QAA (2019) *Subject Benchmark Statement – Education Studies. December 2019*, pp. 1–12. Available at: https://www.qaa.ac.uk/docs/qaa/subject-benchmark-statements/subject-benchmark-statement-education-studies.pdf?sfvrsn=3ae2cb81_5 (Accessed 26 August 2021).

Ribolits, E. (2011) *Bildung – Kampfbegriff oder Pathosformel. Über die revolutionären Wurzeln und die bürgerliche Geschichte des Bildungsbegriffs*. Wien: Löcker.

Smith, B. (1992) Zur Nichtübersetzbarkeit der deutschen Philosophie. In D. Papenfuss and O. Pöggeler (Eds) *Zur philosophischen Aktualität Heideggers, Band 3: Im Spiegel der Welt: Sprache, Übersetzung, Auseinandersetzung*. Frankfurt a.M: Klostermann.

Snow, C.P. (1959) *The Two Cultures. With introduction by Stefan Collini*. Cambridge. Cambridge University Press.

Standish, P. (1995) Why We Should Not Speak of an Educational Science, *Studies in Philosophy and Education*, **14**, pp. 267–281.

Standish, P. (2007) Rival Conceptions of the Philosophy of Education, *Ethics and Education*, **2**(2), pp. 159–171.

Trotman, D., Willoughby, R. and Lees, H.E. (Eds) (2017) *Education Studies. The key concepts*. London: Routledge.

Tubbs, N. and Grimes, J. (2001) What Is Education Studies? *Educational Studies*, **27**(1), pp. 3–15.

Uljens, M. (2002) The Idea of a Universal Theory of Education: An impossible but necessary project? *The Journal of the Philosophy of Education Society of Great Britain*, **36**(3), 353–375.

Weiß, E. (2013) Krise der Allgemeinen Pädagogik und allgemeine Krise der Pädagogik. Ein Versuch über Gegenwartssituation und Zukunftsperspektiven der Erziehungs- und Bildungswissenschaft. In D. Salomon and E. Weiß (Eds) *Krisendiskurse*. Frankfurt a.M: Peter Lang.

Winch, P. and Gingell, J. (2008) *Philosophy of Education. The key concepts*. London/New York: Routledge.

Preface to Section II

Learning to become a 'whole' human being

Tom Feldges

The previous section was about the uncomfortable experience, almost the pain, of having to critically assess oneself or one's previous outlook on the world and to alter or even dismiss parts of it. This was introduced in Chapter 2, elaborating on the German concept of *Bildung* as a way of initiating a challenge that could, when skilfully posed, lead to the reflective thinking that can bring about this change of perspective. The notion of 'cultural situated-ness' was discussed along with the requirement that, in the context of language learning, the educator must make these 'painful' challenges carefully and in alignment with a (developing?) theoretical background.

This section is about one of these possible goals for education: becoming a 'whole' person and, from a European perspective, contributions from Norway, Italy, Germany and Belarus/Lithuania engage with different versions of this 'becoming'. Under normal circumstances no further contribution from Germany would have been accepted. However, the author of this text is a professional Creative Writing Coach, working with school dropouts and juvenile prisoners and in that context the notion of 'becoming' gains a completely different dimension. Because of this and because of his unusual but gripping writing style this interesting text was included.

To start the discussion off, one may want to remember the title of John Dewey's (1942 [1916]) seminal work on *Democracy and Education*. This title links two major topics: first, democracy as a specific form of organising social life, one which allows for as much individual freedom as possible, but with the limitation that an individual's freedom should not unduly infringe upon the freedom of others (see also Chapter 5). The second topic, of course, is education. With a title linking both concepts, Dewey makes his reader aware that the freedom of a democratic society is not something that is achieved by the people now and for all eternity. Freedom is rather something that is in continuous need of being preserved and that newcomers to a society – the young generation – have to be initiated into it. Hence the pairing of society's political organisation to the pursuit of education.

However, similar thoughts around the need to educate the young, and even education as a compulsory exercise, had already been formulated by Emmanuel Kant (1978) around a hundred years earlier in the context of the Enlightenment (see Chapter 2). These two examples from Modernity clearly advocate that a responsible and reasonable exercise of personal freedom is not something that should be left to chance. The preservation of the freedom that a free society grants its citizens requires a certain type of citizen, one who is willing and able to engage with the challenges and the responsibilities that such freedom brings along with it. So the question arises as to whether those who are not able to bear the responsibilities of their freedom should still be entitled to these freedoms? The current legal *status quo* is that a set of human rights is granted to all human beings *qua* being human: not one living human being is left out. But it comes with problems not foreseeable by those who drafted and codified these human rights. Human beings can be defined as belonging to a certain genus within the biological-scientific classification of all life forms. However, when using such an all-inclusive classification, one runs into problems when approaching the fringes of a biologically defined concept, and it might be helpful here to draw on an issue in medicine and psychiatry. Is someone who is brain-dead still a human being? Most certainly: yes! But is it necessary to grant that person all the rights that emerge from his/her belonging to the biological species when he/she cannot have a view on these nor exercise them? To engage with such problems, some scholars suggest a distinction between a 'human being', i.e. someone who belongs to the biological species, and a 'person'. The 'person' as a concept is dependent on the underlying concept of a 'human being'. Hence a 'person' is a human being with the additional essential feature of having its own wishes and – very importantly – who is also capable of acting upon those wishes (Radoilska, 2012) (see also Chapter 5).

It is now time to reflect upon this distinction and its potential implications for education in the light of Dewey's thoughts. Human beings are born as that. Two human beings procreate an offspring and that will be another human being. However, this young human being will display, as Freud (2020 [1909]) called it, a 'polymorphous perversity', and thus not be able, in the early stages of development, to take up a mutually rewarding place in society. This is where socialisation and education are supposed to do their work (see Chapter 1) to turn the human being into a person or, even better, into a *reasonable and responsible* person. It could thus be argued that one of the goals of education is to turn life-forms that belong to the biological species of *homo sapiens* (which means: wise or knowledgeable man) into 'whole' human beings in the way that they become what the biological species-name suggests, i.e. a wise and knowledgeable being. Viewed from such a perspective, education would need to initiate and support the transition from the mere biological functioning of a human being towards becoming a whole person who is able to take its place in a (democratic?) society. So far this discussion should not have raised too many – if any – objections. But it is always easy to draw a compelling argumentative arch by hopping from one big idea to the next. The problem begins when assessing what these ideas actually entail and whether they, when read in detail, still fit the particular case one wishes to make. This is where a close analysis of the literature can build a well-founded and logically coherent argument. To highlight this point, here is an introduction to Dietrich Benner (2001) and his thoughts on *Bildung und Demokratie* (forming education and democracy). All direct quotes from Benner's German Text are translated by the author.

Benner takes the concept of *Bildung* (see Chapters 1 and 2) and discusses it in relation to democracy. As *Bildung* could be seen as a sub-set of overall educational efforts, the impression might emerge that Benner has a probably up-dated version of Dewey's (1942 [1916]) *Democracy and Education* in mind. But this is where the backgrounds of the theorists come in and where caution is needed in making comparisons and establishing connections. Dewey belongs to a philosophical tradition called 'pragmatism'. This school of thought emerged in the late nineteenth century in the United States and is characterised by a) a scientific methodology, b) an initial focus upon empirical phenomena of the everyday world, c) a strong orientation towards democratic ideas (as in Dewey) and finally d) the acknowledgement of the forces of biological evolution. Benner, on the other hand, has strong idealistic roots in a philosophical tradition called 'idealism' for which the objects of human cognition are not real objects that exist independently of cognition and are nothing but ideas and presentations *about* these real existing objects (see also Chapter 4). For clarity, it must be added here that this idealistic perspective does not rule out the existence of these objects but maintains the position that one simply cannot know about them for sure (Feldges, 2021). With this slight detour, it already appears as if Benner would be very unlikely just to run a re-make of Dewey; their starting positions are too different to allow for something like that. Benner's main point is his argument that a free democracy (*freiheitliche Demokratie*) has to limit itself in terms of its normative demands regarding the life of its citizens and that education should not be part of a political practice that defines the educational goals to be achieved by the learners.

However, Benner takes on Dewey's thoughts and engages critically with some of them. First Benner (2001: 53) mentions Dewey's distinction between traditional societies and modern ones. The latter ones are in a constant shift, aiming to strive for the betterment of society's current state. Modern societies are the ones in which democracy can emerge. Dewey (1942 [1916]: 101) explains his concept of democracy as '… more than a form of government; it is primarily a mode of associated living, of conjoint communicated experience', and continues:

> A society which makes provision for participation in its good of all its members on equal terms and which secures flexible readjustment of its institutions through interaction of the different forms of associated life is in so far democratic.
>
> (1942 [1916]: 115)

In the light of these thoughts about democracy, Dewey can then focus his view specifically upon the task of education in such a society:

> Such a society must have a type of education which gives individuals a personal interest in social relationships and control, and the habits of mind which secure social changes without introducing disorder.
>
> (1942 [1916]: 115)

Benner engages critically with Dewey, and his main points are that Dewey's concept of democracy is used in an ambiguous manner. It allows for a far-reaching application, but also one that has not enough conceptual clarity to distinguish between modern and classical societies, a distinction that Dewey himself introduced. Hence, his concept might not be sharp enough to assess current questions as they emerge around the topic of education, economy, social life, science and politics. A second objection is made by criticising Dewey's underlying (pragmatist) optimistic assumption that Benner (2001: 55) paraphrases as '[w]ithin a democratic society everyone will find his suitable purpose (*Bestimmung*) in accordance with his natural predispositions (*Anlagen*)'.

With this recourse to a ubiquitous and naturally occurring harmony between individual predispositions and actual social life, Dewey clearly reveals his pragmatic background. Contrary to that, Benner points towards an ever-increasing dynamic of what *Bildung* is supposed to entail. This dynamic is characterised by an established link between

> … an undeterminable capacity to gain from *Bildung* [central is here Benner's concept of *Bildsamkeit* as an individual aptitude to be susceptible to forming efforts, T.F.] or perfectibility of modern human beings together with the openness and the unfamiliarity of one's future destiny.
>
> (2001: 58) [my translation]

Hence, Benner sets himself in direct opposition to Dewey's assumed harmony and rather claims that the modern individual is more of an 'uncertain project'. A project in which it must remain impossible to a) ascertain how much an individual learner will be able to benefit from attempts to form (*bilden*) a perfect result to eventually fit societal needs, and this in the light of b) an invariably unpredictable and uncertain future path of an individual's life (see also Preface to Section I). Quite contrary to Dewey's pragmatic assumption that, to put it plainly, *every Jack has his Jill*, Benner advocates the immanent openness of human existence, one that – inherently – remains unpredictable. But while Dewey could leave the pairing of democracy and education as one that will sort itself out somehow, Benner faces a problem due to the undeterminable future horizon of an individual life. If no natural harmony is safeguarding a fit between individual and society, the question will invariably arise as to what education is supposed to achieve with the individuals in its care in preparing them for society. By way of a negative determination, Benner (2001: 60) claims that democratic societies are characterised by a self-imposed prohibition of attempts to create a 'new human being' according to the state's goals, as well as staying clear of efforts to bring about the 'political new' through education. This is, by the way, also a clear criterion by which to distinguish appropriate educational efforts from inappropriate indoctrination, as discussed in Chapter 1. In opposition to Dewey's natural-harmonic conception of democratic societies, Benner engages in a question of what could/should be a valid virtue, one that education should evoke in its learners to prepare them to become citizens in such democratic societies. After dismissing some examples, Benner (2001: 60) claims that the only valid virtue could be a willingness and ability to make use of

> ... one's civil courage to argue in a non-fundamental manner and with the individual duty to actually exercise one's freedom to form an opinion to be utilised in the public domain.

Benner is thus advocating a reason-guided form of argumentative engagement with what is going on in the public sphere. The influences of Habermas' (1981) discourse-ethics as outlined in his *Theory of Communicative Action* are clearly present here. However, the capacity to form a reason-guided opinion assumes already that fundamentalist positions are excluded. But Benner does not stop there; instead of just claiming this to be the right of an individual, he insists that it is also a duty, one for which one needs the civil courage not only to think but also to utilise the results of this thinking-engagement to contribute to relevant discourses in the public domain. These much-extended demands are the basis upon which Benner then concludes that the task of education is to prepare the young to approach

> ... questions with conflicting economic, ethical, political, aesthetic and religious problems, to discuss and to reflect upon these in the light of their multiple perspectives. The gains of an enabling *Bildung* in this sense cannot exhaust themselves in that knowledge is known and skills are mastered. These gains must also be questioned in terms of what they [the gains T.F.] can contribute to a reasoned pursuit of public debates.
>
> (2001: 63)

Benner is thus not only outlining what education in a democratic society is supposed to *do* with its learners; but he also, albeit implicitly, provides a matrix according to which the success of these gains of *Bildung* are to be rated. This is, interestingly enough, not the knowledge or the skills mastered, but an achieved ability to form reasoned judgements regarding complex and interrelated problems and to communicate these judgements based upon logically coherent reasoning. However, such an outcome measure of educational efforts would need to come with a completely different set of assessment strategies as opposed to the rating of a few (quantitative) performance indicators. In that respect, Benner's idea of what education – and specifically the sub-concept of *Bildung* – is supposed to achieve reaches far beyond the preservation of a status-quo in the interplay of individual and democratic society. (See here also the discussion in Chapter 4 about the philosophical differences of educational theorising.) Benner's concept demands that an individual uses reasoned reflections and exercises freedom not only to preserve but equally to challenge (even on the danger of social disorder – as in the case of the current debate about climate change) by contributing to the public discourse about the direction society should take.

Without engaging any further here with Benner's thoughts on the specific form of education known as *Bildung*, it is already evident that any attempt to follow his theoretical considerations is riddled with ambiguities. Instead of hoping for a balancing harmony, one would need to outline what would/could count as 'civil courage', 'non-fundamental arguing', 'the exercise of forming an opinion', 'the utilisation within a public debate' and, of course, the extent of the 'duty' of which Benner speaks. How much individual effort would need to go into the forming of a reasoned opinion to qualify as having done enough to fulfil this duty? These requirements of Benner's theory reveal how different his philosophical-theoretical background is from Dewey's pragmatic approach that seeks to develop an empirically founded basis of phenomena in the pursuit of everyday life. However, even acknowledging these differences, the question remains as to whether one approach could be superior to the other or which of these two approaches would yield the most beneficial outcome. Here one faces yet another problem: what would be deemed to be a benefit? How would it be assessed? When would it be assessed (increased life chances or exit assessments)? Who would define 'good' as opposed to 'not so good' in this context? So it is basically about who commands the power to determine the values of education. Would that be a kind of a system-immanent process of natural harmony as Dewey implied it, or rather politics, to which Benner is strictly opposed, or even education itself? But if that were the case, then upon which competence and theoretical underpinning should such a claim be founded?

This section's introduction ends with five questions – again, not to be answered straight away or at all. The questions should serve as prompts to encourage the reader to think about the becoming of a 'whole' person in relation to the theoretical discussion of this introduction and in reading the following chapters.

- Does it make sense to try and teach democracy or the presumed values that go with the pursuit of a democratic society in a content-orientated manner, or would an experience-based approach yield better results?
- Why would 'educational poverty' yield negative effects on a learner's chances of becoming a 'whole person'?
- Is the reader able to trace authoritarian-like practices and attitudes in her/his own work environment?
- Could the change of a theoretical background improve one's ability to recognise these practices and attitudes – probably even alter these?

- Underpinning theories cannot be transferred from one cultural context into another. But if Tatiana Shchyttsova (see Chapter 8) can make use of the contributions of Kierkegaard (Danish), Merleau-Ponty (French), Heidegger and Fink (both German) to apply these authors and their thoughts to a problem in current Belarusian educational reality, then there is obviously the possibility of such a 'theory-transfer'. By carefully reading the text, is it evident what kind of care must be taken to achieve a successful application of theory beyond the society in which it emerged?

References

Benner, D. (2001) Bildung und Demokratie. *Zeitschrift für Pädagogik*, **43**, pp. 49–65.
Dewey, J. (1942 [1916]) *Democracy and Education*. New York: Macmillan.
Feldges, T. (2021) *Neurophenomenology and Cognitive Science*. Mauritius: Lambert Academic Publishing.
Freud, S. (2020 [1909]) *The Theory of Sexuality*. London: Big Nest Publishers.
Habermas, J. (1981) *Theorie des kommunikativen Handels*. Frankfurt a.M: Suhrkamp.
Kant, E. (1978) *Werksausgabe – Band 12. Schriften zur Anthropologie, Geschichtsphilosophie, Politik und Pädagogik*. Frankfurt a.M: Suhrkamp.
Radoilska, L. (2012) *Autonomy and Mental Disorder*. Oxford: Oxford University Press.

5 Perspectives on democracy, citizenship and value education in the Norwegian school

James McGuirk

Introduction

The Norwegian Directorate for Education and Training launched its long-anticipated new *Core Curriculum for Norwegian Schools* (UDIR, 2018a) which is being implemented in classrooms. In addition to a revision of curricula for the core school subjects themselves, the new plan includes a preamble that lays out the central values upon which the curriculum as a whole revolves, along with, interestingly, the introduction of three transdisciplinary themes to be integrated in all school subjects in the years to come. Drawing their inspiration partly from the UN Sustainable Development Goals (UN SDGs), the themes are: public health, democracy and citizenship and sustainability. This chapter focuses on issues related to the second of these transdisciplinary themes. Very specific claims are made in relation to these sources, and it might be a worthwhile educational exercise to read some of the original texts. While the referenced material is not quoted directly, the page numbers are included to guide the reader to the relevant sections.

The chapter structure is as follows: I will begin by contextualising the transdisciplinary themes in terms of the UN SDG, as well as the Core Curriculum's overall educational goals. I will explain how the integration of these themes is envisaged across subjects such as Social Science, language instruction (Norwegian and English), Mathematics and Natural Science and Religion and Worldview education. I will show that the net effect is to make these themes concrete rather than merely aspirational. While I believe this approach is broadly successful, the second part of the chapter will focus on a potential tension of visions with regard to the second of the transdisciplinary themes, democracy and citizenship. Specifically, the document seems to give voice to two competing conceptions of what is essential in democracy and citizenship education. On the one hand, there is a commitment to the procedural values that ensure autonomy and self-determination and, on the other hand, a commitment to substantive values embedded in specific traditions. I suspect that this tension of visions is not just a Norwegian phenomenon and is one that will be recognisable to school researchers in other parts of the globe. It is my hope that bringing this tension to light can contribute to the furtherance of critical reflection about the aims and goals of democracy and citizenship education.

DOI: 10.4324/9781003223528-7

The new curriculum and the transdisciplinary themes: Theory and practice

The new Core Curriculum (henceforth CC) launched in 2018 comprises a preamble as well as a rearticulation of the goals that define the teaching of the various school subjects, and of the school's personal and social mission in general. It does this in an elegant fashion by unfolding abstract values and commitments in ever more concrete and practical terms.

Beginning with the preamble, the stated purpose is to elaborate the value foundation of the school and of education in Norway (UDIR, 2018a: 1). The preamble explicitly anchors its mission in the cultural heritage of the Christian and Humanist traditions, a move whose significance is threefold. Firstly, Norwegian cultural heritage is described in terms of an historical situated-ness with which pupils should be familiar. Secondly, this heritage is seen as a transmitter of central values which the pupils are expected to appropriate and share. And thirdly, the open nature of these values should connect Norwegian pupils with a wider international community, committed to human rights and solidarity across ethnic, national, religious and other boundaries (UDIR, 2018a: 2–3). The central values of this cultural heritage are further identified as (1) human dignity, (2) identity and diversity, (3) critical thinking and ethics, (4) curious engagement (*skaperglede*), (5) respect for nature and (6) democracy. The authors of the CC draw several careful distinctions in articulating these values to make clear that they are understood both as meta-level commitments endorsed in their own right, as well as values that are to be manifested in the everyday practice of the school. For example, pupils will be expected not only to espouse the value of nature and the environment but also to experience engagement with the natural world as a source of joy, health, and learning (UDIR, 2018a: 7).

Questions for discussion

How important are values for our understanding and practice of education?

How should values be taught in the practice of the school?

As the preamble progresses, it crystallises these six value commitments into three transdisciplinary themes which should connect up with the various school subjects on offer. These themes are (1) public health and personal responsibility, (2) democracy and citizenship and (3) sustainable development. While the UN's SDG (2015) are not mentioned explicitly here, it is easy to draw a line between these themes and several of the areas covered by the SDGs. Public health can, for example, be connected with SDGs 3–6, democracy and citizenship with goals 4 and 16, while sustainable development can be connected with goals 7–9, 11 and 12. It is arguable that the first two themes are somewhat more practical than the third. The emphasis on public health, for example, attempts to foster the capacity of the pupil to take responsible choices concerning his/her own life and health (UDIR, 2018a: 12), while the theme of democracy attempts to give pupils a grounding in the rules of democratic engagement as well as fostering a lived commitment to human rights, freedom of speech, and freedom of organisation (UDIR, 2018a: 13). Some commentators have lamented a discrepancy in the CC between democracy as a theme and democracy as practice, accusing its authors of speaking *about* democracy without a corresponding commitment *to* democratic processes within the school (Johanessen, 2018). This seems a little unfair. Whether the school really will be inspired to practise democracy in the light of the CC is a matter that cannot be adjudicated here, but we can at least say that the document expresses a genuine commitment in this direction. In contrast with the first two themes, however, the theme of sustainable development mostly describes the need for the pupil to understand the problem of sustainability in the light of climate change and other global crises. This theme operates to a greater extent at the meta-level, but given the constraints of the practice of the school, this is surely understandable.

In a final specification of the value foundation of the practice of schooling, the transdisciplinary themes are then discussed in some detail as to how they can and should be realised in all school subjects. The purpose here is specifically to avoid the temptation to treat these themes as topics of abstract discussion which are only spoken about. Rather, their import should be made visible in everything from Art and Design to English and to Mathematics. And, ambitiously, each of the three themes should be made explicit in each subject.

It would take us too far afield to try to cover the way this appears in each of the school subjects, but by way of example, we can note that Natural Science should give the pupil insight into her/his own physical and mental health (theme 1), an ability to weigh scientific and non-scientific truth claims (theme 2), and to understand environmentally conscious choices in the light of global challenges (theme 3). By contrast, Art and Design teaches the pupil to develop creative problem-solving skills (theme 1), to reflect over the role of art as a bearer of culture (theme 2), and to gain insight into the flexibility and re-usability of materials (theme 3).

Elsewhere, the approach aims to impart knowledge about fundamental rights such as voting, free speech, and political organisation (Social Science), tools for developing the student's capacity for self-expression (Norwegian), perspectives on religious and political diversity (Religion and Worldview), and democracy in a global perspective (English). In sum, the proposal is impressive and far-reaching both in terms of themes covered and in terms of the realisation of each curriculum's goals in a transdisciplinary setting.

The double movement of the transdisciplinary themes

In this sense, the trajectory of the CC constitutes a steady unfolding downwards into more and more concrete arenas of application, from a statement of the values of education in general to an explication of the meaning of the transdisciplinary themes for education in specific subjects. But the CC also has another trajectory which aims at synthesising the experience of the pupil in the school. It does this along at least three axes.

Firstly, the transdisciplinary themes constitute a *unity* in the pupil's school experience. While specialisation into discrete school subjects is necessary for the school and for inquiry in general, the transdisciplinary themes mitigate the fragmentation by showing that each subject provides a unique perspective, or way into interests, that transcend disciplinary boundaries, and thereby reveal the inner unity of the subject. As such, it is possible to respect the integrity and difference of subjects as diverse as Natural Science and Norwegian, while demonstrating that both bring to light aspects of democratic engagement that can be singularly and mutually enriching.

Secondly, this unity is constituted as a unity of *value*. Educators, parents, and pupils are all at times guilty of falling into the language of instrumentalism when justifying the practice of schooling. We go to school so that we can learn, so that we can get a job, so that we can be happy and so on. There is, in principle, nothing wrong nor especially instrumentalist about thinking that school has a purpose, but we err when we describe that purpose as wholly external to the object of study, as though what we are studying is arbitrary and only a means to doing well on a test that will open certain doors for our future selves. By explicating the school's mission in terms of the transdisciplinary themes, the CC shows that, at bottom, we are always engaged in a value exercise. Not only does the study of Mathematics have intrinsic value, but this intrinsic value is nested within more comprehensive networks of value that are ultimately anchored in our humanity and our natural and social co-existence. The meaning of what we do in school is indexed to the cultivation of the personhood or subjectivity of the individual pupil (Biesta, 2013: 128), while also orienting us towards the community to which we belong.

Thirdly, the transdisciplinary themes bring our value consciousness into regions of *contemporary* concern. While all three of the themes in question can be considered transhistorical, transcultural and context-transcending in the sense of being enduringly relevant, they also give voice to challenges that are felt to be especially pressing in our cultural (locally and globally understood) moment. Whether in terms of health challenges such as pandemics, threats to democratic engagement, or natural catastrophes, the transdisciplinary themes bring the enduring mission of the school, and of education, into dialogue with the specific challenges facing our societies. Of course, we must tread carefully when making education relevant in this thematic way. Hannah Arendt rightly cautions us against irresponsibly transferring the task of solving social ills to the next generation through the school: it overburdens the child and destroys the school as a space of creative exploration at the same time as it entails an abdication of responsibility by the adult generation (Arendt, 2006). For the adult generation to entrust specific tasks, for example, climate change, to the next generation for Arendt would be an abdication of responsibility. In so doing, we effectively say to our children: 'Here is a problem for you to solve that we could not'. At the same time, specific problems of this kind constrain the school as a space of world inquiry and inhibit the possibility of new ideas and initiatives to come from unexpected places. At the same time, the enduring values of the school will only become visibly meaningful when they also address the world outside the school. I contend that the delicate balance enacted in the CC between the world inside and outside of the school avoids the pitfalls of isolating the school too much or too little from the society in which it is anchored.

As far as the practice emerging from the new CC is concerned, it is not always obvious that this will be radically transformed. Many have claimed that both the values espoused and the transdisciplinary themes are obvious, and their implementation describes a practice that has already existed for many years. Teachers have long been concerned with transmitting and enacting the value of democracy and self-responsibility for their pupils, and have been concerned with environmental issues since long before 2018. Nevertheless, there is value in articulating and re-articulating the purpose of education, its contemporary relevance and its unity across subjects and disciplines. For both teachers and pupils, re-engaging with core values and their embedding in relation to current problems has, or at least can have, the effect of arresting the kinds of fragmentation, instrumentalism and loss of relevance described earlier.

Questions for discussion

To what extent should teachers address current affairs in the classroom?

Are there dangers associated with doing too much or too little of this?

On the value of democracy: A tension in visions

In the second part of this chapter, and notwithstanding my generally positive estimation of the CC, I want to draw attention to a tension in the CC document, especially in relation to theme 2, Democracy and Citizenship. What I will suggest is that the document's articulation of the value of democracy gives expression to at least two different overarching paradigms which I will call the Libertarian/self-determination model, on the one hand, and the Traditional/hermeneutical on the other. My claim is that this tension involves ambivalence about the relationship between democracy and substantive ideas about the good life. This tension is not one that necessarily mires the document in self-contradiction, but it can give rise to queries that the document itself struggles to answer.

The Libertarian/self-determining vision

What do I mean by libertarian vision of democracy and citizenship? I should, at the outset, be clear that I do not mean that the document explicitly endorses any specific political vision or takes a position in terms of left- or right-wing politics as these are understood in Norway or anywhere else. The document aims to endorse the value of democracy as a form of government rather than any specific political vision that forms or has formed within a democratic society. So, the document is not libertarian if by 'libertarian' we understand it as alignment with any of the political parties at home or abroad that label themselves with this term. At the same time, the attempt to be positive to democracy, while agnostic about substantive questions regarding the good life or the good society, can be considered a libertarian orientation. The CC frequently endorses the values of self-determination, autonomy and liberation from so-called grand narratives, in so far as they would curtail the individual's right to make decisions about the meaning and purpose of her/his own life.

So, the CC document is libertarian in that it argues for the value of democracy as a form of political rule that vouchsafes the individual's right to self-determination. This is evidenced in the repeated emphasis on facilitating the pupil's capacity to 'make responsible life choices' (UDIR, 2018d: 12). The pupil should, of course, be aware of her/his cultural situated-ness, but the exact role of this situated-ness is often left ambiguous. At times, culture is presented as a nourishing source that has 'contributed to the development of our democracy' (UDIR, 2018a: 5), while at other times, it appears as an object of study with which the pupil need only be thematically familiar. For example, religious and philosophical cultural formations are to be taught in 'an objective and critical way' (UDIR, 2018b: 2) and never explicitly espoused by teachers. Pupils are expected to understand that culture plays a role in the formation of identity (UDIR, 2018a: 5) and that our perception of the world is always culture-specific (UDIR, 2018c: L 3). The tone of several of these passages tends to 'externalise' culture and gives the impression that, while we all come into the world with cultural baggage, we need to treat this baggage with a degree of scepticism to avoid our individuality being swallowed up by cultural norms and expectations.

It is not surprising, therefore, that the CC mostly forefronts the formal aspects of democracy and the democratic rules of engagement such as freedom of organisation, freedom of speech and the right to vote (UDIR, 2018a: 13). In turn, these rules of engagement are described as important for ensuring the democratic values of respect, tolerance and the rights of others to make choices concerning their own lives (UDIR, 2018a: 8).

This is the clearly libertarian voice in the CC that encompasses both egocentric (self-regarding) and allocentric (other-regarding) moments. Its egocentrism is visible in its scepticism about cultural hegemony and its attempt to protect the sovereignty of the individual to make decisions concerning the meaning of her/his own life. Its allocentrism is seen in fostering tolerance and respect for the perspectives and worldviews of others (UDIR, 2018d: 4). The total effect of this emphasis in the document is the valorisation of democracy as a form of rule and a form of life that ensures a social space which is non-invasive to the individual's pursuit of her/his own autonomous self-determination.

Readers familiar with American jurisprudence may be put in mind of US Supreme Court Justice Anthony Kennedy's famous definition of freedom as 'the right to define one's own concept of existence, of meaning, of the universe, and of the mystery of human life'. According to this understanding, the pursuit of and attempt to articulate the meaning of the good life is intrinsic to human reality, but there are no objective standards or norms that determine what the content of this life is or should be. As such, the purpose of democratic forms of organisation is to ensure that each one of us is able to explore this neutral space on her/his own terms. This is why the procedural side of democracy, concerning freedom, tolerance, respect and autonomy, is so heavily weighted in the document, since these are the values that will ensure that both I and all others can determine what the good life is.

Compelling reasons in support of the libertarian model

The libertarian argument of the CC is not a difficult one to make, of course, and aptly captures many of the foundational intuitions modern audiences will have about democracy. We live in a time that is scarred by the horrific excesses of the twentieth century and remains deeply sceptical about 'grand narratives' (Lyotard, 1984) that would compress all of the complexity of human experience into a single overarching framework. Perhaps more importantly, recent years have witnessed increasing awareness of and sensitivity to cultural diversity, not only as a global phenomenon but also as a local one. Like the vast majority of Western countries, the Norwegian population is no longer of exclusively European ethnic origin, let alone Christian. While the majority of Norwegians (ca 70 per cent) are members of the Norwegian Lutheran Church, less than half (47 per cent) claim to be religiously affiliated and only about 2 per cent of the population are regular church attenders (Statistisk sentralbyrå, 2021). What is more, Norway has seen an increasing focus in recent years on its troubled history of the oppression of its indigenous Sami population.

As such, there is greater emphasis placed on the provision of space for individuals and marginalised groups to determine the meaning of their own lives free of overarching societal norms. This is not to say that a diverse society is one without norms, but rather that it comprises a plurality of norms. This is viewed in the CC document as a resource both at the level of society as a whole and in the light of the individual's engagement with questions of value and meaning (UDIR, 2018a: 14). The fact that the school does not attempt to endorse a specific cultural view of the good life is precisely what makes it possible for the individual to explore these questions for herself, and it simultaneously allows traditional minorities a space to give expression to their own cultural insights and intuitions.

Ambiguities in cultural embeddedness

Now, of course, a pluralist starting point will itself need some kind of meta-level framework within which pluralism can operate, and this is seen in the previously discussed weighting of the procedural democratic values of openness, mutual respect, and tolerance. In other words, while the libertarian voice in the CC does not seek to endorse a specific historical vision of the good, it does endorse the kind of framework that allows the competing visions room to breathe.

As an aside, it is interesting that this approach entails a strange contradiction that depends upon one's own situated-ness. For minorities, it seems as though the point is to guarantee representation for one's culturally embedded intuitions. For members of the indigenous Sami population in Norway, for example, the open inclusiveness of the CC will ensure that one's religious and cultural practices and beliefs are properly represented and representable in the school. For majority pupils, the point seems rather to be that one is guaranteed an unconstrained space within which one can engage the question of the good life on one's own terms. While it is likely not to be the intention, this suggests that cultural minorities are more locked in their traditions than cultural majorities, and that while these minorities want to be allowed to preserve and cultivate their traditional roots, cultural majorities wish only to be free of theirs (Åberg, 2020). Now, one might wish to counter this suggestion by pointing to the clear emphasis on the Christian and Humanist heritage of Norway in the initial framing of the CC document. This is true enough, but it is equally clear that such heritage is most often presented in a thematic rather than existential light. That is to say, they are the subjects of objective and critical study, rather than sources of insight and inspiration.

> **Question for discussion**
>
> To what extent is our understanding of and commitment to democracy anchored in our cultural traditions?

Traditional/hermeneutical

All of which brings us to the second voice in the document which I am calling 'the traditional or hermeneutical'. This aspect of the CC emerges from precisely the ambivalence in the document's understanding of the meaning of cultural heritage. As I have argued, the CC is simply unsure of what it means by saying that the values of the school and of education in Norway in general are rooted in the Christian and humanist heritage of the country. The sense is often that this heritage can be divided into two parts: on the one hand, a substantive set of metaphysical claims about what is true and good and in what the good life consists; on the other hand, a commitment to freedom and self-determination that insists on the value of the individual's pursuit of these questions on her/his own terms. The idea appears to be, further, that these are separable and that, while the first should become an objectified thematic question, the second should become a framework baseline around which the school is organised and is a condition of possibility for its success for all pupils.

Thus, the specific metaphysical claims or beliefs of Christians or humanists should become objects of critical study that are presented as sociological or anthropological facts, one among many examples of the materialisation of fundamental questions within human culture. At the same time, the commitment of this culture to the procedural norms through which questions of truth and goodness are pursued are non-negotiable foundations that everyone in the society must commit to endorsing. Again, there is nothing especially new or surprising about this. It is nothing short of the kind of classical liberal position, articulated in the Kennedy ruling, that is sceptical about all material claims to truth, while robustly protecting the formal pursuit of these questions through democratic norms and practices. But there are two potential problems in this approach.

Majorities, minorities and cultural (dis)embedding

The first is the already mentioned tendency to differentiate between members of majority and minority cultures where the former are depicted as free, autonomous, and self-determining as individuals, and the latter are depicted as free and self-determining only insofar as they are members of a group. That is, ethnically Norwegian Maria can extricate herself from her cultural embedding and take a neutral starting point from which she can explore questions of value and meaning. Indigenous Mikkel, on the other hand, is free to give expression to the traditional norms of the group to which he belongs. This potentially overestimates the radical neutrality of Maria's starting point, while bizarrely assuming that Mikkel is only interested in articulating the value norms of his group. Another way of putting the point would be to say that the majority pupil is portrayed as a culture-less agent, while the minority pupil is reduced to a cultural token (Appiah, 1994).

Procedural and substantive values: The reef of tradition

The second problem has to do with a perceived naivety in the aforementioned separation between formal and material or substantive and procedural aspects of cultural heritage. What I mean is something like this. In framing the theme of democracy and citizenship, the authors are careful to espouse only the formal or procedural dimensions of democratic co-existence, such as the freedom to express oneself, to pursue the true and the good and to respect similar pursuits among other fellow citizens. At the same time, the CC anchors this endorsement of procedural democracy in a series of inherited core values, the first and most important of which is human dignity. The CC takes as given the idea that 'human dignity is inviolable and that each human being is worth as much as every other' (UDIR, 2018a: 4). It goes on to flesh out this idea in terms of commitment to the individual's duty of respect to him/herself and others, the intrinsic value of nature, the inborn desire to know and the corresponding possibility of the world to be known (6–7). The document takes these commitments as given, but are they? Are they not, rather, commitments to the possibility of truth, goodness, and harmonious co-existence that are only possible in the light of more fundamental material value commitments?

For example, the commitment to human dignity and inviolability is a central motif of both the Christian and humanist traditions and one that historically came to expression most prominently in the idea of the person (Joas, 2013; Maritain, 1971; UN, 1948). In both of these traditions, 'the person' is a deliberately more robust term than the more neutral 'individual' (Joas, 2013: 51; Maritain 1971: 34). Pretty much anything can be an individual – a tree, a rock, a plastic bottle – but what makes the individuality of the human being important is that here individuality is a kind of ground zero for the manifestation of value. The person is a value in herself (Kant, 1993: 35) and also the kind of being for whom what is valuable in itself can become visible. It is the human person that can not only insist on her/his own intrinsic worth but can also articulate the value of others, the value of nature, the value of art and so on (Hildebrand, 2020: 37). This is not something obvious with regard to our being individuals, but resides rather in our being persons. It often appears as though a commitment to human personhood is operating as a background assumption in the CC. This becomes most visible in the document's emphasis on the developmental, social and ethical aspects of education.

> **Question for discussion**
> Do we all mean the same thing by democracy?

To be a person is to be the kind of being that becomes or unfolds over time. This again distinguishes the person from the mere individual. It is not clear that we could ever become more or less individual. This seems rather to be a constant state as long as we are living. But the idea of the person is the idea of one whose potential *to be* is nourished and fostered. What is more, this idea is usually one to which educational theories have been especially attuned. Our personhood is not achieved once and for all, but is the inviolable seed in our individuality that emerges in ever fuller manifestations during the process of formation (Arendt, 2006: 178). It is cultivated and maintained in the pursuit of knowledge, virtue and social and civic engagement (Maritain, 1971: 10). It is precisely this kind of idea that alone can make sense of the CC's commitment to curious engagement and the pursuit of truth and knowledge.

The idea of the person is also foundational for the interpersonal and social values that the CC takes as given. While the idea of the person invests the neutral term 'individual' with fundamental value, it is also an idea that bespeaks vulnerability and porosity. Since the personhood of the person requires care in order to emerge and be maintained, the person can only be herself in the company of others. To be a person is, therefore, to be irreducibly bound up with others in relations of concern and love. So, while ethical consciousness could conceivably be considered something added to our individuality, it must be considered intrinsic to our personhood.

The porosity of the person is also something that becomes manifest over time in society and in social institutions (McGuirk, 2021). This materialisation of the commitment to the person is, of course, fragile and contains always within it the risk of corruption, but at their best, our institutions express the centrality of the person as both of intrinsic value in him/herself and one whose existence makes no sense in the absence of others. Our democratic institutions like law courts, and above all schools, are anchored in the idea of dialogue. To enter into dialogue is to acknowledge that the other sees something I have not seen, and that I see something s/he has not. As such, to dialogue is to enter into a process of mutual calling to attention in a way that widens and enriches the world for each member of the exchange (Buber, 1971; Lévinas, 1969). Dialogue, so construed, is not about shallow compromise or versions of relativism that deny the truth of all positions and thereby lock each of us into the narrow confines of our own experience (Giussani, 2019: 80). Rather, it is about testifying to the overdetermined nature of our common world. As they have been formed over time, our institutions give physical form to the idea of the truth of things as revealing itself across agents, cultures, and histories and thereby requiring attention and dialogue in ways that expand and deepen our perspectives (Masschelein and Simmons, 2013; Bengtsson, 2011; Giussani, 2019).

> **Question for discussion**
> How does/should the school balance commitment to individual subjects with commitment to the common good?

This is, in fact, what I mean by the traditional or hermeneutical approach. It is not at all about prioritising one cultural standpoint or tradition above all others, but rather of fleshing out the substantive ideas that lie at the heart of the kinds of intuitions that shape the CC document. Here is the idea of a tradition that is itself porous and whose identity is essentially an identity of growth and inclusion (Brague, 2002). This means that pupils learn from others who have gone before them, and those with whom they share the world now. It also means that, by incorporating what is said to them, they enrich the world by the uniqueness of their own appropriation of it. This is not necessarily in opposition to the libertarian voice's weighting of freedom. In fact, the personalistic view is the context in which commitments to freedom and autonomy make sense. It is because we are persons that we must be allowed to explore questions of truth and meaning freely. And yet, the two voices can come into conflict if the libertarian comes to be conceptualized only in terms of a naïve and unconstrained form of self-determination. To be free, on the personalistic view, is not about creating myself from out of myself, but about being freed towards the world, others, and my own capacity to be more than I presently am.

Conclusion

I conclude not with a resolution of the tension in the CC document. Perhaps what we have seen is not so much a tension as a multiplicity of emphases. And yet one cannot escape the sense that there is something uncertain in the document's sense of the meaning of the cultural heritage and how it shapes the starting point and goals of education in the Norwegian school, and perhaps in education in general, both locally and globally. The document wants to remain agnostic about specific forms of cultural expression concerning the good and the true, and yet its reliance on core values is only possible in the light of precisely the substantive commitment to the kind of personalistic view I have outlined in the latter part of this chapter. This is not a problem in the document as such, but rather a problem in the self-understanding of its authors, and perhaps many of us that are involved in policy development of this kind. We tend to be torn between the necessity of substantive value commitments and the desire to avoid these in a pluralist society. But, if my development of the personalist idea here holds water, this is perhaps not a choice we need to make. If I am correct in suggesting that the personalist standpoint is essentially pluralist, without being relativist, then perhaps this is the kind of commitment those of us engaged in education at all levels can feel freer about espousing. If there is a resolution in this chapter, let it be that.

Summary

- The chapter discusses the new Norwegian core curriculum, which has tried to articulate the mandate of the school around three transdisciplinary themes. These are public health, democracy and sustainability.
- Democracy education is often identified as one of the major challenges for contemporary schools. This chapter looks at some difficulties associated with understanding what this entails.
- The UN Sustainable Development Goals have identified global challenges that concern all areas of society, including the school. This chapter discusses how these come to expression in policy documents.

- This chapter identifies two major concepts, tradition and freedom, which often define our understanding of democracy and democracy education. It looks at how these are weighted in current Norwegian policy documents.
- The chapter discusses personalism as a way of bringing the commitments to individuality and community into constructive engagement in the context of the school.

Recommended reading

Arendt, H. (2006) The Crisis in Education. In H. Arendt *Between Past and Future*. London: Faber and Faber.
Biesta, G. (2013) *The Beautiful Risk of Education*. London and Boulder, CO: Paradigm Publishers.
Maritain, J. (1971) *Education at the Crossroads*. New Haven, CT and London: Yale University Press.
UDIR (2018a) *Norwegian Directorate for Education and Training: Preamble*. Online. Available at https://www.udir.no/lk20/overordnet-del/ (Accessed 30 September 2021).

References

Åberg, I. (2020) Diversity Is the Others: A critical investigation of 'diversity' in two recent education policy documents. *Intercultural Education*, **31**(2), pp. 157–172.
Appiah, K.A. (1994) Identity, Authenticity, Survival: Multicultural societies and social reproduction. In A. Gutman (Ed.) *Multiculturalism*. Princeton: Princeton University Press.
Arendt, H. (2006) The Crisis in Education. In H. Arendt *Between Past and Future*. London: Faber and Faber.
Bengtsson, J. (2011) *Educational Dimensions of School Buildings*. Bern: Peter Lang.
Biesta, G. (2013) *The Beautiful Risk of Education*. London and Boulder, CO: Paradigm Publishers.
Brague, R. (2002) *Eccentric Culture*. South Bend, IN: St. Augustine Press.
Buber, M. (1971) *I and Thou*. New York: Simon & Schuster.
Giussani, L. (2019) *The Risk of Education*. Montreal: McGill-Queens University Press.
Hildebrand, D.v. (2020) *Ethics*. Steubenville, OH: Hildebrand Project.
Joas, H. (2013) *The Sacredness of the Person*. Georgetown: Georgetown University Press.
Johanessen, M. (2018) *The Teacher's Blog*. Online. Available at https://martinjohannessen.blogspot.com/2018/10/om-demokrati-og-medborgerskap.html (Accessed 30 September 2021).
Kant, E. (1993) *Grounding for the Metaphysics of Morals*. Indianapolis, IN: Hackett Publishing.
Lévinas, E. (1969) *Totality and Infinity*. Pittsburgh, PA: Duquesne University Press.
Lyotard, J.-F. (1984) *The Postmodern Condition*. Manchester: Manchester University Press.
Maritain, J. (1971) *Education at the Crossroads*. New Haven, CT and London: Yale University Press.
Masschelein, J. and Simmons, M. (2013) *In Defence of the School: A public issue*. Leuven: Education, Culture, and Society Publishers.
McGuirk, J. (2021) Embedded Rationality and the Contextualisation of Critical Thinking. *Journal of Philosophy of Education*. https://doi.org/10.1111/1467-9752.12563
Statistisk sentralbyrå (Central Bureau of Statistics) (2021). Online. Available at https://www.ssb.no/kultur-og-fritid/faktaside/religion (Accessed 30 September 2021).
UDIR (2018a) *Norwegian Directorate for Education and Training: Preamble*. Online. Available at https://www.udir.no/lk20/overordnet-del/ (Accessed 30 September 2021).
UDIR (2018b) *Religion and Worldview Curriculum*. Oslo: Norwegian Directorate for Education and Training.
UDIR (2018c) *Curricula in English*. Oslo: Norwegian Directorate for Education and Training.
UDIR (2018d) *Norwegian Subject Curriculum*. Oslo: Norwegian Directorate for Education and Training.
UN (1948) *Universal Declaration of Human Rights*. New York: United Nations.

6 Educational poverty as a challenge for the future

Concepts and criteria for combating non-material child deprivation in Italy

Daniele Bruzzone and Simona Finetti

Introduction

Thanks to initiatives by Save the Children and other organisations, the question of educational resources for children and adolescents has come under increasing scrutiny in recent years. It has prompted the Italian government to adopt key social policy measures, including setting up a dedicated financial fund to support children and families. The explicit aim is to counter and prevent the various forms of 'educational poverty' which are often associated with material poverty, but sometimes entail circumstances of cultural and relational deprivation that can also affect the economically better off.

Given its specific nature and relative independence from economic factors, the notion of 'educational poverty' undoubtedly includes pedagogy; yet, to date, the concept has not been systematically reviewed or theoretically analysed from a pedagogical perspective. This chapter represents an initial attempt to fill this gap and to identify future lines of development within research and educational action. It does so by utilising a good number of Italian sources whenever these sources are quoted, they are translated by the authors.

Children and new forms of poverty

Social science researchers have long acknowledged the complex and multifactorial nature of poverty. Gradually, since the second half of the twentieth century, the traditional conception of poverty as the lack of a specific type of resource has come to be flanked by a multidimensional view that sees poverty as a state of life characterised by severe distress and the overlapping of different kinds of need. Since the mid-1980s, much of the discourse has revolved around the so-called 'new poverty' which is typically elusive and invisible, and is underpinned by the risk of material want and social exclusion in variable proportions.

Consequently, the notion of poverty has been revisited, such that levels of income and consumption remain key but are no longer the only possible indicators. As noted by Nobel laureate Amartya Sen, 'there are good reasons for seeing poverty as a deprivation of basic capabilities, rather than merely as low income' (2000: 26). Since the 1990s, the concept of inadequate resources has been extended to cover the entire set of material and intangible goods that a person requires to 'function' properly. As a result, efforts have been made to ensure that all members of society have access

DOI: 10.4324/9781003223528-8

to education, healthcare, and housing and to help them lead, or return to, active lives that facilitate the full enjoyment of their rights and protect their human dignity.

In 2010, the United Nations Development Program (UNDP) introduced *the Multidimensional Poverty Index (MPI)*, associated with *the Human Development Index (HDI)* (UNDP, 2010). This index measures poverty by taking into account multiple potential deprivations, including the lack of basic opportunities in the domains of health, education and standards of living. The AROPE – 'at risk of poverty or social exclusion' – indicator, which has been adopted by Eurostat to monitor the European Commission's Europe 2020 strategy, also assesses non-material aspects of poverty and considers those living under any one of the following three conditions to be at risk: financial poverty, severely materially and socially deprived, living in a household with a very low work intensity.

Perceived poverty evolves as a function of changes in lifestyles and standards of living. Today, it is measured against the parameters of the consumer society. Nevertheless, economic standards are not the only measure of poverty or exclusion. In our contemporary era of uncertainty, which is characterised by fragile and unstable bonds, and relationships that are 'increasingly less reassuring and increasingly more conflictual' (Cheli, 2013: 9), it is also possible to suffer and, paradoxically, to feel poor due to the superabundance 'both of objects of desire and objects of knowledge and the amazing speed with which new objects are born and old ones exit the stage' (Bauman and Mazzeo, 2012: 43). Poverty is therefore also experiential, and in this sense, has come to be perceived differently over time.

In 2011, the European Commission emphasised early childhood education and care as 'the essential foundation for successful lifelong learning, social integration, personal development and later employability' (European Commission, 2011: 1). Forms of poverty affect children twice over: first by making their living conditions challenging, and second by limiting their future possibilities (Saraceno, 2002). There is often a worrying circular correlation between material and immaterial poverty, which affects families and has a negative impact on children and their futures. However, socio-economic disadvantage does not always condemn an individual to a lifetime of poverty and exclusion. According to PISA-OECD, socio-economic status predicts academic performance, but there are exceptions. Disadvantaged children can rank in the top quartile for performance. This is a clear signal that we should not underestimate the importance of the encounters and significant experiences that children have from their earliest years, nor the educational resources available to families and communities. Quality of experience and interpersonal environment plays a key role in children's learning.

> The care and affection of parents, [...] encouraging teachers, help with homework, the presence of friends ... are all experiences that can minimise or eliminate the negative effects of exposure to risk factors, increasing resilience, the capacity to respond positively to traumatic problems and events, and the ability to *cope*, that is to say, to speedily and successfully address and overcome stressful situations by deploying one's mental energies and problem-solving skills and managing one's emotions.
> (Giustini and Tolomelli, 2012: 126)

Hence the need to identify not only the causes of deprivation and distress but also the protection and resilience factors that can help children and young people to tackle these issues constructively.

Educational poverty can also lurk where we would least expect to find it, in families objectively viewed as educated or financially well-off. Even such settings can harbour forms of poverty that are less frequently recognised, but no less harmful, such as neglect, lack of concern, lack of care, lack of time, and lack of listening, as well as multiple forms of violence and abuse, including those that are most difficult to identify. Forms of relational poverty and emotional illiteracy among adults, as well as parental vulnerability and confusion around parenting, inevitably impact on children's development and rights. Educational poverty is a deep wound which only sometimes comes to light at school under the guise of poor academic outcomes, or forms of difficult behaviour that are often dangerously overlooked.

In our community, there are children or young people who are 'without' and children or young people who are 'against'. Being *without* does not necessarily culminate in being *against*. *Without* may mean 'I have not been given an opportunity', 'I feel the lack of something inside of me', 'I am experiencing an inner void', regardless of how much a child has in material terms and how much he or she seeks surrogates to fill this lack, including engaging in deviant behaviour. Being *without* and being *against* are not always associated with, or symptoms of, educational poverty. Now, children who are *without* may certainly be considered deprived when they do not read, play no sport, never go to the theatre or the cinema, have never seen the sea, have no relationships with peers outside of the school setting, do not have a Wi-Fi connection, or do not know what a museum or archaeological site is (Save the Children, 2019). Children who are *against*, on the other hand, engage in antisocial or precocious criminal behaviour, reflecting 'the close relationship between educational poverty and violent juvenile delinquency' (Iavarone and Girardi, 2018: 23) and the absence of effective educational models.

Whether growing up on the streets behaving like adults, or overprotected and inhibited in their own home-cum-shelters, many children today experience a time without play, without stories, and sometimes without any friends or with very few, and are therefore daily denied valuable developmental resources. They can suffer irreparable damage not only in cognitive terms but also from the emotional, relational, moral and spiritual points of view. Those in the *without* condition can also suffer the loss of their vital energy: when perennially at home, indoors, in the semi-darkness – or for those who can afford it – the blue light of a screen, the flame can easily be snuffed out. When poverty becomes existential, when it becomes difficult or impossible to find meaning in life, children can be driven to extremes such as depression and social isolation, self-harming behaviours (which are dramatically on the increase among adolescents), substance abuse, forms of addiction or suicide.

Children, however, are never born *poor*, but rather are *deprived* of the resources they need to grow and develop: someone/something deprives them of what they are entitled to by law. Hence the urgent need for intervention.

Questions for discussion

What do you think are the possible forms of poverty that children can suffer from in your social environment today?

What do you think are the most difficult forms of poverty to recognise?

What kind of long-term consequences can these different forms of deprivation have?

Educational action as a strategic investment

An early definition of 'educational poverty' was provided by Save the Children Italia in the report *Aladdin's Lamp*, as part of *Let's Lighten the Future 2030*, a campaign informed by the United Nations Sustainable Development Agenda: 'educational poverty means the depriving of children of all ages of the possibility to learn, experiment with, develop and give free rein to their abilities, talents and aspirations' (2014: 4). This definition echoes the *Convention on the Rights of the Child (CRC)* – approved by the United Nations General Assembly on 20 November 1989 – which, in Article 29 (1)(a), calls for 'the development of the child's personality, talents and mental and physical capabilities to their fullest potential'.

Save the Children Italia also explicitly invoked *the capability approach* of Martha Nussbaum and Amartya Sen who have argued that human beings require a 'capacitating' environment that allows them to develop *capabilities*. Nussbaum conceptualises capability as the answer to the question: 'What is this person able to do and to be?' (2011: 20), including what Sen refers to as 'the real freedoms that people enjoy' (2000: 3), 'substantive freedoms' that allow one 'to choose a life one has reason to value' (2000: 74). The term 'capability' means a capacity that society endows upon (or denies) an individual. Preventing and combating educational poverty requires combined capabilities, the sum of the internal capacities that a person has acquired and developed since early childhood, and the socio-economic and cultural conditions that facilitate development.

Nobel prise-winner and economist James Heckman has noted that capabilities are underpinned by both cognitive and non-cognitive skills (Kautz *et al.*, 2014). The latter are among the 'most important predictive factors for educational development, with substantial effects beyond childhood' (Save the Children Italia, 2018: 18). *Non-cognitive skills* are personal attributes that cannot be measured via intelligence (IQ) tests. They include what the literature terms soft skills, personality traits, character or social-emotional skills or cross-functional skills, which predict an individual's developmental trajectory and adult life no less powerfully than do cognitive skills. Motivation, self-esteem, perseverance, self-confidence, trust in others, ability to deal with complex situations and manage conflict positively, autonomy, self-effectiveness, optimism and realism, are only some of the non-cognitive aspects that are salient in educational experience.

In adults, a good level of capability fosters social inclusion, employment access, economic and social mobility, productivity and well-being, and enables the acquisition of additional capabilities over time. Early childhood, in particular, is a crucial time for the development of both cognitive and non-cognitive abilities. Both sets of skills have a genetic basis: they can be influenced by events during the prenatal period, but they are shaped above all by the relational environments and the care and experiential settings that the child encounters throughout his or her development. Investing in education during the first three years of life appears to have more positive effects over the long term and to yield greater benefits than investing in later years. Nevertheless, there is evidence that quality intervention during adolescence, targeting non-cognitive skills, can significantly help minors who have been affected by severe disadvantage or educational deprivation in early childhood (Kautz *et al.*, 2014).

The popularity of the *educational poverty* construct has been underpinned by European scholarship in the field of socio-politics and economics since the 1960s. Since Gary Becker's (1964) studies on human capital, a general consensus has built up among economists that education is a decisive factor in the development of individuals, national economies and global society. Investing in education is predictive of positive economic development and lower social costs, because it ensures, among other outcomes, better health, longer life expectancy, greater existential satisfaction, greater civic engagement and less deviant behaviour.

If education is viewed as a strategic investment, then we may use the term 'poverty' to indicate a total or partial lack of it. As far back as the 1990s, when the term 'educational poverty' had not yet been coined, this insight had already become a focus of attention for the European Union, as borne out by documents including the *White Paper* edited by Édith Cresson (European Commission, 1996) and the Delors (1996) *Report* in which education was defined as 'a treasure for all' members of the knowledge society.

As explained in a report entitled *In It Together. Why Less Inequality Benefits All* (OECD, 2015), inequality of educational opportunity among children represses talent and blocks key skills for economic and social development. A deprived educational and recreational-cultural environment during childhood, influenced by inherited factors such as familial socio-economic status and geographical location, generates disadvantage, with potentially negative effects over the long term, including intergenerational chains of poverty, a vicious cycle that undermines both individual well-being and national growth. Nevertheless, PISA-OECD (2019) data suggests that disadvantage is not destiny: quality educational interventions can compensate effectively for negative impacts on the cognitive skills and development of personal and social skills in at-risk minors. The quality of educational offerings for children and adolescents, therefore, is what makes the difference.

The EU guidelines have been prompting greater attention to the issue of educational poverty. The considerations of the Transatlantic Forum on Inclusive Early Years in 2013, as well as those of the Italian forum and virtuous grant scheme *Infanzia, Prima* (Fondazione 'Emanuela Zancan' onlus, 2019), together with the advocacy of Save the Children, have led to the setting up in Italy of the *Fondo per il contrasto della povertà educativa minorile* (Child educational poverty fund), a dedicated fund for tackling educational poverty among children. This government programme was introduced via the 2016 finance act, and is supported by the banking foundations, with the state participating indirectly by providing tax relief to the foundations. The potentially revolutionary novelty and political value of this fund lie in the original approach underpinning it: a joint commitment by the public and private sectors to finance or co-finance projects that must necessarily be implemented by networks of schools and third sector actors through grant schemes run by the social enterprise Con i Bambini which was set up *ad hoc* to manage and execute the fund's activities. Over the first three-year period of the fund's existence (2016–2018), €360 million in grant monies were made available. The 2019 finance act confirmed the fund for the following three-year period 2019–2021, with a budget of approximately €240 million to be distributed via grant schemes and co-financing projects. The projects approved up to June 2021 numbered 384 and involved some 500,000 children and 6,600 organisations.

Educational poverty is not therefore an abstract concept, but rather a concrete locus of investment with the potential to catalyse planning and change, with the result, in recent years, of contributing to the revitalising of both the social fabric and educational interventions for children and young people. The underlying logic is that 'people's resources cannot be exclusively read in terms of material assets and economic possibilities, but rather as a pool of interdependent factors in which educational opportunities and the vitality and quality of educational environments play an important role' (Triani, 2018: 21). Hence the need to identify possible future directions for effective political action and socio-educational intervention in support of the capability to cope with the complexities of life at both the individual and community levels.

Measuring educational poverty: A process still being defined

Save the Children Italia has suggested that there are four core dimensions of educational poverty that need to be addressed. These echo the four pillars of UNESCO's International Report on Education for the twenty-first century, *Learning: The Treasure Within* (*Learning to Know, Learning to Do, Learning to Live Together, Learning to Be*) (Delors, 1996) and emphasise the need to educate the whole person, as previously flagged in the 1972 report *Learning to Be. The world of education today and tomorrow,* edited by Edgar Faure (1972):

1. Understanding: Cognitive and problem-solving skills;
2. Existing: Development of the mental and emotional sphere;
3. Living together: Social and interpersonal life;
4. Knowing the world: The educational community beyond school.

In order to measure educational poverty with respect to each of these dimensions, Save the Children Italia has worked to identify existing regional data with a view to developing an Educational Poverty Index (IPE). The first IPE consisted of the following 14 indicators (2014: 8–9):

1. public provision of early childhood education and care services;
2. full-time classes at primary school;
3. full-time classes at lower secondary school;
4. school complexes with a school meal service;
5. schools with a certificate of occupancy;
6. classrooms with internet access;
7. school drop-out rate;
8. children who have been to the theatre;
9. children who have been to a museum or exhibition;
10. children who have visited a monument or archaeological site;
11. children who have been to a concert;
12. children who regularly practise a sport;
13. children who use the internet and
14. children who have read a book.

Save the Children Italia has itself raised the need for a more comprehensive measure, given that this IPE does not consider, for example:

> .... the qualitative aspects of the early childhood services provided, access to these services, data on the human resources in the school system, the training received by staff, the extent of inclusive, participative pedagogical practices, the presence of green spaces and public libraries, frequency of school trips, and access to summer camps.
> (2014: 25)

The IPE indices from 2014 make it clear that effective action to prevent and combat educational poverty must necessarily be conducted systematically. Educational welfare demands collaborative intervention by a network of institutions, services and settings, while availing of opportunities in the community for free and open forms of extracurricular education. Given the lack of a comprehensive Italian database, the social enterprise Con i Bambini is working on mapping existing educational resources at the municipal level in parallel with administering the current grants scheme.

In 2015, three goals were identified in the context of the *Let's Lighten the Future 2030* campaign (Save the Children Italia, 2015: 45–47):

1. All children should be able to learn, experiment, develop skills, talents and aspirations.
2. All minors should have access to quality educational offerings.
3. Child poverty should be eradicated in order to foster educational growth.

As a result, in 2016, two new indices were devised: one reflecting 'educational poverty at the level of individual competence' (Goal 1) and the other the 'poverty of the educational offerings available in the community' (Goal 2). The composite index IPE 2016/2018 could not be compared with the previous IPE introduced in 2014 as it was based on ten new indicators (Save the Children Italia, 2016: 13–14):

1. percentage of 15-year-olds who fail to attain the minimum levels of competence in maths;
2. percentage of 15-year-olds who fail to attain the minimum levels of competence in reading;
3. percentage of school drop-outs;
4. percentage of 6- to 17-year-olds who have not done four or more of the seven recreational and cultural activities listed (the same seven activities that comprised indicators 8–14 in the IPE 2014 index);
5. percentage of 0- to 2-year-olds without access to publicly funded ECEC services;
6. percentage of primary school classes that do not attend full-time;
7. percentage of lower secondary school classes that do not attend full-time;
8. percentage of students that do not use the school canteen service;
9. percentage of students attending schools without an adequate learning infrastructure and
10. percentage of classrooms without a fast internet connection.

As indicators 5, 8, and 9 make clear, Save the Children Italia did not just collect data on coverage, availability or certification, but recorded the actual accessibility, attendance and state of the various educational services.

In 2017, Save the Children Italia (2017) called for children to be involved in the development of new indicators that include information about children's subjective well-being and the quality of educational services, both of which should be monitored annually. This was an attempt to remedy another gap: the failure to listen to children, despite the fact that Article 12 of the UN Convention states that children have the right to be listened to in relation to all matters concerning them.

On February 2018, the first report on educational poverty in Italy was published (DEPP srl, 2018). This document analysed four thematic dimensions:

1. availability of daycare and early childhood education centres;
2. distribution of libraries;
3. availability of sports halls in schools and
4. state and accessibility of school buildings.

The second report on educational poverty in Italy, *Scuole e asili per ricucire il paese* (Schools and kindergartens to mend the country), published in April 2019, supplemented this snapshot with data on the availability of child services in all Italian municipalities (Openpolis, 2019). Save the Children Italia focused on early childhood. *Il miglior inizio* (The best start) (2019) documented experimental research conducted to assess the efficacy of infant-toddler centres and quality time in the home for 0- to 3-year-old children with a view to reducing inequalities among children in terms of their acquisition of skills and competences prior to beginning compulsory schooling. The indicators used were four activities with parents: reading books, experiencing music together, physical outdoor activity and going to the theatre. The importance of investing in early education was borne out by the results of the IDELA (*International Development and Early Learning Assessment*) test, administered in over 40 countries to assess the progress of 3- to 6-year-old children across four dimensions of competence and development: physical growth, mathematics, language ability and social and emotional learning.

In May 2020, given the exponentially increased risk of educational poverty caused by the COVID-19 public health emergency, Save the Children Italia emphasised the importance of protecting children's non-cognitive – 'motivational, emotional, and social' capabilities (2020: 10), which were in danger of being undermined by forced isolation measures. With a view to adopting an increasingly participatory approach, a study was conducted on the impact of the COVID-19 lockdown on educational poverty, as perceived by families and children/adolescents between the ages of 8 and 17 years. The following five indicators were used to map the areas of Italy at greatest risk of educational poverty (2020: 16–23):

1. availability of publicly funded daycare for 0- to 2-year-olds;
2. explicit school drop-out: *Early School Leavers*;
3. percentage of minors aged 14–16 years (attending second year of high school) who belong to the most socioeconomically and culturally disadvantaged quintile;
4. implicit school drop-out: percentage of minors aged 14–16 years (attending second year of high school) who fail to attain the minimum levels of competence required to pass the Ministry of Education INVALSI tests in maths and Italian and
5. percentage increase in successful applications for basic income payments.

In recent years, the Italian National Statistics Institute (Istat) has also conducted multiple studies on educational poverty: it has reviewed the educational poverty indices (EPI) in use around the world, proposing new indices for assessing educational poverty that measure a combination of the material, relational, cultural and environmental issues that can hinder children from acquiring the capabilities they need to live in our complex contemporary society. Istat devised indicators for four areas or dimensions deemed to be interdependent: (1) cognitive capabilities; (2) non-cognitive capabilities; (3) material determinants, standard of living, health and security and (4) resilience. The complete set of selected indicators was as follows (Quattrociocchi, 2018):

1.1. Does not have books at home or has less than 25;
1.2. Does not have friends, or does not spend time with friends;
1.3 Low digital skills;
1.4 Low literacy skills;
1.5 Low numeracy skills;
2.1 Does not do voluntary work;

2.2 Does not engage in and is not interested in political activism;
2.3 Does not read newspapers, even online;
2.4 Does not use internet, or only rarely;
2.5 School drop-out;
2.6 Does not attend language, computer, art/culture courses, etc.
3.1 At risk of poverty and social exclusion;
3.2 Does not practise sport either continuously or occasionally;
3.3 Lives in an area with characteristics of urban decay;
3.4 Lives in an area without public green spaces;
3.5 Physical health index;
4.1 Mental health index;
4.2 Does less than four out of the six cultural activities listed;
4.3. Does not read books or has read less than three;
4.4 Does not do activities that involve being active during free time;
4.5 NEET (Not in Education, Employment or Training).

As this account of all the different indices of educational poverty and their evolution over time suggests, the process of establishing how best to measure the construct is still underway. One of the first gaps identified in 2014, a lack of data on the location of libraries, has been partially filled thanks to the efforts of the social enterprise Con i Bambini (DEPP srl, 2018). Meanwhile, the EPI index adopted by Istat includes access to green spaces, reflecting efforts to broaden the construct to encompass the mental, physical and social spheres. Indeed, those setting out to measure educational poverty in children have increasingly focused on the multiple dimensions that can contribute to making a subject *educationally* poor, yielding a more flexible construct that includes, alongside traditional variables (mainly individual cognitive capabilities and effective access to services and opportunities), additional – no less important – indicators concerning the emotional-relational sphere and culture in the broader sense.

Concluding remarks on the concept of 'educational poverty'

Reviewing the theme of educational poverty as it is treated in the international literature is a complex exercise. The signifier of the term *educational poverty* overlaps to a large degree with *academic poverty*. Now while poor schooling is surely a core component of educational poverty, the qualifier *educational* is not exclusively pertinent to the sphere of formal preschool or primary/secondary school education. Thus, the Italian version of United Nations Agenda 2030 Sustainable Development Goal 4, *Ensure inclusive and equitable quality education and promote lifelong learning opportunities for all*, explicitly translates *education* as both *educazione* (i.e. education in the wider sense) and *istruzione* (i.e. schooling) (although not all languages have two distinct terms for these concepts) in acknowledgement of the fact that the former entails a broader and more diverse field of experience.

To date, in European and Western contexts, the themes most frequently associated with the concept of *educational poverty* are: *early school leaving*, the phenomenon of NEETs (*Not (engaged) in Education, Employment or Training*), and new forms of poverty. In poor or developing countries, however, the concept of educational poverty is linked to the phenomenon of the exclusion of children from the school system (*out-of-school children*), and to the problems of child labour, illiteracy, disability, street children, child mortality and gender discrimination in access to education.

Since 2017, scholars in other countries who are in communication with Italian researchers have been investigating the concept of *educational poverty*, drawing on the definition of educational poverty proposed by Save the Children Italia and analysing the situation in their country from this perspective. TreeLLLE and Con i Bambini Impresa Sociale have collected papers from France, England, and the Netherlands (2017), and the 'Emanuela Zancan' Foundation from China, Australia, Spain and the United Kingdom (2019).

Istat too is contributing to the international dissemination of this revisited concept of educational poverty as 'deprivation in education, read also as deprivation of opportunities and rights i.e. health, culture, participation, social relations' (Pratesi *et al.*, 2020: 1), thus encouraging an understanding of the construct of *educational poverty* as deprivation of non-material rights and opportunities. However, the question remains as to what the dimensions making up educational poverty actually are and what indicators should be used to measure its impact on the lives of children and adolescents. A set of issues urgently needs to be addressed if we are to answer these questions.

A first question is whether educational poverty may be viewed as a form of poverty that is *distinct* from material poverty, that is to say, a type of poverty that is *sui generis*, and to some extent independent of, economic determinants. While educational poverty is certainly made more likely by material poverty, which undeniably reduces opportunities, we nowadays perceive the former as a broader phenomenon that is not always, or necessarily, related to material deprivation.

This raises numerous themes for reflection. Is it possible to be materially rich, but *educationally poor*? And vice versa: Can one be poor in terms of economic resources, but nevertheless rich in educational stimuli and opportunities? Is it appropriate to describe children living in rural areas or village streets and squares – who are poor materially yet grow up within a social fabric that is relationally rich and are well integrated into their local communities – as *educationally poor*? Does this term not apply more so to city children whose lives are highly organised and may even be overloaded with educational opportunities, yet whose social lives are severely limited, and who may not even have time to play or to engage in free play?

It might even be claimed that there is a form of material wealth and a level of well-being and consumption that hinder development: children's difficulties are not always caused by deprivation, but in some cases, even from an 'excess of donations' (Scaparro and Pietropolli Charmet, 1993: 6); in contrast, there are children who, having been exposed to problematic conditions, have developed more resources and resilience for this very reason. Is an opulent society not perhaps *educationally poor* when it presents money and success as the main measure of personal achievement and value, or when it fills the daily calendars of its children with commitments, forcing them to forego boredom (and the creativity that often accompanies it), or bombards them with information without letting their desires and talents emerge, or holds them hostage to their parents' fears by preventing them from having the experiences that they need to develop a healthy level of independence?

On the other hand, might poverty that fosters the development of children's latent potential be viewed as *educational*, where material want is not (as unfortunately is often the case) a source of brutalisation or deviance, but rather strengthens social ties and stimulates proactivity and resilience? In the latter scenario, education (both formal and informal) is likely to be a decisive discriminating factor. Street children are often 'intelligent subjects, endowed with decision-making skills and a spirit of independence, highly organised, capable of living within a social system characterised by precise roles and rules' (Vico, 2005: 110). Growing, maturing, and developing resilience and a love of life can simply be the outcome of coping positively with adversity and even deprivation.

Perhaps, therefore, rather than defining (educational) poverty in terms of needs that can sometimes be frustrated, we should begin to frame it in terms of the resources and rights that children require to provide for their own needs and address their own frustration. From such a perspective, a truly pedagogical approach would avoid the error of producing interventions, targeting only those sectors of the population traditionally viewed as disadvantaged and forgetting that the various forms of educational poverty are actually more complex and cut across social class.

A second key question is whether educational poverty can be properly assessed based on the indicators currently in use in Italy and Europe, or whether it should include less objectifiable or measurable forms of need, which are destined to remain latent or *even invisible*, despite being significant from an educational point of view.

Here, we cannot overlook the importance of parenting, which is children's first great, yet sometimes problematic, resource. Families who are 'poor' (from a cultural or moral or emotional-relational point of view) can be a source of educational deprivation, in that they provide a developmental context that influences how their children learn to attribute meaning to the world, and to organise thoughts, objects, and emotions. The affective poverty that sometimes lies behind the security doors of apartments, along with – unfortunately still widespread – forms of neglect, abuse, maltreatment, violence (whether witnessed or experienced as a victim) and suffering can play a role in educational poverty, often permanently conditioning the traits of developing subjects.

The relational dimension, aside from these extreme situations, also plays a key part in cognitive development. According to studies on brain plasticity, 'learning is not so much due to inherited biological characteristics, as to the offerings of the environment, which facilitate, through experience, new trajectories and the activation of new circuits' (Milani, 2018: 29). Receiving attention and love also seems to affect IQ and the thickness of the cerebral cortex. Longitudinal studies bear out the highly protective value of a family that reliably provides the child with environmental stimulation in the early years of life (Avants *et al.*, 2015). What is more, neuroscience has recently established that disadvantaged children, born in a materially poor environment, when exposed to adequate environmental stimuli, develop reasoning skills that are comparable to those of children who grow up in the wealthiest families. The cognitive and motivational stimuli offered by the educational agencies that children encounter make a far greater difference to their education than the socio-economic status of their families (Leonard *et al.*, 2019). Nevertheless, the greatest gap that persists in the measurement of educational poverty (perhaps because it is challenging to objectivise) concerns precisely the quality of children's relationships and the child's own perceptions. This is an unjustifiable gap, given that *education* always takes place within *a relationship*.

We often hear talk about the importance of good schools in combating child educational poverty. However, 'educational poverty must not and cannot be reduced to academic poverty and school-related issues, but rather is something far wider and more radical' (Casartelli and Dodi, 2018: 106). The work of Howard Gardner (1983, 2005) paved the way for a new conception of intelligence: no longer unique, but multiple. To ensure harmonious development and the sensitive valuing of individual traits, 'school curricula, from primary school onwards, should offer differential trajectories and contents' (Cheli, 2013: 105). Yet, if educational investment continues to focus on certain modes of intelligence to the detriment of others, this will be unfairly penalising towards children with other propensities.

When we discuss *intelligence,* we tend to associate it with the cognitive sphere, but we should not forget the essential role of the child's emotional life. Emotions are an integral part of all cognition and powerfully filter our interpretation of experience. The polarised separation of the affective and cognitive dimensions of education is thus misleading.

There is an entire range of non-cognitive skills that tests of academic performance fail to adequately assess, such as perseverance, conscientiousness, self-control, confidence, attention, self-esteem and self-effectiveness, resilience, openness to experience, empathy, humility, tolerance, cooperativeness and the propensity to engage in constructive relations: all traits that are valued in society at large and in the workplace, and which foster integration and a satisfactory quality of life. The International Association for the Evaluation of Educational Achievement (IEA) has shown a laudable commitment to evaluating selected soft skills in conjunction with cognitive skills in different areas, focusing on reasoning, valuing, enjoyment and self-confidence. Failing to take these skills into account (and to view neglect of them as an expression of educational poverty) can have negative repercussions at the moral and social levels also, as the now large body of studies on emotional illiteracy shows. Equally deficient is a model of education that excludes the existential-spiritual dimension and does not offer children tools for embarking on their personal quest for meaning. Neglect of this aspect places children at risk of existential frustration (Frankl, 2010), with significant repercussions for their well-being and future life planning.

> Education should always try to simultaneously involve the planes of sensitivity, affectivity, intellect, and will, using different languages, and never disjoining the head from the heart or the spirit from the body. Indeed, phenomenology teaches us that the human person is a unified bio-psycho-socio-spiritual whole.
>
> (Bruzzone, 2012: 60)

An education that does not work on all of these planes at once might therefore be defined as *poor*.

Perhaps, in acknowledgement of the multifaceted nature of education, we should replace the term 'educational poverty' (in the singular) with 'educational poverties' (in the plural). This would also help to convey the fact that there is no one form of poverty, in this case, *educational*, of which individuals are victims, or to which they can be completely immune; rather there are multiple potential forms of deprivation that can co-exist with equally numerous resources. From this perspective, all children (even those who appear to be the most privileged) are potentially poor, and at the same time, all (even those generally considered disadvantaged) possess resources that are sometimes undervalued. The task of education is, precisely, to ensure that both groups produce an optimal response to their own peculiar needs and desire for growth and realisation.

Questions for discussion

In what ways, in your opinion, can 'educational poverty' manifest itself?

What dimensions of educational poverty do you consider more dangerous for the future of our children?

Are there any aspects of educational poverty that have not yet been considered in your opinion?

What actions do you view as key to preventing and fighting against educational poverty in children and/or adolescents?

Summary points

- Poverty does not uniquely coincide with material or socio-economic disadvantage: it can also involve intangible dimensions that may be symbolic, cultural, relational, affective, moral and spiritual in nature. Deprivation, therefore, can take multiple and often interdependent forms. The exclusive identification of 'poor' subjects with those living in poverty or marginalised contexts is no longer sustainable. Even 'privileged' segments of the population can suffer from various forms of poverty, which often remain invisible precisely because they are intangible.
- The concept of 'educational poverty' implies life and developmental conditions that do not facilitate (or even severely impede) the development of children's and adolescents' cognitive, emotional, social and existential resources. The various forms of educational poverty thus include a lack of cultural stimuli, affective deprivation, a lack of ethical and value-based models, etc.: indeed, any factor that can somehow slow down or prevent the full deployment of a developing person's potential, and adversely affect their future and ability to cope with life.
- In recent years, in Italy, increasing attention has been paid to the theme of educational poverty, leading to the allocation of significant financial resources to hundreds of community projects designed to support the rights, education, socialisation and participation of children and young people. This investment in preventing and countering educational poverty has sparked a debate on the nature and significance of the concept *per se*: there has been a consequent shift in the focus of intervention from disadvantaged socio-economic conditions and exclusion to the cultural, relational and symbolic conditions that can also affect the children of non-marginalised families.
- A series of indices for the measurement of educational poverty have been implemented, with a view to detecting its presence and impact on the development trajectories of children and adolescents. However, some spheres of educational poverty remain largely overlooked, despite their decisive importance, because they are challenging to objectify and measure. We need to find ways to make these aspects more visible and measurable, and to integrate quantitative and statistical methods with selected qualitative and phenomenological approaches, so as to more fully grasp the subjective and intersubjective dimensions of experience.

Note

Both authors researched and wrote this chapter together; Simona Finetti wrote the first and second sections, Daniele Bruzzone wrote the third and fourth.

Recommended reading

Nussbaum, M.C. (2011) *Creating Capabilities. The human development approach*. Cambridge (MA) and London: Belknap Press of Harvard University Press.

OECD (2015) *In It Together: Why less inequality benefits all*. Paris: OECD Publishing. Online. Available at: https://www.conibambini.org/en/ (Accessed 4 October 2021).

Save the Children (2014) *Aladdin's Lamp. Save the Children's index to measure educational poverty and illuminate the future of children in Italy*. Rome: Save the Children.

References

Avants, B.B., Hackman, D.A., Betancourt, L.M., Lawson, G.M., Hurt, H. and Farah, M.J. (2015) Relation of Childhood Home Environment to Cortical Thickness in Late Adolescence: Specificity of experience and timing. *PLoS ONE*, **10**(10), e0138217.

Bauman, Z. and Mazzeo, R. (2012) *Conversazioni sull'educazione*. Trento: Centro Studi Erickson.

Becker, G.S. (1964) *Human Capital: A theoretical and empirical analysis, with special reference to education*. New York: National Bureau of Economic Research.

Bruzzone, D. (2012) *Farsi persona. Lo sguardo fenomenologico e l'enigma della formazione*. Milano: FrancoAngeli.

Casartelli, A. and Dodi, E. (2018) *Povertà educativa, povertà, dispersione scolastica, competenze. Cosa significa oggi investire sull'educazione?* Online. Available at: https://welforum.it/poverta-educativa-poverta-dispersione-scolastica-competenze/ (Accessed 15 June 2021).

Cheli, E. (2013) *L'epoca delle relazioni in crisi. (E come uscirne). Coppia, famiglia, scuola, sanità, lavoro*. Milano: FrancoAngeli.

Delors, J. (Ed.) (1996) *Learning: The treasure within. Report to UNESCO of the International Commission on Education for the Twenty-First Century*. Paris: UNESCO Publishing.

DEPP srl (2018) *Povertà educativa. Servisi per l'infanzia e i minori*. Roma: DEPP.

European Commission (1996) *Teaching and Learning: Towards the learning society*. Brussels-Luxembourg: Office for Official Publications of the European Communities.

European Commission (2011) *Communication from the Commission. Early Childhood Education and Care: Providing all our children with the best start for the world of tomorrow*. Brussels: European Commission.

Faure, E. (Ed.) (1972) *Learning to Be. The world of education today and tomorrow*. Paris: UNESCO Publishing.

Fondazione 'Emanuela Zancan' onlus (2019) *Studi Zancan. Politiche e servisi alle persone*. **XVII**(3–4).

Frankl, V.E. (2010) *The Feeling of Meaninglessness. A challenge to psychotherapy and philosophy*. Milwaukee: Marquette University Press.

Gardner, H. (1983) *Frames of Mind: The theory of multiple intelligences*. New York: Basic Books.

Gardner, H. (2005) *The Development and Education of the Mind: The selected works of Howard Gardner*. London and New York: Routledge.

Giustini, C. and Tolomelli, A. (2012) *Approssimarsi alla povertà tra teorie, esperienze e buone prassi. Riflessioni di pedagogia sociale*. Milano: FrancoAngeli.

Iavarone, M.L. and Girardi, F. (2018) Povertà educativa e rischio minorile: fenomenologia di un crimine sociale. *Rivista di Studi e Ricerche sulla criminalità organizata*, **4**(3), pp. 23–44.

Kautz, T., Heckman, J., Diris, R., ter Weel, B. and Borghans, L. (2014) *Fostering and Measuring Skills: Improving cognitive and non-cognitive skills to promote lifetime success*. Cambridge (MA): National Bureau of Economic Research.

Leonard, J.A., Romeo, R.R., Park, A.T., Takada, M.E., Robinson, S.T., Grotzinger, H., Last, B.S., Finn, A.S. and Gabrieli, J.D.E. (2019) Associations between Cortical Thickness and Reasoning Differ by Socioeconomic Status in Development. *Developmental Cognitive Neuroscience*, **36**, 100641.

Milani, P. (2018) *Educazione e famiglie. Ricerche e nuove pratiche per la genitorialità*. Roma: Carocci.

Nussbaum, M.C. (2011) *Creating Capabilities. The human development approach*. Cambridge (MA) and London: Belknap Press of Harvard University Press.

OECD (2015) *In It Together: Why less inequality benefits all*. Paris: OECD Publishing.

OECD (2019) *PISA 2018 Results*. Paris: OECD Publishing.

Openpolis (2019) *Scuole e asili per ricucire il paese. La presenza dei servisi per i minori in tutti i comuni italiani*. Roma: Osservatorio Povertà Educativa #Conibambini.

Pratesi, M., Quattrociocchi, L., Bertarelli, G., Gemignani, A. and Giusti, C. (2020) Spatial Distribution of Multidimensional Educational Poverty in Italy Using Small Area Estimation. *Social Indicators Research*, **156**(1), DOI:10.1007/s11205-020-02328-5.

Quattrociocchi, L. (2018) *Povertà educative: (non) finirai come tuo padre). Popolazione, istruzione, mobilità*. Online. Available at: https://www.slideshare.net/slideistat/lquattrociocchi-d-irezione-centrale-per-le-statistiche-sociali-e-il-censimento-della-popolazione-i-stat-povert-educativa (Accessed 15 June 2021).

Saraceno, C. (2002) Cittadini a metà. Le nuove forme della povertà e dell'esclusione sociale. *Italianieuropei*, **5**(28).

Save the Children (2017) *Sconfiggere la povertà educativa in Europa*. Roma: Save the Children.

Save the Children (2019) *Il tempo dei bambini. Atlante dell'Infanzia a rischio 2019*. Roma: Save the Children.

Save the Children Italia (2014) *Aladdin's Lamp. Save the Children's index to measure educational poverty and illuminate the future of children in Italy*. Roma: Save the Children.

Save the Children Italia (2015) *Illuminiamo il futuro 2030. Obiettivi per liberare i bambini dalla povertà educativa.* Roma: Save the Children.
Save the Children Italia (2016) *Liberare i bambini dalla povertà educativa: a che punto siamo? Un'analisi regionale.* Roma: Save the Children.
Save the Children Italia (2018) *Nuotare contro corrente. Povertà educativa e resilienza in Italia.* Roma: Save the Children.
Save the Children Italia (2019) *Il miglior inisio. Disuguaglianze e opportunità nei primi anni di vita.* Roma: Save the Children.
Save the Children Italia (2020) *Riscriviamo il Futuro. L'impatto del coronavirus sulla povertà educativa.* Roma: Save the Children.
Scaparro, F. and Pietropolli Charmet, G. (1993) *Belletà. Adolescenza temuta, adolescenza sognata.* Torino: Bollati Boringhieri.
Sen, A.K. (2000) *Development as Freedom.* New York: Anchor Books.
TreeLLLe and Con i Bambini Impresa Sociale (2017) *Pratiche di contrasto alla povertà educativa minorile. Casi di Francia, Inghilterra, Paesi Bassi.* Roma: TreeLLLe and Con i Bambini Impresa Sociale.
Triani, P. (2018) *La collaborazione educativa.* Brescia: Morcelliana.
UNDP (2010) *Human Development Report 2010. 20th Anniversary Edition. The real wealth of nations: Pathways to human development.* New York: Palgrave Macmillan.
Vico, G. (2005) *Erranza educativa e bambini di strada. Teoria e narrazioni.* Milano: Vita e Pensiero.

7 Everything, but a teacher
Notes from creative writing workshops within liminal space

Ronny Ritze

Introduction

I admit that this chapter is, in the context of this book, an unusual one. This is because I use a rather journalistic style to capture the reality of the liminal spaces in which I try to initiate reflective processes in school drop-outs and male juvenile offenders. This liminal space was defined by Gennep (2019 [1909]) as a metaphorical space in which a transition happens as for example, the transition from a girl/boy to become a woman/man. In the current context, it is a field where the young people I meet during my 'writing workshops' embark on an ambiguous and disorientating journey. A journey where what they have been before they no longer are, while what they might become – as a result of their efforts – they are not yet. This is basically a journey into the self, trying to develop an awareness of one's body and its expressive capabilities, i.e. a mindful, reflective endeavour regarding one's own embodiment (Varela *et al.*, 1991). This allows the youngsters not only to align their bodily expressions to their affective experiences but equally to gain clarity about these affective experiences themselves, allowing them to recognise them under concepts (Feldges, 2014) and to start utilising them in their own reasoning. In this respect, these 'writing workshops' constitute nothing less than a genuine opportunity for the participants to embark on a transformative journey (Koller, 2018) to become – if it works – a different person. After their often traumatic school experience (Wuttig, 2016), these youngsters have the opportunity to alter their relation towards themselves, others and their surroundings. An opportunity sadly not taken up by all of them, showing the general unpredictability of efforts to initiate the processes of *Bildung*. My chosen writing style reflects the often disrupted, haphazardous nature of living in a continuously developing and potentially chaotic situation.

School drop-out project, ten minutes before the break

Two participants are alone in the room. The rest of us, a group of ten youngsters and myself, are standing outside in front of the door. 'What is it that a sculptor does?' I ask, grab someone by his arm and move it into a position while asking the person to whom it belongs to keep it that way. 'A sculptor chisels a stone until that stone turns into a figure. Behind this door, we have two people. One is a sculptor the other one is the stone that will be turned into a statue. When we later go back into the room, we can see how this happens in slow motion'.

DOI: 10.4324/9781003223528-9

The task of the participants is to find out what kind of representation it could be and to explain which feelings and emotions are expressed in the character. The participants can relax while getting an idea about the expressive capability of the body – of their bodies. A writing workshop unit lasts 90 minutes, which means there are 15 minutes to write. The rest of the time consists of listening and talking. Praise, praise and more praise. To do this, we bring these group exercises together, like the sculptor, releasing the blockages and filling the togetherness, the space between us while also learning about a body's – their body's – expressive capabilities.

> **Question for discussion**
>
> Can you see how such a sculptor/sculpture game is yielding benefits in increasing the participants' ability to put a name (concept) to their emotions?

The coaching personality

I'm a creative writing coach and I'm responsible for opening these youngsters up to the world of literature. I am also to show them how to express themselves. How they formulate life goals and recognise themselves. There are always catchphrases in the concepts that are made for this at the beginning: creative writing serves to process stressful experiences, promotes mindfulness, self-efficacy, emotion regulation, the preservation and improvement of cultural techniques, social integration; it protects against depression and negative thought circles, particularly important in drug withdrawal (Seligman, 1972). That is the conceptual approach when such a 'creative writing workshop' is initiated.

But how can you explain relationship work when you have to *feel* it? How can the preventive aspect be measured at all? And how do you convince people who are scared of school that a pen and paper aren't so bad? How does creative writing work in the context of self-determined learning? What are the rules? Can writing alone change a life, even heal it (Jagusch, 2013)? And what am I doing here in these groups where every second participant is a drug addict, has a criminal record, has been expelled from school, or is about to slide into a social support system that later will need state funding, time, therapy, a place in prison, and social benefits?

I'm 42 years old and I didn't choose the job. It just came up on me. I was actually a bookseller when a juvenile detention centre opened in the neighbourhood. It was more by chance that I started giving writing workshops there. Back then I was wearing an old coat, beard and had a cig in my mouth and looked like a crisis myself. In debt, I had just quit drinking. That's how I got to know the first group. And I had no idea what I was doing, I just did it. Apparently that was a good thing, and word got around. In the further course I accompanied hundreds of adolescents and young adults in their (re-)socialisation process. Some of them didn't come back because they made it: education, family, housing and a halfway decent life without having come into contact with the law. They write me emails, telling me how writing stories changed and affected them, showing me pictures: of a new girlfriend, the child or their employment contract. But there is still something left: the experience of working with them.

Eight years after my first encounter with juvenile delinquents, my catalogue of methods consists of 300 pages. It ranges from introductory exercises for people with mental disabilities to writing games for group formation with school-outs and prisoners to lecture techniques for readings. But all these exercises and the reports from the groups and the lectures cannot be reduced to a few sentences on. So here's the story.

The rules

Everything that is initiated in a writing workshop revolves around relationships, approaching each other in a non-judgemental and relaxed manner. This is of key importance with my work with male juvenile delinquents. It doesn't matter how a participant writes, whether the spelling is correct or not. First, everything he learned in school he has to forget. You have to convince him that he can break the rules. We're not in class here! And whoever taught him to spell a word 'exactly like that' did not get the point. It is important to overcome the trauma of school. That's why the little things are taken seriously right from the start. If someone manages just one sentence, one scribble on the margins, maybe just one remark, any form of expression is valued positively and everyone who contributes gets support. Tasks are presented in small, achievable steps. I make the quiet, passive participant the secretary: he makes sure the rules are followed, organises things when I'm not in the room, and tidies up. Ultimately, however, I will get to know everyone and can put my finger on their potential. And in the end, everyone has to put up with it.

The next most important thing is that they can read their own handwriting. Grammar, spelling and punctuation are secondary. It also doesn't matter how the participant starts writing, whether large or small, on paper or chalk on the floor, or whether he sprays it with a can on the wall.

> **Question for discussion**
>
> Why would you think it is possible to ignore the forms of 'correct' writing in these classes and under these circumstances?

The subsequent text production itself can be understood as an intimate and mindful act. The act of writing needs slowing down and pausing (Heimes, 2015. The participants rehearse being alone with themselves and the paper. And no matter what they produce, whether it's a diary entry, a short story, poetry, rap or dramatic texts. It's often about getting rid of stressful experiences (vom Scheidt, 1989) which creates space for new experiences.

The text can be presented and evaluated in the group. The need for appreciation that is satisfied in this way also opens up space for the perception of others and can increase the ability to empathise. In addition, dealing with the text in this way promotes self-confidence; at best the participants understand that they do not need substances or advice, but are able to help themselves. The result is not the finished contribution, but the experience of having mastered a difficult task and, even better, a strategy derived from it for dealing with challenges. The text can break soon ground in the first or second lesson. And this can become the most important moment during our joint cooperation. The participant must dare to pick up a pen, and keep it in his hand.

The main thing is not the result, although this is important, it is always the process and the relationship that develops between the coach and the participant. If I manage to build enough confidence to write the first few lines, the rest of the text often comes overnight.

When a therapist subsequently works with the text, there is more 'space'. Classic writing training tends to pay attention to theoretical aspects, to style, tension, characters, to a certain literary penetration. Instead, I guide the participants from A to Z, evaluate the text and, although a result is always desired, it is the free form that takes centre space. The text is not evaluated.

The topics

All the content of the conversation around the writing process takes place on a deep emotional level, regardless of whether we are talking about music, food or the weather. Every single text depicts a tension between love and hate. As a writing coach, I therefore have to reveal myself without tearing down the wall between us, maintaining my position in the liminal space and allowing closeness without it being explicit (cf. von Werder, 2007). Conversations in advance, games like the sculptor and the common break in the yard, can all be important prerequisites for later writing about feelings.

Even then, the group 'senses' a frightening amount of what is happening on a personal level. If I'm not careful, participants may ask me how much money I'm making. If I'm too euphoric, the group may suggest taking a break. When I'm sad, the group is strangely quiet, without me saying a word about my personal life or event, even though I consider myself a good actor. Mutual respect determines working together. Respect for the personalities and the life stories behind them.

The truth resides within man

A characteristic of creative writing is that it engages with the whole person more than other approaches to writing. It connects cognitive, emotional and imaginative processes (Spinner, 1993), releases from inner paralysis, relieves from powerlessness, anger and hate. This reactivates self-protection and strengthens the sense of self. And where else could it be more useful than in prison? A place where the individual is on their own in an omnipresent, omnipotent institution, a 'total institution' as Goffman (1961) called it: a place where a personality is reduced to simple processes and ways of thinking, but where the inmate as an author can ultimately allow himself to preserve his own personality to a certain extent through the text.

> **Questions for discussion**
>
> Is it possible to transfer some of the here mentioned benefits of writing into 'normal' classroom activities as well? What kind of problems could you envisage?

A change of scene: A youth offenders prison in Germany with a special station for drug-addicts

It is difficult to quieten the participants down. Maybe I'm too nervous. Maybe I'm breathing too heavily, sorting my papers for too long. Maybe there is too much clutter in my head, maybe the bars are irritating me. Maybe it's the weather. I'm looking for a hundred reasons and they blur with the words in space. This writing workshop is going to be one of my craziest, I think. Any text will be gratefully received. Because whatever happens, the results don't come from outside but from and with these imprisoned junkies.

First, we try it in a room that is meant for something like that. There are no tables, only space for a circle of chairs and a flipchart. If we want to take a break and smoke, the way to the cells is too far. So we're moving. The next workshop meetings will take place on their patch, the guarded area. Always after lunch. It smells of coffee, detergent and impatience. The cells are opened when it's time to get going, things are sorted out between the doors and hinges, then everyone sits down around a square arrangement of dark tables at which they previously ate. It is the third floor, the window overlooks the yard where the free period takes place, for everyone else, just not for these guys here. A special feature of the programme is that they are not supposed to have any contact with other prisoners. They're all here for numerous crimes, but it was mostly drugs that got them in here. There is a glimmer of hope in all of them that they could have the rest of their lives without punishment, for an existence free from intoxication, a little humility and trust. The cornerstones are to be created with various therapeutic approaches. Behavioural therapy, art, reflection, talks, coming to terms with it. That's why it's not the really tough cases that end up here and get this eight-month special programme, but rather those who could still understand what they did to themselves and those around them.

The officers play along, saying it's getting harder and harder not only to keep young prisoners in custody but somehow to reach them in an educational way. The reign of 'Crystal' (class A drug: methamphetamine) makes any educational approach a daily battle against windmills.

Aggression, delusions, fears and power structures that this invisible enemy called 'Crystal' creates are more unpredictable situations than the war against 'smack' (class A drug: heroin) once did. The prisoner who used crystal meth before entering prison and is now in forced rehab reacts more aggressively than a pack of inmates in a comparable group without crystal contact. In this special ward, a psychiatrist, an art therapist, a social worker and a psychologist join the team. The participants, all come from the local region, are between 19 and 26 years old, and have been on the radar from an early age; some are addicted to several substances and have mainly been convicted of drug-related crime. You can smoke tobacco here, that's all. Anyone who smokes weed or drinks is excluded. Now they have slung themselves onto the chairs and are scraping the remains of the scooped goulash from their teeth. The summer air shimmers around the barred windows. Behind the prison fence, lemonade-coloured fields wither. Short-sleeved uniforms run in front of the fence.

First of all, we start talking calmly about other lyrics, about the weather, music and conspiracy theories, about Mickey Mouse and skin diseases, television and drugs, of course. Everyone has a turn in speaking out. Rules are difficult to instil in the heat. After an hour I hand out notebooks and pens. The notebooks will remain and to be filled up over the next few months: with scribbles, tags, annotations, with things torn out, text and calculations. The pens wear out like the sun burns the grass outside. Two hours later, the first day dissolves into happiness. I come again and again. During the summer, I accidentally repeated a sample text three times. They keep laughing quietly to themselves. The fourth time they grumble that we already had the text: 'Hey, we already had that'. I'm grateful that they think along with me.

Three jump off. Eight participants remain. Sometimes it's extremely loud and the boys ask: 'Tell me, Mr. Ritze, what kind of lousy group is this today?!'

I'll bring more examples, books and short stories. Poems are subject, characterisation, topic-finding and perspectives. I soon realise that I don't get very far in guiding the group as a whole. I notice that I have to take care of the individual participants: here a poem, there a biographical fragment, there displeasure and resignation, someone writes wildly and lashes out verbally like a wild bull. But somehow we manage to get a few presentable results out of the emotional chaos. And the summer, this hot, unbearable summer goes on.

I don't intervene with their texts, I just transcribe them. The content is anonymised, done. Whatever it wants to be, it's authentic as can be. In the end, the boys give their collection the title 'Prefabricated Building Philosophy' and write their names underneath it with a swan feather – they take ownership.

Then it's autumn and still much too hot. The texts have been copied and printed out. They don't claim to be perfect, let alone a whole book. But they give an impression of what is going on in the young prisoners. They are attempts to deal with the immovable past, rub against the present and to endure the pain and to take a deep breath. If all the lyrics were written at the same time, there would have been an hour of silence in everyday prison life. So the silence took place in hesitant moments, in small moments of time when they were allowed to be authors.

We meet again to review the prefab philosophy before it goes to print. The programme will also end in a few days, and then the open prison, and finally their release is waiting for them. They find a few more mistakes, nag about them and finally give the thumbs up. Then everyone wishes each other luck and quickly they vanish back to their cells. Saying goodbye is not their thing.

Secret messages

Boundaries, respect, language. Some participants are very grateful for this. Another rule, especially when working with delinquents, is: Do not accept gifts in any shape or form. Also, as a writing trainer, I must not allow myself to be seduced by offers that appear to come from outside. Sometimes after a prison workshop, when everyone has left the room, I find a scrawled piece of paper on the table. Not only can the prisoners make things disappear, they can also make them appear. And if someone doesn't dare to speak in the workshop and wants to get rid of something, it can be found among my documents, even if I'm careful with my stuff, making sure that nobody gets too close. Mostly the clandestine contributions are about violence, neglect, depression, sometimes about outsiders. I make these notes disappear, unless they are indications of suicidal intent or imminent danger.

There is a clear boundary: here I stand, there they stand. And anyone who does not comply with this rule will be severely punished by my withdrawing my attention from them. But what remains? What does creative writing trigger, for example, in relation to the re-socialisation process? Did a criminal become a better person because he is now also an author? It's a problem of causality. What writing has opened up, moved, changed cannot be measured by future actions. What worked and how can neither be proven nor investigated methodically afterwards. What is certain is that the relationship work alone is worthwhile and has an effect on the future path of the participant.

Change of scene: Adult prison system

Overall, the building seems run down. A dilapidated concrete block in the middle of the provinces. Well fine! This prison lives from the region, the region from the prison. The prison officer opens a door and leads me to a room. It's a sort of common room, with a rectangular table long enough for a company of twenty people. You could also celebrate an engagement party here or even a fortieth birthday. But the walls are high and drab, the windows are barred.

Notes from creative writing workshops within liminal space 89

Danny is standing in front of the table, wearing an undershirt over his sweatpants. I give him my hand, he shakes it without breaking it. He seems a bit like Shrek to me, comes across as charming and has the upper arms of a lumberjack. I say that I will sit at the end of the table. Danny says he'll bring me a chair. Disappears outside and a few seconds later carries in an office swivel chair with the left index finger. I say thank you Danny.

Meanwhile, other inmates appear. Some say they have already written something. Others murmur as they draw. There is coffee. A volunteer brought cookies. Confidentialities are exchanged. Then everyone sits down. Introductory words follow, formalities, now I may explain what I intend to do. I jot down their names or pseudonyms and find myself nagging that the group is 'much too big', so please forgive me if I can't remember their names. I'm also sorry that we're rushing through this week together. 'This is the time you have, but I don't'.

At the end of the first session, I ask for trust, the basis for everything that comes with the relationship between the participants and me. Sure – it's not that easy. 'But just pinch your butt cheeks together and make it work', I demand, and try not to judge your neighbours as bums 'who just want to annoy you'.

We start with the round of introductions. Makes us realise that everyone has to give something of themselves. The group has to find each other. By the break everyone had processed that and it became clear that the training means something for most of them. We go outside, drink coffee and smoke cheap tobacco. Then we start with the properties of fictional and biographical texts. Rough classifications, a small compass before the first outpourings happen. The group is too big, I think to myself. There is unrest and noise. When the two groups meet, I notice that there are no other officers present, and that the officer is alone with me. Great personnel cover, I think. But it's not uncomfortable: you could almost forget that it's a prison. Considering the fact that over thirty inmates meet here, the situation is relaxed. The smell of coffee, wonderful. On the second day, we move. Table tennis tables are pushed together in an adjoining room. I'm going through everything in quick succession; it's going to be difficult to do justice to everyone. The first participant arrives, dragging pages and pages of text: pure brain cell massacre for me. But the group stays cool. Stable types, just very thorough.

There's Sisko, for example, who remembers his childhood, things that took away his courage, who always wanted to be a pilot, but was only managing to fly thanks to drugs. Or Hubert, who describes himself as a misanthrope and thinks about genetic material and pharmaceutical cartels. Or Christian, the professional burglar who regrets so many things. Life is built on sand. They are given a chance to experience forgiveness and humility once more in this stinking place. They have short sentences of up to five years and are still young. When the next storm comes, they might be prepared, provided they find a rock to build on.

Achim sits there lost in himself; he has just lost his mother and realises what pain means when it has to be endured behind bars. Next to him Paul, who pays homage to the bosom of the leisure officer in a text and bursts out laughing about it: Fat things that are poetically processed. The group engages in the game. I suggest a title and we associate terms that have to do with the settled life outside. Everyone knows that outside is not a spatial classification, but a temporal one.

Jim, the 'walking screen', sits on a chair in front of the blackboard and we try to capture this tattooed man with all his characteristics and in all his qualities. The prisoners explain that a person can have a hundred different sides. Whoever Jim really is, we'll probably never know. But that's not the point here – or is it?

At the end, we take a photo on the steps in the yard. The guys are raising their hands in the air, I'm standing on the side, happy about their achievements. It looks like a class photo at a vocational school that was just taken during the break. If it weren't for the barbed wire at the edge of the picture. Finally, we draw a good conclusion. Everyone hums contentedly. Even if I babble too much, Danny says, 'it goes well with the writing'. One says: 'In the time that I was here, I forgot where I was'. Precise landing. When walls and bars blur and dissolve, the imagination breaks chains, one questions the shackles of freedom, everything else is void and the writing has had its effect: I think so, but don't say it. Therapists would like that sentence, but I don't want to get my face smacked. But I can hear myself say that I sometimes forget where we are. 'And that', I say, 'is the dangerous thing'. We meet on a level where it seems unimportant that there are serious reasons why our paths crossed. I'm the writing coach in this backcountry gaol. You are the participants, inmates, who are deprived of their freedom, since they have been convicted. The borders are clear, I'm going again now.

When I packed my stuff and slung the bag over my shoulder, Danny showed me his cell. Four of them sleep here. It's a showpiece, he says. And still, he was in gaol 'only for theft'. His colleagues sleep in the cell. I quickly retreat, but I find it a bad situation. Everyone should have the right to more space if they are willing to be reintegrated into society. But who am I to decide or talk about it? The gate closes. The workshop closes, leaving lots of text.

Perception and feedback

Another book with fringe group contributions has just been published. In addition to a few radio plays and radio features, plays and photos, the general public can see the texts created with the prisoners and those who refuse to go to school. And the general public is interested. As the editor, I'm interviewed, asked why I'm doing this, what it's like to 'work with them'. I answer cordially, aware that I'm satisfying a certain voyeurism. People on the supposedly good side of society like it when the curtain rises, when they can get a glimpse of the bad inside. After all, the texts give an insight into the drag of prison life and the realities of life for delinquent young people. It is material ready for a film – and yet very close to reality, which already frightens readers and listeners. When I then also state my core theses in the sessions, namely (1) that young people are not as bad as they seem, that only five per cent commit really serious crimes (cf. Ritze, 2021), that (2) the punishment should be milder and a prison is the worst possible place to take a young person up into society again. And that (3) everyone bears responsibility and can become a perpetrator at any time – most people duck away and prefer to buy a crime thriller in the bookstore or hide in front of the television. A few stay and listen when I read short stories from prison and from my sessions done with school drop-outs. Most often, these are educators. And often enough they book me for their schools and classes to read there. And so I stand in a different school every week. And there it is: 13 to 16-year-olds who soak up these stories and find them more exciting than any school education on addiction. They come to my lectures voluntarily and even forget their mobile phones for two hours. And then one or the other comes and says: 'Now I don't want to be a drug dealer anymore'.

Question for discussion

From an educational point of view, should sentences be milder and what kind of changes would the prison system need to achieve re-socialising effects? Make sure the argument is developed from an educational point of view!

It's interesting what really goes on in prison. So far they knew all this from YouTube and from hearsay. Then they buy such a book; I often give one to them as a present. They crouch in a corner or at the bus stop and read the texts of others, of those who have already fallen out of the system, who are already 'inside'. I can only guess why this excitement arises: since these stories are genuine, do not exhort, sugar-coat or proselytise; the authors do not pay attention to the pedagogical impetus or the age rating. And for the students, that's like watching Netflix, only for real. Sometimes, after an event, on the way to the car, I am stopped by the young people and their teacher and asked if I would like to be their teacher, something with German lessons. No, I say without thinking: Anything but a teacher!

Mona Lisa and Superman – Back to the sculptor and the sculpture

My group of youngsters is getting restless. They want to take a break, they want their cell phones and they want to smoke. Standing here in front of the classroom door and being told something about sculptors can be exhausting. You breathe heavily. Seven of them won't find their way back into the system any time soon. With three of them, I'm sure that they will somehow manage to catch up. It's a little bit of math, a little bit of physics that they're missing. None of them went to school, for most of them, it was fear of the teacher, fear of their classmates, of the material. Add to that the trouble in the family, the drugs, a divorce. So seven of them will remain in this project for school drop-outs for another year and have substitute lessons, for example, with me. After that it will either work or not. In all likelihood they will cost us money. The EU Commission estimates that around 1.8 million Euros are caused by a single school drop-out over a lifespan of 40 years (Nairz-Wirth et al., 2012). This is also one of the reasons why the other three are now getting everything they need to find their way back to school and to still graduate. It's a good yield when there are three.

'Okay', I say and release the door, 'let's go! What do you see?' We enter the room where the two participants are waiting for us, the sculptor and the statue. They had four minutes to rehearse. We sit and watch in silence as an arm is raised, a foot is twisted, and a nose is wrinkled. Some call out 'Superman', 'Mona Lisa', 'Pope'. Sculptor and statue standstill. What feelings are being expressed? It's hard to find words, but it works. Then there is a break.

Summary points

- These writing workshops provide an opportunity for the participants to explore the expressive capability of the body and their own body.
- Writing has to start as freely as possible with as little demands on style or correctness as possible.
- Writing facilitates for the emergence of a reflective space where the writer can re-visit parts of his past and work through these, probably even by applying a different perspective.

Recommended Reading

Goffman, E. (1961) *Asylums: Essays on the social situation of mental patients and other Inmates.* New York: Anchor Books.

References

Feldges, T. (2014) Understanding Pain and Neuroscientific Approaches to Pain. In T. Feldges, J.N.W. Gray and S. Burwood (Eds) *Subjectivity and the Social World*. Newcastle upon Tyne: Cambridge Scholars Publishing.
Gennep, A. (2019 [1909]) *The Rites of Passage*. Chicago, IL: University of Chicago Press.
Goffman, E. (1961) *Asylums: Essays on the social situation of mental patients and other Inmates*. New York: Anchor Books.
Heimes, S. (2015) *Kreatives und therapeutisches Schreiben*. Göttingen: Vandenhoeck & Ruprecht.
Jagusch, B. (2013) Schreiben als Copingstrategie bei psychischen Belastungen im Beruf und Arbeitsleben. Ein Konzept für die gewerkschaftliche Bildungsarbeit. In S. Heimes, P. Rechenberg-Winter and R. Haußmann (Eds) *Praxisfelder des kreatives und therapeutischen Schreibens*. Göttingen: Vandenhoeck & Ruprecht.
Koller, C. (2018) *Bildung anders denken – Einführung in die Theorie transformatorischer Bildungsprozesse*. Stuttgart: Kohlhammer.
Nairz-Wirth, E., Feldmann, E. and Wendebourg, K. (2012) *Professionalisierung von Lehrerinnen und Lehrern im Bereich der Prävention und Intervention von Schul – und Ausbildungsabbruch. Entwicklung einer auf der Theorie von P. Bourdieu und internationalen geprüften Modellen beruhenden Konzeption*. Wien: Bundesministerium für Bildung, Wissenschaft und Forschung Österreich.
Ritze, R. (2021) *Texttäter, Therapie oder Tod*. Gera: Garamond der Wissenschaftsverlag.
Seligman, M. (1972) Learned Helplessness. *Journal of Abnormal Psychology*, **87**(1), pp. 49–74.
Spinner, K.H. (1993) Kreatives Schreiben. *Praxis Deutsch*, **119**, pp. 17–23.
Varela, F., Thompson, E. and Rosch, E. (1991) *The Embodied Mind*. Cambridge, MA: MIT Press.
vom Scheidt, J. (1989) *Kreatives Schreiben. Texte als Wege zu sich selbst und anderen*. Frankfurt a.M: Fischer Verlag.
von Werder, L. (2007) *Handbuch des kreativen Schreibens*. Wiesbaden: Matrix Verlag. 32.
Wuttig, B. (2016) *Das traumatisierte Subjekt – Geschlecht – Körper – Soziale Praxis*. Bielefeld: Transcript.

8 Without hierarchy
A phenomenological contribution to the antiauthoritarian approach in pedagogy

Tatiana Shchyttsova

Introduction

Hierarchical relations and communication between adult and child may seem something natural as they are, indeed, 'unequal' in cognitive development and moral accountability. Yet this chapter aims to show that developmental differences between adult and child are not the reason for building intergenerational communication on the principle of the adult's superiority. Due to the developmental differences, it is the adult subject who is in position of *having to* educate the child, and not vice versa; but this in itself is not sufficient to justify a hierarchical structure, nor that the educational relationship should take the form of top-down instruction. To discuss and to clarify this issue today is relevant in the context of the recent strengthening of authoritarian tendencies in socio-political life in a number of European countries. As history shows, authoritarian regimes tend to lead to the spread of authoritarian patterns and style in various social institutions, including education. The chapter will indicate the historical connections between authoritarian patterns in contemporary social institutions. It is suggested that phenomenological philosophy can contribute to the development of an anti-authoritarian approach to pedagogy. Using phenomenological philosophy clarifies the constitution of *existence* as a particular mode of being characteristic of a human being. The chapter will use the approach to reveal that a primary meaning of upbringing is deeply rooted in the emotional constitution of human existence. Modes of communication relevant to that primary meaning of upbringing will be considered.

Modernity and authoritarian patterns in education: A view from Belarus

Belarus is a European country that gained state independence with the dissolution of the USSR in 1991. After the collapse of the Soviet Union, Belarus enjoyed a brief democratic period, ended by the 1996 ratification of constitutional amendments that dramatically expanded the scope of presidential authority. Since then, an authoritarian regime has been established in Belarus, and social life in the country is to a large extent defined by the soviet institutional and ideological legacy. This also – or even primarily – holds for schooling as, in Belarus, a school is predominantly a state institution providing free education and considered to be one of the key elements in the official politic ambition of building a so-called welfare state. The reproduction of soviet institutional patterns in Belarusian schools means, firstly, a constant state control resulting in increased bureaucratisation of teachers' work and, secondly, the predominance of an authoritarian approach to education: education 'from

DOI: 10.4324/9781003223528-10

above', receptive modes of learning, and inflexible teaching methods. Furthermore, the state ideology whose pragmatic goals are political friendship with Russia and the cultivation of 'loyal citizens' has a doubly restrictive effect on school education. On the one hand, it prevents the acquisition of knowledge about the very rich and multi-dimensional, or the history and culture of the Belarussian people. It hinders the development of children's self-activity, agency and ability for critical thinking. In other words, the current authoritarian regime in Belarus is incompatible with a vision of the school as a place where a child can envision both national-historical and global horizons, given that such ambitions are required for the learner's reflexive self-determination and creative self-realisation in the contemporary world. The reform of education has been a core government agenda for many years, including the control of all relevant non-governmental organisations, Belarussian experts in education, and teachers. A massive democratic protest movement in 2020 in Belarus sparked a new wave of discussions concerning educational reforms designed to overcome the authoritarian system in all educational institutions. Today, such discussions continue online against the background of the strengthening ideological pressure of state control over educational institutions at all levels, including primary schools.

It must be stressed that overcoming authoritarian – and cultivation of anti-authoritarian – approaches in pedagogical theory and praxis is at once a political, ethical, methodological and epistemological task that appears relevant not only in the post-Soviet Eastern European region but also in a broader European context, given the recent authoritarian political movements in Poland and Hungary, and the strengthening of right-wing conservative tendencies in some other European countries. Therefore, it makes sense to raise questions about socio-historical and intellectual (conceptual) roots of contemporary authoritarianism in Europe that promulgate authoritarian patterns and approaches in educational institutions. One may notice in this regard that, despite certain significant differences between them, the forms of authoritarian rule that exist in Eastern and Central Europe are essentially associated with patriarchal norms and values, in particular the centralisation of power in one authority (person, party), rigorous subordination, obedience and reproduction of the *status quo*. Since schooling is one of the key institutions of European Modernity, we have to ask how are Modernity's conceptual grounds consistent with patriarchal assumptions? Or: What features of Modernity are a 'condition of possibility' (i.e. *a priori* conditions) for the development of authoritarian pedagogy?

There is a consensus in modern scholarship (in humanities and social sciences) regarding the critical judgement about the concept of the autonomous rational subject developed in classical Modernity by thinkers such as Descartes or Kant. The concept gave rise to a homogenising rationality which, despite its claims to universal validity, produced knowledge and epistemological frames that could not acknowledge any *otherness* beyond the (seemingly) abstract concept of the subject. In other words, the classical concept of the subject excluded the possibility of the existence of an *Other* whose *otherness* would be irreducible to – i.e. inconceivable in terms of – the homogenising rationality implied in that classical concept. Merleau-Ponty (2010) explains that the *otherness* of the female subject or the *otherness* of the child subject cannot be conceived by the classical concept. Thus, through the philosophy of Enlightenment, by advancing the idea(l) of the moral and intellectual maturity of the fully fledged subject, Kant had introduced a new paradigm of adult-centred thinking (Shchyttsova, 2014). Within this paradigm, the child had been conceived of as not-yet-a-subject. Correspondingly, the adult-child relation had been understood in terms of the rigorous moral and intellectual subordination, which meant that the ultimate pedagogical task of the fully fledged adult subject is to help the child to become likewise autonomous and rational – to become an adult. Such an approach made the teacher's authority unquestionable. The only paradigmatic difference of the teacher's superiority over the child from the (male) adult's superiority over children in pre-modern societies was that teaching had to be built on a corresponding scientific basis (physiology, psychology or pedagogy) relevant to the general logic of modernisation.

Preparing the child for the future – namely, his/her future as an adult – defined the pedagogical paradigm of the child's socialisation (Corsaro, 2005) prevailed both at school and in everyday life. In its everyday use, the paradigm was reflected in corresponding attitudes and patterns: didacticism in adult-child communication and children's social segregation in both public and in private spaces. In the western societies of late Modernity, there have been promising – both theoretical and practical – shifts towards changing away from the perspective of the child as a deficient form (or stage) of human being (Piaget, 2001) and, correspondingly, in the adult-child relation as that of rigid subordination and top-down instruction. It is not surprising that such a democratisation of intergenerational relations develops much faster in theory than in ordinary life, and much faster in the liberal-democratic societies than in authoritarian ones. Overcoming patriarchal-authoritarian codes and patterns in education, and in adult-child relations in general, needs critical thinking on the one hand and a phenomenological description of the corresponding experiential field on the other hand (Brinkmann and Friesen, 2018). The last one provides an access to the experiences of child and adult as they themself experience their surroundings and relations. It can help to reveal a mode of adult-child co-existence alternative to the rigid hierarchical mode that so easily becomes a channel for establishing and reproducing authoritarian patterns in education.

The phenomenological perspective on primordial emotions and communication in adult-child relations

In what follows I will take my bearings from the authors whose theories allow seeing the asymmetry in the adult-child relation, not in terms of subordination based on the concept of (adult) subject, but in terms of primary mutual inter-personal relatedness and open complementarity that lie beyond the subject-centred ontology. First of all are the Danish thinker Søren Kierkegaard and the German philosopher Eugen Fink. Kierkegaard in his existential phenomenology succeeded in tracing a connection between the experience of freedom, anxiety and mode of communication in the adult-child relationship. Fink was a pupil of Edmund Husserl, the founder of phenomenological philosophy who suggested an innovative methodology of clarifying the relation between experience and the constitution of meaning. Like Heidegger (another prominent pupil of Husserl), and under certain influence of his thought, Fink criticised Husserl for a particular sort of subject-centred thinking that does not allow for a genuine complexity of relation between the subject and the world. Therefore, Fink (2016) developed his own version of phenomenology, a speculative one that views the world as a permanent cosmological event that cannot be grasped from the perspective of a single consciousness. His new theoretical approach had very significant implications for philosophical anthropology, social philosophy, and pedagogy. In particular, the co-existence of the adult and the child has to be viewed as a cooperative equal constitution of the world by different generations. He tried to develop a new conception of pedagogy grounded on the idea of an intergenerational *sharing* of the world in which none has an absolute advantage (Shchyttsova, 2019).

Authoritarian pedagogy presupposes an inherent interconnection of a rigorous emotional atmosphere, constituted in the adult's didacticism and the child's obedience, a top-down mode of communication, and framed by the fixed vision of preparing an appropriate *future* adult subject who will conform to social norms. To unmask the patriarchal-authoritarian misuse of this asymmetry in the adult-child relationship, we have to clarify a genuine connection between fundamental existential feelings and upbringing, and to identify the modes of communication relevant to the anti-authoritarian pedagogy.

Anxiety and curiosity

Many challenges and difficulties in education are rooted in the fact that education deals with a child's freedom. In existential phenomenology, first in Kierkegaard and then in Heidegger, the phenomenon of freedom as a constitutive of human existence is seen to correlate with anxiety as an existential mood or feeling. Both thinkers differentiate between anxiety and fear, stating that, while fear has a definite object – we are fearful of *something* – anxiety has no object because it relates to the individual's existential task of 'having to be'. Anxiety originates from the self's relation to itself as the capability of being. In other words, to be anxious is an existential form of a being becoming aware of its being. Self-relation is revealed as a virtual site of freedom and anxiety at once. Thus, anxiety is seen in existential phenomenology as a fundamental affective disposition that thoroughly attunes human existence in its totality, regardless of the age of the human being. Kierkegaard, however, pointed out a difference between the adult's and the child's experience of existential anxiety: whereas Heidegger's interpretation of anxiety, while claiming universal validity, traditionally took the adult human being as a human 'norm'.

According to Heidegger's existential ontology, human 'being-there' (*Dasein*) is of such a kind that 'in its very being, that Being is an issue for itself' (Heidegger, 1962: 32). This definition clearly implies a non-indifferent relation of the existing self to itself, and is valid both for the adult's and the child's existence. However, adult and child as concrete anthropological forms of embodied human existence (being-in-the-world) are characterised by different forms of fundamental self-relation. In other words, Heidegger's formula can be revised this way: the adult's 'being-there' and the child's 'being-there' are of such a kind that their very being is an issue for them *differently*. It means, adult and child experience their respective ontological openness differently – i.e. the existential task of becoming a self. Heidegger defines the existing individual's fundamental self-relation as *care* (Heidegger, 1962). Kierkegaard, when addressing the child's existence, indicates that much more relevant would be another definition, namely, *curiosity*. What is crucial here is that this differentiation of the forms of fundamental self-relation depending on the respective life-stages of a human being is essentially connected with a corresponding difference in the experience of existential anxiety.

As mentioned earlier, anxiety is regarded by Kierkegaard and Heidegger as a fundamental existential feeling precisely because it is part of the very structure of human existence as being-in-the-world. Moreover, Heidegger's and Kierkegaard's accounts of such emotional disclosure concern various life-stages of the human being. Whereas Heidegger addressed only the adult form of human existence, Kierkegaard considered human existence in its different life-stages, including the child. Kierkegaard's analysis of anxiety presented in his famous work *The Concept of Anxiety* is very complex. This chapter touches only upon his reflections on the child and not his theological thinking. Kierkegaard describes how anxiety discloses the respective forms of self-relation relevant to adult and child as different life-stages of the human being. According to Heidegger, anxiety discloses to the existing individual that her own existence is a burden to be taken on. He interprets this 'burden' as an ontological 'being-guilty', not for this or that specific fault, but being-guilty due to the fact that the (adult) existing individual is always responsible for how her being-in-the-world looks. It appears consistently when Heidegger conceptualises self-relation using the term 'care'. The adult's human existence is care – both structurally and emotionally – as the adult's self-understanding includes, if only in a latent or concealed form, a fundamental responsibility for what already has been done, what is being done and what will be done. Thus, 'being-guilty' is a precondition for any self-realisation of the adult individual. It is anxiety that reveals this disturbing existential truth to the individual. That anxiety and care appear essentially complementary and dependent on each other is peculiar to the adult human being.

Kierkegaard identifies a decisive existential difference of the child from the adult: the child 'has no conception of what he is able to do' (Kierkegaard, 1980: 44). For Kierkegaard, the child in his ignorance is incognito to himself. He exists in ignorance of his self. The child experiences that he has an ability to be. It is a part of his original vitality, of his very basic self-understanding. However, initially he has no idea of himself as a concrete self. It is an open question he faces as a *being-in-the-world*: what he is, namely, what he is capable of. Because it is obscure to him, the child's existential condition, unlike the adult, is characterised by *innocence*. Indeed, if he does not know himself (what he is able to do), how could he be responsible for what he is? It is notable that Kierkegaard considers the Biblical Adam as a mythological figure symbolising the innocent mode of existence. In this connection, Kierkegaard uses the gendered pronoun 'he' while developing the phenomenology of anxiety.

As mentioned above, anxiety arises out of the relation of the self to its own possibility of being able. This statement pertains both to the adult's and the child's existence. However, due to the child's constitutive ignorance, anxiety experienced by the child is essentially connected not with the primordial being-guilty (which is relevant for the adult), but with the primordial innocence. The child, while being aware of his/her being, is not yet defined as a concrete self which he/she could be responsible for. Therefore, unlike the adult's anxiety, the child's anxiety concerns becoming a self that does not yet know itself as a definite form. In *The Concept of Anxiety*, Kierkegaard addresses the phenomenon of anxiety that is characteristic of the existing individual in the state of innocence and explores transformations of the self that happen in its transition from innocence to being-guilty. He gives a very sophisticated definition of the anxiety experienced in the state of innocence: 'a sympathetic antipathy and an antipathetic sympathy' (Kierkegaard, 1980: 42). It means that the child's existential anxiety is inherently dialectical, meaning that it is constituted by two opposite affective directions: turning away from and being attracted to the 'possibility of being able'. The child's possibility of being able when 'filled' with anxiety is something both attractive and repulsive.

The child as an individual *being-in-the-world* marked by the existential ignorance is in constant search for itself. An emotional equivalent of this search is curiosity. The child is deeply curious about himself as an open possibility. However, the existential curiosity at issue is an anxious curiosity, because a possibility of being able that the child is curiously searching for is uncertain, hidden, 'dark'. Therefore, we may define the fundamental existential feeling of the innocent self as 'anxiously curious'. What is crucial here is how such anxious curiosity – or curious anxiety – manifests itself in the child's everyday life. Kierkegaard notes in this regard: 'In observing children, one will discover this anxiety intimated more particularly as a seeking for the adventurous, the monstrous, and the enigmatic' (Kierkegaard, 1980: 42). Thus, the adventurous, monstrous and enigmatic things (events, scenarios, images, objects, etc.) are a vehicle for the child's primordial existential feeling of 'anxiously curious'. They appear attractive for the child as they are associated with danger, risk and the unknown. They indirectly indicate and reflect the child's fundamental emotional disposition in the world. The search for them is a manifestation of the peculiarity of the child's existential anxiety.

The existential task of upbringing and relevant modes of communication

We have to ask now: What does all the above imply with for the tasks of upbringing? As the child is 'anxiously curious' about himself/herself as a *being-in-the world* it seems reasonable to assume that upbringing must first of all correlate with and be relevant to the child's primordial existential feeling. To put it in a more concrete way: upbringing has somehow to calm that anxiety and to satisfy that curiosity. Thus, a primary existential task of upbringing is to respond to the child's ambivalent request, to meet his/her primordial existential need.

Kierkegaard suggests a very simple notion that defines how upbringing should look in order to fulfil its primary task of meeting the child's existential-emotional need described above. It is the notion of 'intellectual-emotional nourishment'. The notion means first of all that upbringing must address the child's existence *in toto,* not in some particular and separated faculties. Furthermore, being addressed in its 'wholeness', the child's existence is considered in terms of freedom, so that to 'bring up' appears somewhat paradoxical. To bring up means to help the child to be and to become himself/herself as a free individual, given his/her freedom is originally rooted in the child's relation to him*self/*her*self* as to a 'possibility of possibility'.

As mentioned earlier, existential phenomenology reveals an essential connection between freedom and anxiety in human existence. Upbringing as a particular kind of interpersonal relation and communication is thus about communication between two freedoms that differ essentially with regard to their anxiety dimension. In the child's existence, the actuality of freedom is experienced anxiously curiously precisely because the child relates to him*self/*her*self* as to a 'possibility of possibility'.

Thus, to be calmed-and-satisfied as an anxiously curious self, the child has to be intellectually and emotionally nourished in an appropriate manner. From this perspective, the seemingly trivial pedagogical task of cultivating and maintaining the child's curiosity is not a cognitive task but, indeed, an existential one that is related to the child's uncertain (hidden) self. It follows that 'bringing-up' is about helping the anxiously curious child to maintain a kind of dynamic balance that will allow her/him to remain open to the world, i.e. to further explore his/her *being-in-the-world* as the issue to be defined in the child's becoming a self.

Let us focus now on modes of communication that would be relevant to the existential task of upbringing. To do this, I focus on narration or telling a story to child because this form of communication allows for the child's uncertain (hidden) self to be continually concentrated and thereby to be indirectly addressed in its unknown wholeness. Kierkegaard gives in this regard two very concrete examples that indicate that there are basically two main modes of narrative-communicative approaches (addressing) the child's self. The first example is 'the stories of the nanny' that are characterised by a sincere conviction of the truth of the story from the narrator. The second example is the stories of someone who knows 'how it is to be a child' and tells a story to a child, taking into account what a child's life needs and what is good for it. The former makes children attuned to a calm fantasising. The latter makes children want to ask, provokes their passionately concentrated questioning. Therefore, we may call the first mode of narration 'immediate-atmospheric' and the second one 'reflective-inquiring'.

Given that the primary existential task of upbringing is calming anxiety and satisfying curiosity we can now identify a role for each of the modes of narration. While both modes fulfil in their own ways the double task of upbringing, they differ in their combination of the calming and satisfying functions. It seems intuitively evident that the *immediate-atmospheric* mode of narration will foreground the calming role and the *reflective-inquiring* mode will foreground the satisfying role. Both modes engage and encourage the child's imagination, yet they do it differently. For the *immediate-atmospheric* mode of narration, it is crucial that child believes that the narrator believes what he is telling. It allows for opening up a whole world of fantasy for the child and brings a wholesome calmness. For the *reflective-inquiring* mode, it is essential that the communicator constantly nurtures the child's 'intellectual-emotional mobility' (Kierkegaard's term).

Thus, the child's becoming a self is intrinsically marked by the anxiously-curious searching for himself/herself. It is this searching that is manifested in the characteristic intellectual-emotional mobility of the child and, in particular, in the child's loving fairy stories. As Kierkegaard (1967: 118) puts it: 'Not to tell children such exciting imaginative stories and tales leaves an unfilled space for an anxiety which, when not moderated by such stories, returns again all the stronger'. Furthermore, the adult's mode of communication – in order to perform upbringing in its very basic existential meaning – has to allow for the child's searching for himself/herself to be genuinely expressed in free questioning.

Conclusion

Phenomenological philosophy may significantly contribute to the development of an anti-authoritarian approach to pedagogy in trying to consider human self and interpersonal communication through immediate everyday experiences. As we saw in this chapter, the human self is not a fixed entity, but rather an open structure that is experienced differently depending on the life-stage or age of the individual. In particular, adult and child have different experiences of existential anxiety which, according to Kierkegaard and Heidegger, reflect the individual's being-in-the-world. It was shown that from the existential-phenomenological point of view, the task of upbringing is emotionally and communicatively to support the child's becoming a self. The primary support of this sort consists of moderating a child's existential anxiety by satisfying his/her anxious curiosity about himself/herself by means of appropriate narrations and communicative modes (Egan, 1986). There were identified two such modes, namely the immediate-atmospheric mode and the reflective-inquiring one.

Thus, upbringing is primarily not about instruction but about the keeping up the balance and openness of the child's existential constitution. Upbringing should be understood first in terms of a particular art of communication and only secondly in terms of delivering certain knowledge. *What* is taught must be built on *how* it is taught. The art of communication under concern presupposes a kind of democratic – non-hierarchical – attitude as it must allow the child's self to freely find itself. The communication between an adult and a child is *sharing* a certain experience in which no one has superiority. To sum up, phenomenological analysis of the existential constitution of adult and child reveals that upbringing requires relational rather than authoritarian style. The relational (anti-authoritarian) approach seems very promising and relevant to today's demands in modern European societies as it overcomes the traditional obsession with making a child into a fully fledged adult subject, and instead focuses on vivid intergenerational communication between adult and child as a non-hierarchical performance of their cooperative being-in-the-world.

Summary points

- Authoritarian patterns in education refer to the natural developmental differences between adult and child. However, as a social phenomenon, authoritarian approach in pedagogy can arise on various ideological bases. It can be either patriarchal-conservative values, the concept of subject elaborated in classical Modernity, or a particular combination of these two sources.
- Phenomenological philosophy – in particular the ideas of Kierkegaard and Eugen Fink – contributes significantly to overcoming adult-centred thinking and to development of the anti-authoritarian approach in pedagogy. Phenomenology tries to consider human self and interpersonal communication following the indications of immediate everyday experiences.
- Anxiety is a primordial existential feeling (mood) that is constitutive of the self's relation to itself as a capability to be. According to Kierkegaard and Heidegger, existential anxiety is essentially connected with the phenomenon of freedom. Heidegger and Kierkegaard describe how existential anxiety shows the self-relation relevant to adult and child as different life-stages of a human being. Kierkegaard shows that, due to the child's constitutive ignorance, anxiety experienced by the child is essentially different from that experienced by the adult.
- The child's becoming a self is intrinsically marked by anxiously-curious searching for himself/herself. It is this searching that is manifested in the characteristic intellectual-emotional mobility of the child and, in particular, in the child's love of fairy stories.
- From the existential-phenomenological point of view, the task of upbringing is to emotionally-communicatively support the child's becoming a self. The primary support of this sort consists in moderating the child's existential anxiety by satisfying his/her anxious curiosity about himself/herself by means of appropriate narrations and communicative modes. There were identified two such modes, namely the immediate-atmospheric mode and the reflective-inquiring one.

Questions for discussion

Why is the authority of the teacher losing its traditional basis in the modern world? What could be a basis for the teacher's authority if we reject the authoritarian approach in pedagogy?

From the phenomenological perspective, education has to address the child's becoming a self. It presupposes certain integrity in pedagogical methods and efforts. What communicative, cultural and administrative principles would be essential for enabling such integrity at different levels in the primary school or secondary school?

Recommended reading

Brinkmann, M. and Friesen, N. (2018) Phenomenology and Education. In P. Smeyers (Ed.) *International Handbook of Philosophy of Education*. Dordrecht: Springer.
Heidegger, M. (1962) *Being and Time*. (Transl. by J. Macquarrie and E. Robinson.) Oxford: Blackwell.

Kierkegaard, S. (1980) *The Concept of Anxiety.* (Ed. and transl. with Introduction and Notes by R. Thome in collaboration with A.B. Anderson.) Princeton, NJ: Princeton University Press.

Shchyttsova, T. (2019) Poetics of Intergenerational Relations. To the importance of Eugen Fink's cosmological substantiation of educational coexistence. In M. Brinkmann, J. Türstig and M. Weber-Spanknebel (Eds) *Leib – Leiblichkeit – Embodiment. Phänomenologische Erziehungswissenschaft,* vol 8. Wiesbaden: Springer VS.

References

Brinkmann, M. and Friesen N. (2018) Phenomenology and Education. In P. Smeyers (Ed.) *International Handbook of Philosophy of Education.* Dordrecht: Springer.

Corsaro, A.W. (2005) *The Sociology of Childhood.* Thousand Oaks/London/New Delhi: Pine Forge Press.

Egan, K. (1986) *Teaching as Storytelling: An alternative approach to teaching and curriculum in the elementary school.* Chicago, IL: Chicago University Press.

Fink, E. (2016) *Play as Symbol of the World. And other writings.* (Transl. with an Introduction by I.A. Moore and C. Turner.) Bloomington, IN: Indiana University Press.

Heidegger, M. (1962) *Being and Time.* (Transl. by J. Macquarrie and E. Robinson.) Oxford: Blackwell.

Kierkegaard, S. (1967) *Journals and Papers.* Vol. 1: A-E. (Ed. and transl. by H.V. Hong and E.H. Hong, assist. by G. Malantschuk.) Bloomington, IN: Indiana University Press.

Kierkegaard, S. (1980) *The Concept of Anxiety.* (Ed. and transl. with Introduction and Notes by R. Thome in collaboration with A.B. Anderson.) Princeton, NJ: Princeton University Press.

Merleau-Ponty, M. (2010) *Child Psychology and Pedagogy: The Sorbonne Lectures 1949–1952.* (Transl. by Talia Welsh.) Evanston, IL: Northwestern University Press.

Piaget, J. (2001) *The Language and Thought of the Child.* (Transl. by M. Gabain and R. Gabain.) London/New York: Routledge.

Shchyttsova, T. (2014) Asymmetry and Gift. On ethical implications of the adult–child differentiation. In A. Kraus, M. Buhl and G-B. v. Carlsburg (Eds) *Performativity, Materiality and Time. Tacit Dimensions of Pedagogy.* Münster/New York: Waxmann.

Shchyttsova, T. (2019) Poetics of Intergenerational Relations. To the importance of Eugen Fink's cosmological substantiation of educational coexistence. In M. Brinkmann, J. Türstig and M. Weber-Spanknebel (Eds) *Leib – Leiblichkeit – Embodiment. Phänomenologische Erziehungswissenschaft,* vol 8. Wiesbaden: Springer VS.

Preface to Section III

How would we ever find out about 'learning'?

Tom Feldges

The previous section was about the becoming of a 'whole' human being, i.e. a subject or person. This is an individual struggle that the subject has to negotiate and navigate for itself. It is only reasonable to assume that such an individualised process of becoming could thus only yield genuinely individual results, i.e. the becoming is accomplished for everyone in an individual fashion. And that makes sense in relation to the notion of sense-giving cultural frames that allow the individual to sort its own experiences under concepts to make them available to reason and cognitive deliberation, but also to communicate about them with others (Feldges, 2021). However, the more individualised the emergence of sense gets, the more difficult research into the relevant psychological processes becomes. And, of course, an additional problem appears with the assessment of educational gain: when would a person be a 'whole' one, able to partake sufficiently in society? This is the focus of the current section. Chapters 9 from the Netherlands and 10 from Greece utilise a 'classic' qualitative approach to researching the experience of individuals, while Chapter 11 from Austria suggests a genuinely novel approach.

Teaching is a job that requires the skill to manage what is going on within another person so that this person learns. This rather bland statement about the inaccessibility of another person's thoughts is not at all invalidated by, for example, Bruner's (1990) concept of a 'theory of mind', the common human ability to attribute mental states to another person. This is also known as 'folk psychology' (Horgan and Woodward, 1990). Theories like these work from the assumption that if someone desires D and believes that B would get him/her D then s/he will act according to this belief B to secure getting D. However, and this will be picked up again later in this introduction and in the following chapters, on reading the previous sentence again it must be clear that these theories are based upon assumptions in terms of a) humans being more or less equal, b) what their current desire and belief in any given situation are and c) that it is possible to deduct from their (observable) action what must be going on in their minds. Hence, folk psychology provides a theory of other minds, but such a theory is – in scientific terms – nothing but a veil behind which it is possible to hide the fact that the relevant states – inside another mind – still remain inaccessible. Hence, even with such a 'theory of mind', one would still have to face the initial problem: How would we find out how learning happens? Teaching is the practice of bringing about learning. It is, of course, a goal-orientated effort. Hence, teaching needs to yield distinguishable progress from the learner's previous state of skill, knowledge or insight towards one that has been advanced as a result of what was taught. It is exactly this necessity of yielding accessible results that leads to the danger of focusing exclusively upon accomplishments, i.e. the results of learning. But with such a shift one remains blinkered with a fundamental problem, one that is

DOI: 10.4324/9781003223528-11

often absent from discussions about education, educational assessment and/or research. The problem concerns the question that emerges in relation to the statement at the beginning of this introduction. If learning is supposed *to happen within* the learner, how can we ever find out that *something* was really learned and – even more so – *how* that learning has occurred. The question could be answered superficially merely by pointing to existing and widely used assessment strategies and research methods. But such an answer must remain superficial simply because it tries to answer the question of how individual learning can be measured while leaving the concept of learning undefined, and to utilise theories of learning and learning assessment and research that are in themselves built upon an undefined concept of learning. It draws on theories that are – often uncritically – borrowed and (often mis-)appropriated from other academic disciplines of sociology, psychology and the neurosciences as the supposedly 'contributory' disciplines of education (Feldges, 2020: 171).

However, interdisciplinary efforts of this kind, well intended as they might be, often neglect the theoretical underpinnings and inherent limitations of those disciplines. This practice entails the danger of inconsistent or even contradictory use of borrowed theories or theory-snippets in an ill-founded attempt to enrich educational theorising (Feldges, 2017; Feldges and Pieczenko, 2020). Its most annoying epitome is in narratives that appear to draw from neuro-psychological research, claiming that the brain *does this or that*, or that the neo-cortex *thinks*. The neo-cortex, as an evolutionary rather recent brain structure, is associated with thought and speech (Bear *et al.*, 2007) and is often subject to a 'mereological fallacy' in the uncritical transfer of neuroscientific research to educational theory. A mereological fallacy is where one part (the neo-cortex) of a whole (the human being) is singled out and has functional properties ascribed to it. In the case of the brain, or the neo-cortex, one has to be clear about the fact that, despite the fact that the function of speech is supported by the neo-cortex, the neo-cortex does not speak at all and would certainly have nothing to say for itself. The same holds for the brain: it is not the brain that thinks! Certain brain functions are the necessary pre-condition for thinking, but thinking itself is an act of the *whole person*. When claiming 'I am angry' someone is expressing a mounting or existing emotion about some matter of fact that one finds him/herself in, and one that has caught his/her attention, probably in relation to previous encounters or future expectations. Hence, it is the person who is angry, not the brain where such an emotional state is registered and probably acted upon. It is equally not the neo-cortex that is angry, although this structure provides the neurological pre-conditions necessary to form this feeling or thought into a sentence. This slight detour illustrates how difficult any kind of theory transfer might be. It is so, even in topics that appear straightforward, like the psychological research regarding the human ability to retrieve items from memory by Atkinson and Shiffrin (1968). Their 'tiered system' of memory, with the organisation of memory recall along a set of cognitive structures, has become a mantra for learning and learning motivation (c.f. Spence and Spence, 1968; but also in an applied form: Bartlett and Burton, 2016). However, when Atkinson and Shiffrin designed their research, it was about the cognitive structures of memory. Learning only figured in their research as far as it was intended to provide a valid benchmark across a sample of participants in order to reveal the sought-after structures. (For a more detailed critique, see: Feldges, 2017.) In that respect, some care is needed when utilising Atkinson's and Shiffrin's research results in a well-meaning theory transfer to apply them to 'learning'. Here we find ourselves back at square one. There is no way to avoid asking: What is that activity that is commonly referred to as learning? It sounds like a strange question, as everyone knows what it is supposed to mean. But when put on the spot hardly anyone can say exactly what is meant by it or how to clearly define the concept. If one does not know where the concept begins or ends, or what it is supposed to cover, how can we ever hope to research the phenomenon itself?

This is where part of the problem is to be found: the meaning of terms in common use such as 'learning', is often ambiguous. To work slowly towards a better understanding, and in an attempt to define the concept of 'learning', it is first necessary to place it into a wider context. Perhaps the widest context is in the statement that 'to be alive means to be learning' (Treml and Becker; 2010: 104). This is by no means an all-inclusive plea for a life-long learning agenda but rather a cruel biological fact. Living organisms have to master the challenge to secure their survival in a mostly hostile environment. This process of self-maintenance is known as 'autopoiesis', i.e. a 'system's ability to maintain and recreate itself over time and within a changing environment' (Feldges, 2021: 51). In order to secure survival such organisms have to utilise previous experiences to be able to apply them to similar situations or to conceive likely assumptions about a possible future. Hence, the ability to retrieve previously acquired behavioural options to react to current environmental challenges surely comes with the possibility of enhancing survival chances. On accepting such an

> ... ability of living systems to cater for a continuous alteration of the current state it finds itself in one has gained a first, very general concept of what learning is.
>
> (Treml and Becker, 2010: 104)

Such a general definition of learning for living systems is much too wide to be applied directly to educational efforts with humans. But on accepting this first approximation as the widest possible definition, every subsequent attempt to capture the concept in a more focused way would always remain within the scope of this first one. Any finer-grained definition would constitute a sub-concept of the overall concept of learning in the sense of this overarching first definition.

As everyone knows, humans learn in relation to the experiences they have and by getting used to their environment to avoid negative and to maximise positive outcomes for themselves. This is due to a certain feature that is known as 'organisational variance' in system theory (Rudrauf et al., 2003: 56). This variability allows a system to adapt to environmental needs by utilising its variance to make a better fit into the ecological niche in which it seeks to survive. The ability for pattern recognition or the perception of space differs depending upon the environment in which one grew up. This was one of the major objections to Piaget's findings in relation to 'the Swiss mountain scene' as brought forward by Dasen (1994). Piaget sought to define universal stages of cognitive development and, in one task, he presented a panorama with three mountains to the participating children. The children were asked what this panorama would look like from a different perspective. Their ability to decentre (or not) their own view from their current perspective and successfully imagine how the scene would look from another angle was – for Piaget – the marker of a specific stage of cognitive development (Gross, 2001). However, Dasen (1994) found that these stages were not at all universal and that their accomplishment depended upon the actual environment in which the children grew up. Those children who grew up in flat landscapes, without mountains, fared worse, although they were not less developed cognitively. These habituating effects have influences upon the neural layout due to the plasticity of the human brain. An individual's neural patterns develop within their environment to 'see' in a specific way. Such patterns influence perception either to singled-out objects or to a holistic perception of situations rather than just that object. In that respect, learning does indeed happen through experience and by 'getting used to' a specific, repeating set of experiences. Undoubtedly, this feature of plasticity is important for learning, as it means that the young learn more easily than older learners, and this is hardly anything new (Hebb, 1949). But if an individual adaptation to environmental needs is possible – and that is what Hebb's seminal text claims – then this plasticity can also be utilised in conscious learning. It is not necessary simply to wait for random events that initiate learning; such learning encounters can be deliberately sought out. This constitutes the form of intended, planned and conscious learning that everyone knows from teaching in schools. But again, it is something that most people could not exactly define. Psychology often refers to learning as an experience-evoked, stable alteration of behaviour. The behaviourist undertone is clearly apparent in this definition, and it also includes the admission that learning – as individual achievement – happens *within* the learning individual. To assess whether learning has taken place, one needs clear empirical markers in the form of responsive behaviour or altered patterns of behaviour. Speech, in this context, is seen as a behavioural expression as well. But – and this is the important point here – being exposed to a stimulus and displaying certain behaviour does not amount to learning. An example might make this clearer: one can think of a stimulus like a teacher asking a learner how much four multiplied by two yields. If the learner is able to display the correct behaviour by answering 'eight', one may assume that something was learned, but the behaviour says nothing about the learning itself and nothing about what went on inside this learner to come up with the correct answer. Treml and Becker (2010: 107) suggest, therefore, that

> … learning is a collective name for all not directly observable processes, mainly brain-processes, that were evoked by experiences and that cause […] relative stable alterations or enhancements of one's behavioural repertoire.

With such increased precision in the definition of learning a basis is established upon which the various learning theories can unfold their explanatory power.

So what was actually gained by this discursive exercise? First and foremost, the fact that learning is experience-dependent, and secondly, that such experience causes change. But the exact form that such a behavioural change takes cannot be predicted due to the 'technology deficit' as discussed in the Preface to Section I. However, this preface to the current section started out with an assertion that teaching-evoked learning is something that happens within the learning individual and cannot be directly observed. By discussing the mis-attribution of capacities to biological structures within a human being it was established that neither the brain nor specific parts of the brain do any thinking on their own and thus cannot learn in isolation. And that also holds for the images now available that make visible increased blood flows in certain brain regions during learning. They are the same as observable behavioural displays: both are clearly associated with learning but they do not constitute learning as such! As much as the correct answer 'eight' did not equal learning, neither is a video sequence showing increased metabolic activities via various imaging techniques when getting right the mental processing of four multiplied by two. Unfortunately, the 'theory of mind' mentioned earlier cannot come to the rescue. Theories are supposed to be corroborated by other theories or empirical evidence.

But if the processes of learning remain inaccessible to scientific evidence-gathering as Treml and Becker (2010) claim, then such a 'theory of mind' would need, in order to be substantiated, exactly that sort of empirical evidence that was lacking in the first place and therefore initiated the formulation of the 'theory of mind'.

So we still find ourselves up against a brick wall posed by the apparent inability to establish what kind of processes constitute 'learning', and despite all the discussion, this wall does not show the slightest crack. But the fact that one is faced with an un-answerable question is, as often in life, not something that should render every further attempt pointless. If an answer to a specific question cannot be found, it might be that the question is wrong. And indeed, if learning depends upon experiences-evoked processes that are not directly observable, it is probably best not to waste any more time trying to observe what – by definition – must remain unobservable. Instead, one could focus upon the experiences to get a hold of the processes of learning? These experiences, as events that have affected the experiencing individual, are individual. They are available in their experiential quality to be experienced by the one who has them. Others can see that someone has such an experience, but the way in which this experience actually affects the one who has it they cannot know for sure. Wittgenstein (1973) called these experiences 'private' in so far as only the one who experiences them has exclusive, or 'privileged', access to them. So, it could be a worthwhile strategy to ask the one having these experiences to report what they do to her/him in an attempt to get a better idea of the otherwise unobservable processes that constitute learning. Of course, not all these learning-relevant processes will be evident to the one who is learning: one might have the actual experience but not be able to apprehend the whole process of learning. However, even if only a limited number of these processes were available to description by the experiencing individual, it could still yield more than a 'beating round the bush' with observations of secondary phenomena (changes of behaviour or biomarkers) that do not really equal learning. This is the thought that is to be parked in the reader's head as an incentive to think along in a slightly different direction when reading the following three chapters. And this thought provides the ground to develop a further set of challenges.

- A subject-centred approach shows that learning can happen even when it is not a goal-directed activity, trying to achieve a pre-described result (see Chapter 9). Can you see the possibility of gaining completely different results when starting off with individual experiences of learning rather than focusing on the results of learning?
- Could you see a similar change of perspective working in other fields of education? Where would you expect to find potential difficulties or limitations – could those be overcome?
- How would you rate the usefulness of qualitative methods to gain insight into the affective conditions as experienced by teacher and learner? (see Chapter 10).
- Can you think of quantitative methods to establish the occurrence of the 'flow' and could a scientific description of such a phenomenon equal the actual experience of such a state of being driven by the completion of the task?
- How do you rate the usefulness of condensing educational encounters (see Chapter 11) to use these vignettes to focus upon learning as a process as opposed to conceiving learning as a result?
- Can such a change of perspective yield insight into learning that cannot be gained by more traditional methods as currently in use?

References

Atkinson, R.C. and Shiffrin, R.M. (1968) Human Memory: A proposed system and its control processes. In K.W. Spence and J.T. Spence (Eds) *The Psychology of Learning and Motivation (Volume 2)*. New York: Academic Press.
Bartlett, S. and Burton, D. (2016) *Introduction to Education Studies*. London: Sage.
Bear, M.F., Connors B.W. and Paradiso M.A. (2007) *Neuroscience – Exploring the Brain*. London: Lippincott Williams and Wilkins.
Bruner, J.S. (1990) *Acts of Meaning*. Cambridge, MA: Harvard University Press.
Dasen, P.R. (1994) Culture and Cognitive Development from a Piagetian Perspective. In W.J. Lonner and R.S. Malpass (Eds) *Psychology and Culture*. Boston, MA: Allyn and Bacon.
Feldges, T. (2017) Motivation and Experience versus Cognitive Psychological Explanation. *Humana Mente: Journal of Philosophical Studies*, **33**, pp. 1–18.
Feldges, T. (2020) Philosophy and Education. In C.A. Simon and S. Ward (Eds) *A Student's Guide to Education Studies*. Abingdon: Routledge.
Feldges, T. (2021) *Neurophenomenology and Cognitive Science*. Mauritius: Lambert Academic Publishing.
Feldges, T. and Pieczenko, S. (2020) Boredom in Educational Contexts – A critical review. *Encyclopaideia – Journal of Phenomenology and Education*, **24**(57), pp. 501–519.
Gross, R. (2001) *Psychology – The Science of Mind and Behaviour*. London: Hodder Headline plc.
Hebb, D.O. (1949) *Organization of Behaviour*. New York: Wiley and Sons Inc.
Horgan, T. and Woodward, J. (1990) Folk Psychology Is Here to Stay. In W.G. Lycan (Ed.) *Mind and Cognition – A reader*. Oxford: Blackwell Publishers.
Rudrauf, D., Lutz, A., Cosmelli, D., Lachaux, J.P. and Vanquyen, M. (2003) From Autopoiesis to Neurophenomenology: Francisco Varela's Exploration of the Biophysics of Being. *Biological Research*, **36**, pp. 21–59.
Spence, K.W. and Spence, J.T. (1968) *The Psychology of Learning and Motivation*. New York: Academic Press.
Treml, A.K. and Becker, N. (2010) Lernen. In H.H. Krüger and W. Helsper (Eds) *Einführung in Grundbegriffe und Grundfragen der Erziehungswissenschaft*. Opladen: Verlag Barbara Budrich.
Wittgenstein, L. (1973). *Philosophical Investigations*. Oxford: Wiley-Blackwell.

9 Attention as the core of education

Collaborative learning from experiences in GP vocational training in the Netherlands

Mario Veen and Marije van Braak

Introduction

In this chapter, we explore the unique value of a form of education at the Dutch training for Medical General Practitioners (GPs): Learning from Experience (LfE). LfE has weathered the test of time despite being quintessentially different from most other forms of medical education. For the past decade, we have systematically studied this form of collaborative reflection on experiences from practice. The value of LfE is widely acknowledged by teachers and GP trainees, but what actually are the 'active ingredients' that contribute to its merit? From a cognitive psychological perspective, which is still prevalent in medical education research, those ingredients remain hidden. They become visible, however, from a phenomenological perspective that describes LfE as 'embodied education', that is closely connected to the profession for which it is educational, including the historical development of this profession. What matters for this educational form, we argue, has less to do with concepts such as 'reflection' which, formally, is what LfE sessions are supposed to be about. It has more to do with the *interaction* that is allowed to emerge in the setting (time, place and participants). The interaction is a site of socialisation, qualification and subjectification that enables trainees' ability to direct and distribute their professional *attention*. This allows the affordances of the profession to shape the educational sessions, instead of the other way around. Rather than 'micro-managing' learning, the GP institute provides a setting, teacher professionalisation training on how to facilitate interaction, and trusts that the participants will use the resources to create and monitor the educational value of the sessions. In that sense, we conclude, the educational philosophy that inspires the doings and workings of LfEs can be a model for meaningful education in other professions and settings.

Learning from Experiences: A unique form of education

The Dutch training for GPs, LfEs is a weekly 45–90-minute session in which a group of around ten GPs in training talk about their experiences in practice. These can be experiences with patients, such as challenging discussions about preferred treatments, training issues, such as struggles in the relations with their supervising GP, or personal issues, such as being called upon as a doctor in case of illness in one's own family. Positive experiences, such as early and correct diagnosis in rare medical situations, are usually explicitly welcomed as well. The sessions are guided by one or two teachers, usually an experienced GP and a behavioural scientist or psychologist. The aim of the

DOI: 10.4324/9781003223528-12

sessions is to create educational value for future practice based on past experiences shared and discussed in the group (van Braak et al., 2021).

What makes this type of education a unique asset? First, none of the Dutch postgraduate medical programmes – and, as far as we know, this situation is similar beyond the Dutch borders – features a form of education specially dedicated to discussing practice experiences. At least, not in the systematic, continuous and persistent way that LfE is part of the training programme of Dutch GPs. Second, it is in contrast with the general trend of educational activities in postgraduate medical education. Over the past years, postgraduate training programmes have become increasingly structured, boarded up in terms of specific learning goals, activities, tasks and assessment of what has been and has to be 'learned' (see the development of Programmatic Assessment, e.g. Schut et al., 2021). This trend has resulted in highly structured curricula, parts of which have been regulated to the extent that they leave very limited room for improvisation and adaptive education. How did LfE, a form of education that runs counter to any such trends and is quintessentially different from many forms of education in other postgraduate medical training programmes, come to exist and then survive?

The history of Learning from Experience

LfE has been an integral part of the GP vocational training since its start in the 1970s. Its introduction was a way of expressing the goals of the vocational training at the time, and it has evolved together with the training ever since. As we will discuss later, perhaps its ability to evolve and be adaptable to changing demands has been part of its success.

Nowadays, most medical training programmes have instituted some form of collaborative reflection as part of their curriculum. In the 1970s, however, this was quite rare. The initiators of the GP vocational training used LfE in order to distinguish and emancipate themselves from other specialisms. At that time, the Dutch GP profession was in an identity crisis: GPs were often seen as doctors without a specialism (Veen et al., 2015). After completing basic medical training, any graduate could become a GP by doing a residency with an experienced GP. The GPs who initiated academic vocational GP training had been participating in 'Balint groups'. Balint was a British psychiatrist who facilitated discussion groups with GPs around what we would today call 'professional identity formation' (Rees and Monrouxe, 2018). GPs in these groups would share patient cases from practice and discuss with the group leader and peers what their own role in the situation was, the patient-doctor relationship, and what questions the experience conjured up. Balint's famous saying that the doctor (or their personality) is the most frequently prescribed drug, and that this drug has side effects, was the core reason for exploring the 'effect of the doctor' on patient treatment.

In the 1950s and 1960s, the search for a distinct GP identity was in part answered through participation in these Balint groups. The idea that GPs are not doctors without a specialism, but doctors who are specialised in the doctor-patient relationship, in communication, and in the effect their own behaviour and personality has on this relationship, became increasingly accepted. GPs build connections with their patients that in many cases last from birth to adulthood, and they are a gatekeeper for the referral of patients to other specialisms. Their gatekeeper role is also manifest in their responsibility for societal health by, for instance, limiting the prescription of antibiotics. In addition, what it means to be a GP differs in each patient case: from psychological help, end of life care or small surgery, to cutting a wedding ring, or 'just reassurance'. It made sense to GPs at that time to create space in their vocational training to share, exchange and give vent to the very diversity of experiences that GPs encounter. It was then that LfE became an essential part of the Dutch GP training.

From the start, the goal of LfE was threefold. First, to bridge practice and theory. The reason why LfE traditionally takes place in the morning is to give trainees an opportunity to talk about and to process their week in residency; they can then enjoy the support of their peers and focus their full attention on learning for the rest of the day. LfE thus facilitate a transition from residency to university, from practice to theory. Second, to gain 'second-hand experience'. Most GPs in training only participate in two different medical practices during their three-year training. They encounter just two different experienced GP supervisors and a limited number of patient cases. LfE provides opportunities to hear from others about patient cases, dilemmas and experiences that they have not yet encountered. Such 'second-hand experience' gives them a head start if they were ever to encounter similar cases or dilemmas in the future. Third, against the background of fostering a sense of community by recounting experiences and learning from each other, LfE is meant to foster reflection on various aspects of the profession. For instance, what does the way I dealt with this patient say about me? What kind of GP do I want to be? How do I want to act the next time I encounter a similar situation?

Although these goals of LfE make sense for the goal of GP training, LfE in many ways has been the odd one out compared to other types of education. Education in the 1960s and 1970s was consistent with the hippie era: it was not uncommon to have these kinds of unstructured, reflective group discussions about psychology, education and values. But in the 1980s and 1990s, medical training programmes, including GP training, became increasingly structured. LfE, however, was an exception. LfE itself is still as unstructured as it was before, although the emphasis is now more on creating educational value instead of 'just sharing', and the GP training institute also increasingly invests in teacher training to improve teaching in terms of several outcomes (Veen et al., 2015) Current trends, especially in medical education, have seen practice becomes increasingly regulated, assessed and scripted. It is indeed quite surprising that LfE has survived, even when it takes considerable time (one or two hours a day) out of the university curriculum. We attribute this to the fact that GP teachers, as well as trainees, regard LfE as valuable. This value comes from LfE's lack of an imposed structure and its being process-based rather than outcome-based, not despite it.

> **Question for discussion**
>
> What are the educational consequences of structured versus unstructured educational activities?

The value of LfE

Fifty years into GP training we now start to get a grip on what actually makes the experience of participating in LfE valuable for participants. In a video-stimulated interview study (van Braak et al., 2021), we asked GPs in training to respond to videos of LfE sessions in which they had participated shortly before being interviewed. We asked them to comment on anything they perceived as valuable or not valuable. The openness of the question resulted in an extensive list of detailed aspects of the recorded LfE-sessions that the interviewees constructed as being valuable or not valuable in one way or another.

It turned out that GPs in training consider an LfE session valuable when during the session, the participants (teachers and trainees) create educational value *for all*. That is, when all participants find in the session something (anything!) that helps them in their future practice as a GP. That 'something' need not be a simple tip that is applicable to tomorrow's activities, but may be 'something' that facilitates personal development in the longer term, 'just' something to think about in the car back home. Contrary to popular theories about reflection in education (de la Croix and Veen, 2018), interviewees did not always consider it necessary to formulate a new course of action, to decide what one is 'going to do differently' the next time, or have any other kind of practical 'outcome' of a case discussion (Veen and de la Croix, 2017). Often, it seemed that just having discussed the case and considered different viewpoints was a sufficiently valuable 'something'.

In our research on LfE (van Braak *et al.*, 2021), it became apparent that, rather than the *outcome* of the discussion, the quality of the *interaction* that takes place is decisive in whether LfE sessions are experienced as valuable. This type of value arises when the interaction about experiences from practice allows for diverse perspectives, includes everyone and anything where appropriate, is a safe environment (e.g. non-judgemental), and features efficient discussion (no extensive digging into personal feelings, no lengthy explorations of issues that don't mean much to the case presenter). In effect, these conditions can be seen as directing teachers of LfE towards facilitating an *open, dynamic* and *only limitedly structured* discussion. Let us now see why.

Working ingredients: Openness and collaborative interaction

So far, we have discussed what LfE is, how it developed, and what is perceived as its value. The essence of the value of LfE, we have argued, is based on empirical evidence, is in its open character and the collaborative, shared nature of the interactions. We now zoom out to discuss these two 'working ingredients' in general terms: how does an open, unstructured form of education and collaborative, shared interaction contribute to educational value?

Open, unstructured education

What can be done in any educational situation depends on the *structures* that govern it. These structures can be anything material or non-material, ranging from the set-up in the classroom to its location, to the materials present, to the time of the day and to the people present (with their specific set of baggage, like knowledge and skills). Such structures influence what can and cannot be done during the educational event. A simple example of such influence can be seen in the way a classroom configuration can allow for particular group activities. Traditional lecture seating, in rows upon rows, affords plenary discussion of content, but does not easily afford group work. Similarly, any structures that prescribe particular ways of teaching or organising the lesson limit the possibility of improvising its content and form.

The structures of an educational situation, both material and non-material, together constitute what has been called the 'sociomateriality' of the educational situation. (For further reading, see Goldszmidt, 2016; and for an analysis of the sociomateriality in a medical training setting, see Burm *et al.*, 2019). Of course, the sociomateriality of any educational situation does not *determine* what happens. Chairs can be replaced, missing materials can be brought in, etc. But what is important here is that any configuration of the educational situation, either material or non-material, has particular possibilities and limitations.

If particular structures facilitate *and* limit what happens in any educational situation, then to allow for anything to happen means to adopt as few structures as possible. That is, leaving an educational situation open in terms of seating configuration, detailed schedules, what is being discussed, and ways to approach relevant topics, creates an open attitude to *what happens* and *what happens to be relevant*. In the case of reflection education, of which LfE is an example, formal reflective activities that follow certain formats (used in many peer-group reflective settings, see e.g. Løvaas and Vråle, 2020; Staempfli and Fairtlough, 2019) restrict that openness. Formal structures and the presence of clear learning 'outcomes' would restrict the extent to which the group can attend to anything, and everything that appears relevant to anyone in the session at any moment during that session (van Braak, 2021). In that sense, then, the open nature of LfE facilitates an in-the-moment construction of value for all.

Collaborative, shared interaction

The second working ingredient we draw attention to is the collaborative, group nature of the interaction during LfE (van Braak, 2021). In line with folk knowledge that 'two heads are better than one', the fact that *groups* of people share and discuss experiences from practice is in itself a powerful factor in creating educational value. Group discussion on experiences is beneficial beyond individual, intrapersonal explorations of such experiences, as research in various professional contexts has shown (van Braak, 2021; Burgess *et al.*, 2020).

So what makes group discussion so beneficial? First, when more than one person discusses a particular experience or issue, it is likely that more than one perspective on the issue is shared in the group. That allows for diversity in searching for ways to deal with the issue. Second, when people with similar professional backgrounds participate in discussion, they can identify with others, relate to others, and engage in mutual recognition. That in turn makes it possible to normalise difficult situations ('I have experienced that as well, that is completely normal at this stage of your training'). As such, being in a group together allows for divergence (diverse perspectives, room for participants to show themselves as unique beings) as well as convergence (recognition of shared norms and values), both of which appear to be very valuable processes in the training of professionals, as in LfE, and for students more generally (van Braak, 2021; Biesta, 2020a).

The value of collaborative, shared interaction is in the sheer *being together* of more than one person, as well as in the fact that those people are *similar but not the same* with respect to relevant topics in the discussion that takes place between them.

Question for discussion

What kind of educational interaction can contribute to educational value in postgraduate education?

Educational theory: Subjectification and attention

So far, we have focused on LfE as an educational form in the Dutch GP vocational training, and distinguished working ingredients that made it so valuable that it survived the increased focus on outcome-based and regulated forms of education. In the remainder of this chapter, we will link the essence of this kind of education to two concepts from educational theory related to a possible goal of this type of education (subjectification) and means to achieving this goal (attention).

Summarising our discussion so far, one of the main insights gained about LfE as a form of education is that its value is mainly attributed to the quality of the interaction rather than an outcome-oriented goal or result. LfE interaction does not follow a pre-set path (as many forms of education do), but nonetheless a recurrent structure does emerge. In that respect, LfE is no different from training in other medical professions or even professional training beyond the medical domain: firefighters, lawyers and teachers also often encounter experiences during their professional practice that might call for 'venting', 'sharing' or even 'learning from'. For each of these, the goal of sharing experiences from practice with fellow professionals is to develop into competent professionals.

But mastery in any profession goes beyond the *standards* that are set by the professional community for what is considered 'competence' and the ability to enact this competence in response to an unpredictable and ever-changing environment. The professional's mastery is also found in the degree to which they are able to act *on their own terms*. Professionals not only distinguish themselves from 'lay people' in that there are certain professional ways of dealing with the world: professional standards, norms and values. However, professionals also distinguish themselves from their fellow professionals as unique subjects within the profession. So, professional competence is about more than following rules and guidelines or mimicking colleagues and mentors. It is also about being visible as a unique professional who is able to question the profession instead or just adapting to it. That is what Biesta, a contemporary educational philosopher, calls 'professional subjectification' (Biesta, 2010).

Professional subjectification

The conclusion that professional competence is both about getting acquainted with the ways of doing and being in the profession, as well as developing a distinct, individual self, leads us to a conceptual description of education in three domains: qualification, socialisation and subjectification (Biesta, 2010). Qualification, which is about gaining the necessary knowledge and skills to competently perform a task, and socialisation, which is about getting to know the norms and values, the ways of being and doing, of a certain group of people or setting, are often associated with educational structures. Qualification, for example, is often seen as systematic attention to particular knowledge and skills in predefined units of 'learning material' or 'learning activities', which is then systematically tested or evaluated to determine whether someone is competent in them. In contrast to qualification and socialisation, which can be done *to* students by having them participate in certain educational activities, subjectification can never be done *to* students and only strives when there is enough space (i.e. literal and figurative *openness*) for those participating in education to *come into existence*. Now, that needs some explanation.

Subjectification can be understood as a process of becoming visible as a subject, a person in your own right, an agent on your own terms (Biesta, 2010). What that means is that students in education, or in the case of LfE, GPs in training, are granted the space to participate in education as subjects, not as objects. That is, education that leaves room for subjectification, for subjects to be subjects, is education that not merely *subjects* students *to* educational activities (Biesta, 2014). That type of education also allows students to enact their 'subjectness' by going against or questioning the educational activities that they encounter when participating in education. Not *fitting in* (as in socialisation), but *engaging with* the norms and values of the community, they are (becoming) part of (Biesta, 2014; Biesta and van Braak, 2020).

Such space for engaging with established ways of doing and being requires openness. First, openness in terms of allowing the established ways to be contested and resisted. In the case of GP training, this entails room for GPs in training to resist established norms, values and practices of being a GP instead of requiring new GPs to walk the well-trodden path of past and current practice. Allowing for such resistance requires teachers to tolerate critical and out-of-the-box approaches to what might be considered well-established and 'good' practice. Second, space for engaging with established ways of doing and being requires openness in the sense of literally leaving room in the curriculum for the 'coming into presence' (Biesta, 2015) of GPs in training. Open space in the curriculum allows GPs in training to *encounter* others in ways that do justice to each individual's way to exist in the world.

What does such open space in the curriculum look like? Biesta's work provides several examples of educational activities that could be helpful here. First, in Biesta (2015), he describes a course that he once taught, where he explicitly tried to *avoid* learning in the sense of gaining a deeper understanding or increased comprehension. That means less structure in the sense of learning goals, explicit knowledge or skills to be mastered. (Compare this to what we have described as the *open* and *unstructured* nature of LfE). Yet, he chose a different 'organising principle' for the course: that of 'adoption'. Students were asked to adopt a theoretical concept and 'encounter' and 'work with' it during the course. This approach may seem to provide less structure to what has to be done during the course, but it apparently opened up various possibilities (*existential* possibilities, Biesta calls them) for the students to engage with the concepts in meaningful ways. Another example is when Biesta (2010) discusses what happens when education leaves room for students to come into being. From that, we could derive suggestions such as: let students speak with their own voice, not as representatives of a community; focus on what is *unique* in students; allow students to *initiate* actions: that is, literally act as agentive subjects. These suggestions all centre around the idea of room for the uniqueness of people participating in education. This uniqueness can never be produced, but it can be prevented:

> It is rather easy to make sure that uniqueness will *not* appear, will have no chance at appearing. This will happen when we prevent our students from any encounter with otherness and difference, any encounter that might interrupt their 'normal' ways of being and might provoke a responsive and responsible response. This is when we let our students become immune to what might affect, interrupt and trouble them.
>
> (Biesta, 2010: 90)

To facilitate uniqueness coming into play, teachers need to organise encounters that confront students, or, in our specific case, GPs in training, with 'otherness'. Encountering 'otherness' means staying with it for a while, scrutinising what is different or new.

So far, we have argued that professional competence is found not so much in the degree to which the professional is able to execute a preformulated plan, but rather in their ability to adapt and improvise in interaction with their professional community and with their professional goals in mind. This, however, may seem contradictory. On the one hand, it requires us to work with trainees in ways that allow them to develop as unique, authentic professionals, while, on the other hand, we provide an educational structure of *peers*, which by default engenders conformity to a norm and socialising into a community (Veen, 2021). This contradiction dissolves, however, when we focus on the role of *attention* in the formation of professionals.

> **Question for discussion**
>
> How can the concept of subjectification help teachers to organise education?

Attention

Attention (both in education and beyond) is a scarce resource that can be trained. Imagine, for instance, a medical emergency. People are screaming, everyone is panicking. For most people, this situation is simply overwhelming. We would not know what to do. A medical professional, however, will be able to focus their attention on what matters: distinguish the signal from the noise, identify the problem and act. Now imagine a situation that seems opposite: an elderly patient sitting opposite a GP, telling a long-winded story. Most of us would get bored and dismiss the patient as 'difficult'. But that same GP may be able to catch a detail – perhaps a certain word or a rise in intonation of the patient – that will alert them to diagnosing what is 'actually' going on and troubling the patient. This has sometimes been described as a 'gut feeling' that professionals develop. In the first case, everything is calling for attention, which makes it hard to distinguish what matters. In the second case, attention risks being lost to mind-wandering. What distinguishes the professional is that they are able to direct and distribute their attention.

In the examples above, the healthcare professional is *situated* in a medical emergency or consultation room, and focuses their attention just as much by noticing phenomena that lay people would not notice, as by 'actively *excluding* all the other things that grab [their] attention' (Crawford, 2015: 15), that are irrelevant to the (medical) goal. Keywords here are *responding to*, *improvising*, *listening* – in short, *paying attention* and *directing attention*. This view of being in the world contrasts with the prevailing notion that to become a competent professional requires the professional to model – as if it is possible to think of all possible scenarios that a professional could find themselves in – and train them into which actions they are supposed to perform in each of these scenarios. In contrast, if we 'throw' ourselves into a situation that requires professional action, as GP trainees are 'thrown' into various practice situations, there will be a wealth of experiences that can provide potential for recognising patterns in what works and does not work in the real world:

> Human beings are exquisitely sensitive to detecting patterns, and this is clearly connected to our drive to *become competent*. [We] achieve competence by becoming sensitive to the

patterns by which the flux of sensual data reveals a stable world. We are able to do this because through our own actions we gain different perspectives on our object; our ability to apprehend reality is intimately bound up with our own agency.

(Crawford, 2015: 103)

As we become more competent, we are not just closer to a pre-established goal, but rather we also become more competent at recognising and formulating more sophisticated goals:

> In the course of your repeated efforts, you find that what you are aiming at is a moving target, because it reveals itself only in the course of your pursuit.
>
> (Crawford, 2015)

If we learn by doing – as GP trainees do in the practical part of their training – and becoming more competent consists of gaining different perspectives on our object, then we start to see how the *collaborative* nature of LfE contributes to the value of this type of education. The key here is that it is a group activity in which one trainee shares an experience that is then made into a *shared object of attention*. This object becomes available for their peers and teachers to comment on, challenge and explore from different angles. It is important that peers and teachers can think and talk about the professional experience from their own lived experiences and shared understandings of professional competence. In doing so, the individuality of each professional (or, as we have described it earlier, the professional as a *subject*), is thus expressed in an activity that, 'in answering to a shared world, connects [them] to others - in particular, to other practitioners of [their] art, who are competent to recognize the peculiar excellence of their work' (Crawford, 2015: 159).

All of this leads us to the conclusion that 'achieving competence [...] has an important social dimension' (Crawford, 2015: 62). Crawford illustrates this by describing how firefighters develop as professionals. We cite an abbreviated version of his account to connect what we have now discussed about the importance of open, collaborative and shared interaction, professional subjectification and the role of attention. Firefighters

> are under mutual surveillance and can criticize one another's mistakes. They can cover one another's blind spots, offering up a third person perspective. [Their] own experience is altered in conversation [...] The fruit of this conversation enters into your ongoing rehearsal of the [professional] experience. If this rehearsed version bears up, and jibes with further experience, it becomes internalized, available to the subconscious mind in coping with future situations. For experiences to become part of the secure, sedimented foundation of a skill, they must be *criticized*. [...] The power of these conversations to clarify your experience, rather than introduce fresh confusions, depends in part on the dialectical abilities of your colleagues. They have to be able to interrogate their own experience of the fire critically, and bring their experience into the conversation in such a way that their initial interpretation is put at risk. [To] be good at this kind of conversation you have to love the truth more than you love your own current state of understanding. This is, of course, an unusual priority to have, which may help to account for the rarity of mastery in any pursuit.
>
> (Crawford, 2015: 63)

> **Question for discussion**
>
> How is the conception of education as 'directing attention' different from other conceptions of education, such as gathering knowledge or learning skills?

Conclusion: Education as turning attention

In this chapter, we have introduced LfEs as a unique form of medical education. We have described its history and analysed its working ingredients: an open structure and collaborative interaction. Linking these ingredients to contemporary educational and philosophical theory, we concluded that open structures and collaborative interaction contribute to professional subjectification by drawing and directing attention in educational activities centring around experiences of practice. As a side note, this conclusion also holds for the professional formation of teachers.

With its open character and room for GPs in training 'coming into presence' as unique subjects, LfEs can provide a model for meaningful education in other types of education and professional training. The above discussion of LfEs and its relation to openness, structure, subjectification and attention, underscores the importance of directing our attention to the act of teaching. It is not *learning* that we are concerned about when we think about the formation of professionals, but *teaching*. As Biesta points out in a recent publication on education in COVID epidemic times:

> What is distinctive about education is not learning—which can happen anywhere, with or without education—but teaching. And the basic gesture of teaching is that of trying to catch and direct the attention of another human being—an act of 'turning,' as Plato already describes it in *The Republic*.
>
> (Biesta, 2020b: 2)

In our COVID and post-COVID times, attention to others and room for ourselves to show how we exist in the world in unique ways, may be more important than ever. With this discussion, we hope to have provided some pointers for designing education that facilitates paying attention and encountering what is fundamentally 'other'.

Summary points

- Medical education in the past decade has seen a trend towards highly structured curricula and assessment.
- Counter to this trend, Learning from Experience, a unique form of education at the Dutch training for general practitioners, has remained an open, unstructured form of education from its introduction in the 1970s and onwards.
- The characteristics of Learning from Experience that facilitate educational value for the ones participating in it are an open, unstructured education, and collaborative, shared interaction.
- Open structures and collaborative interaction contribute to professional subjectification, an important domain of purpose in the education of professionals, by drawing and directing attention in educational activities centring on experiences of practice.
- This model of education can serve as an example for meaningful forms of training of professionals in other disciplines, as well as for medical education across the board.

Recommended reading

Biesta, G. (2010) *Good Education in an Age of Measurement: Ethics, politics, democracy.* New York: Routledge.
Crawford, M. (2015) *The Beyond Your Head: On becoming an individual in an age of distraction.* London: Penguin.
van Braak, M., Giroldi, E., Huiskes, M., Diemers, A.D., Veen, M., and van den Berg, P. (2021) A Participant Perspective on Collaborative Reflection: Video-stimulated interviews show what trainees value and why. *Advances in Health Science Education,* **26**, pp. 865–879.

References

Biesta, G. (2010) *Good Education in an Age of Measurement: Ethics, politics, democracy.* New York: Routledge.
Biesta, G. (2014) *The Beautiful Risk of Education.* New York: Routledge.
Biesta, G. (2015) Freeing Teaching from Learning: Opening up existential possibilities in educational relationships. *Studies in Philosophy and Education,* **34**, pp. 229–243.
Biesta, G. (2020a) Risking Ourselves in Education: Qualification, socialization, and subjectification revisited. *Educational Theory,* **70**(1), pp. 89–104.
Biesta, G. (2020b) Have We Been Paying Attention? Educational anaesthetics in a time of crises. *Educational Philosophy and Theory,* **54**(3), pp. 221–223.
Biesta, G. and van Braak, M. (2020) Beyond the Medical Model: Thinking differently about medical education and medical education research. *Teach Learn Med,* **32**(4), pp. 449–456.
Burgess, A., van Diggele, C., Roberts, C., and Mellis, C. (2020) Facilitating Small Group Learning in the Health Professions. *BMC Medical Education,* **20**, 457. DOI:10.1186/s12909-020-02282-3.
Burm, S., Faden, L., DeLuca, S., Hibbert, K., Huda, N., and Goldszmidt, M. (2019) Using a Sociomaterial Approach to Generate New Insights into the Nature of Interprofessional Collaboration: Findings from an inpatient medicine teaching unit. *Journal of Interprofessional Care,* **33**(2), pp. 153–162.
Crawford, M. (2015) *The Beyond Your Head: On becoming an individual in an age of distraction.* London: Penguin.
de la Croix, A. and Veen, M. (2018) The Reflective Zombie: Problematizing the conceptual framework of reflection in medical education. *Perspectives on Medical Education,* **7**(6), pp. 394–400.
Goldszmidt, M. (2016) When I Say … Sociomateriality. *Medical Education,* **51**(5), pp. 465–466.
Løvaas, B. J. and Vråle, G. B. (2020) The Value of Group Reflection. In H. Askeland, G. Espedal, B. J. Løvaas, and S. Sirris (Eds) *Understanding Values Work.* Cham, Switzerland: Palgrave Macmillan.
Rees, C. E. and Monrouxe, L. V. (2018) Who Are You and Who Do You Want to Be? Key considerations in developing professional identities in medicine. *Medical Journal of Australia,* 202–3. DOI: 10.5694/mja18.00118. PMID: 30157410.
Schut, S., Maggio, L. A., Heeneman, S., van Tartwijk, J., van der Vleuten, C., and Driessen, E. (2021) Where the Rubber Meets the Road – An integrative review of programmatic assessment in health care professions education. *Perspectives on Medical Education,* **10**(1), pp. 6–13.
Staempfli, A. and Fairtlough, A. (2019) Intervision and Professional Development: An exploration of a peer-group reflection method in social work education. *The British Journal of Social Work,* **49**(5), pp. 1254–1273.
van Braak, M. (2021) Joint Construction of Educational Value: Exploring 'teaching' in group discussions on experiences from practice during General Practitioner training. PhD thesis Erasmus University Medical Center Rotterdam, The Netherlands.
van Braak, M., Giroldi, E., Huiskes, M., Diemers, A. D., Veen, M., and van den Berg, P. (2021) A Participant Perspective on Collaborative Reflection: Video-stimulated interviews show what trainees value and why. *Advances in Health Science Education,* **26**, pp. 865–879.
Veen, M. (2021) Wrestling with (In)authenticity. *Perspectives on Medical Education,* **10**(3), pp. 141–144.
Veen, M. and de la Croix, A. (2017) The Swamplands of Reflection: Using conversation analysis to reveal the architecture of group reflection sessions. *Medical Education,* **51**(3), 324–336.
Veen, M., Snijders Blok, B., Bareman, F., and Bueving, H. (2015) Uitwisselen van ervaringen in de huisartsopleiding. *Huisarts Wet,* **58**(1), pp. 6–10.

10 Teaching with flow in the times of COVID-19

Danai Tselenti and Alexandros Tillas

Introduction

Recent technological advancements have triggered radical changes in teaching and learning, not least by introducing a variety of digital learning platforms (e.g. Webex, Zoom) (Schiffman et al., 2007), massive open online courses or classes delivered through handhelds and wearables, augmented or virtual reality and so forth. These novel technologies challenge traditional pedagogical methods to the extent that they allow for new types of interaction between learners and teachers (Decuypere and van den Broeck, 2020; Decuypere et al., 2021). This educational digitisation process has been heavily accelerated by the emergency nature and scale of the measures taken in tackling the current COVID-19 pandemic, including social distancing, public and private school closures all over the world.

A number of researchers provide insights into the particularities and the educational effects of the recently adopted digital learning environments largely imposed as a reaction to COVID-19 (Flores and Swennen, 2020; Zhou et al., 2020). A main line of research focuses on the perceptions and experiences of students and teachers on distance education during the pandemic (Hebebci et al., 2020; Schaefer et al., 2020), while others investigate, for example, the adapting competences of educators (König et al., 2020), the effectiveness of specific platforms in dealing with the imposed challenges, e.g. keeping student motivation high (Noah and Gbemisola, 2020).

Despite this significant amount of work, and given the time required to adjust to the novel and ongoing emergent circumstances, it is hard to pinpoint the levels at which schools have managed closures by providing sufficient communication and learning opportunities for their students, or whether teachers have managed to master the challenges of their new digital 'classrooms'.

One aim of this chapter is to understand the key aspects of the online teaching and learning which have taken place in the context of the current COVID-19 pandemic, and which differ significantly from standard digital learning practices mainly due to their emergency status (cf. Hodges et al., 2020). Specifically, it focuses on educators and investigates how digitally mediated teaching affects their experience and performance. We start from the assumption that 'flow', the state of ultra-focused performance in a given task, is key for effective teaching and learning. We undertake an empirical study in order to show why it is crucial to understand how teachers perceive their online experiences during the COVID-19 crisis, and to shed light upon the conditions that nourish or hinder flow in online teaching. Within an educational context, the source of flow is not always easily identifiable. By using teachers' self-reports, we focus on three closely intersecting directions

DOI: 10.4324/9781003223528-13

of flow: (1) The achievement of flow in teachers; (2) the inducement of flow in the students by the teachers' intent and (3) the crossover of flow from students to teachers. Understanding this three-directional source of flow could promote developing better digital education practices.

In a state of flow

The extant literature on improving learning focuses largely on how students experience flow and on how they can optimise their experience in an online classroom, often within the imposed virtual setting during the pandemic (Han et al., 2020; Habe et al., 2021), while significantly less research has focused on how teachers experience online teaching flow (Basom and Frase, 2004; Bakker, 2005). In an attempt to fill this gap in the literature, we focus on how recent educational developments have influenced the psychology of teaching. Specifically, our goal is to identify the aspects of digital education that hinder or nourish flow, and in turn learning, and make suggestions about how both the positive and the negative aspects of a digital learning environment can be further adjusted in order to improve the experience of teachers and learners alike.

What is flow?

A state of flow has a number of characteristic qualities. For instance, from a phenomenological perspective, one of the major aspects of flow is that performing a task in a state of flow seems effortless for the agent (Moller et al., 2010), as the subject focuses (almost) exclusively on the task in hand (Csikszentmihalyi and Rathunde, 1993). Moreover, while in a state of flow,

1. The agent has a clear view of the goals of the task throughout the task.
2. Feedback from either the environment or subjects involved in the task is immediate, allowing the agent to assess his or her performance and adjust accordingly.
3. The challenges posed by the task match the subject's skills, nourishing a good balance between boredom (too easy) and anxiety (too difficult).
4. The subject is fully and deeply concentrating on the task.
5. Any problem not related to the task is forgotten.
6. The subject has an enhanced sense of control of her actions and environment, so that succeeding in the task at hand is solely down to the subject.
7. The subject loses her reflective self-consciousness.
8. Time perception is distorted -time is often perceived as passing quicker than normally.
9. The activity becomes 'autotelic' in the sense that it is the activity rather than its outcome that becomes rewarding. Subjects are prone to repeat such rewarding activities (adapted from Csikszentmihalyi, 2014).

In this chapter, we compare the experiences of educators in light of the above characteristics of flow and assess whether digital education can in practice nourish flow. For instance, the ecology of digital education is realisable in a multitude of ways as it is conducted in environments where the level of structure is reduced compared to a face-to-face learning environment. As shown below, this has significant implications for entering and maintaining high concentration levels – a prerequisite for flow.

> **Question for discussion**
>
> Judging from your personal experience, how often do you think that educators enter a state of flow?

Methodology

This research focuses on the teaching experiences of ten Greek educators engaged in online teaching during the COVID-19 pandemic, while seeking to address the cognitive features of online teaching experiences, and highlight the experience of flow in online teaching.

Data for this study were collected through in-depth, semi-structured interviews carried out over a five-month period (April–August 2021). Questions were designed to enlighten the experiences of teaching and were structured around the educators' experience of flow. All interviews were audiotaped and transcribed verbatim. In order to focus upon different aspects of the complex, multifaceted experience of online teaching during the COVID-19 pandemic, participants were selected from diverse educational contexts. Specifically, participants were teaching at different levels ranging from preschool to senior high school (Lyceum), as well as in both public and private schools (*frontistirio* – a form of cram school). Participants were teaching a wide range of subject matter, including modern and ancient Greek, mathematics, history, computer science, chemistry and biology. Their teaching experience ranged from one year to over 35 years. The sample was selected using personal networks and the snowball sampling procedure, which mainly relies upon the references and nominations of participants already in the sample (Biernacki and Waldorf, 1981).

The research was conducted from a phenomenological perspective and aimed at exploring lived teaching experiences in rich detail (Vagle, 2018). Interviews were coded and analysed using a qualitative thematic analysis (Braun and Clarke, 2006) with the intention of identifying key and recurrent themes embedded in the material.

In presenting our findings, we have anonymised all identifiers such as teacher and student names, so that no information can directly be connected to any research participant. The passages of the transcripts given here have been translated by the authors.

Data analysis has revealed four common themes throughout the teachers' perceptions and experiences.

Losing connection: Technical challenges and challenges of understanding

In Greece, the outbreak of the COVID-19 pandemic has led to the adoption of online (synchronous and asynchronous) teaching at all levels of education. Educators were called to transition at a very short notice and were given only rudimentary training.

Sara, a 61-year-old preschool teacher, describes her experience as follows: '[W]e were thrown to the WebEx platform, were asked to create an account without having a single clue, and we essentially learned by [ourselves and by] helping each other. The school advisor gave us a seminar for just an hour or two on some basic principles'.

A line of challenges that teachers experienced within this novel situation was related to establishing connection with students, primarily on a technical level, as well as with regards to the level of student comprehension. More specifically, the majority of educators reported that a range of technical issues had impeded receiving the necessary perceptual feedback from students. Low internet speed and connectivity problems had often resulted in rebooting devices or shut cameras and microphones off. The lack of the appropriate technical infrastructure highlighted issues of class inequality among students. Depending on the family setting, not all students were appropriately equipped with computers, while many of them could only connect to class with their mobile phones.

The lack of feedback from the environment is detrimental for flow, as neither an educator nor a student can assess her performance and adjust her actions accordingly. Furthermore, connectivity problems also have significant negative effects with regard to the level of concentration on the task of both educators and students; they distort the clarity of goals to the extent that participants focus on reestablishing connection and other technical issues. Largely, the challenge of losing connection has implications for the majority of the above list of the qualitative characteristics of flow.

Marion, a 55-year-old elementary school teacher, argues that in a lot of cases, more than one family member had to connect to their classes simultaneously, resulting in older siblings connecting using a PC, while younger ones were forced to connect via a mobile phone. 'Most children connected through mobile phones; how is it possible to participate in a class through a mobile phone screen?'

Teachers also report that, within the context of a physical classroom, they have constant access to verbal and nonverbal cues; they can explicitly ask students whether they have understood the material, coupling this with pertinent information including facial expressions, gestures, bodily feedback and so forth. This plurality of feedback allows teachers to continually monitor and assess their students' responses and progress in a variety of ways. In the absence of face-to-face interactions, teachers describe feelings of continuous anxiety and awkwardness regarding their ability to understand student comprehension levels. The absence of cues from the environment prevents the teacher from getting into flow.

In addition to communicating the taught material, teaching in a digital classroom makes it harder to provide students with the appropriate corrective information. Comparing teaching using a blackboard in a physical classroom with just a screen and camera, Marion stresses that: 'It was extremely hard to transmit through a screen something that I would [otherwise] [need] one single move on the blackboard, and be sure that the children get it. It was difficult, and this is very important to me that (in offline teaching) you can bring the children to the blackboard, they immediately see the difficulties facing them, and give them instant, clear and precise feedback. I could not control this online'.

Sara's experience is typical with regard to the lack of feedback from her students: 'It was really stressful not being able to know whether the delivered material was actually getting through to the children. You could not know how it was received'. In this sense, the teacher was lacking environmental feedback and could not get into flow.

In this sense, the majority of teachers were unable to monitor and assess how the delivered material was received and whether the set learning objectives had been accomplished. As Ben, a 33-year-old computer science teacher, points out, the difference [between offline and online teaching] is mainly psychological in the sense that what is missing from online teaching is knowing which information does actually reach the student, whether s/he understands it, and which bits of the delivered material need further elaboration in order for the student to grasp it. Asking the question 'Did you get it?' is simply not enough.

Regarding teachers' and students' flow, technical challenges can impede feedback, which is very important. Moreover, the limitations posed by the various technical aspects of online teaching pose a number of task-unrelated problems, which are otherwise forgotten while in a state of flow.

Losing control: Challenges of student engagement

Further analysis of the material highlights the unique challenges facing educators with regard to controlling student engagement. The technological affordances of the online educational platforms allow individual users to switch their cameras off or mute their microphones, providing them with the ability to control how much they wish to disclose to the classroom. Susan notes, 'Not all the students had their cameras or microphones on. [In fact, m]ost of them declined to switch their cameras on, even though I [repeatedly] asked them to do so'.

The right to privacy has triggered a series of unforeseen deviations from traditional classroom practices, and has raised the issue of control in terms of the educators' abilities to ensure student attendance and engagement. Most of the participating educators distinguish between higher and lower levels of student engagement and expressed feelings of discomfort and incompetence with regard to initiating student engagement. This lack of control in many cases triggered distinct management strategies, forcing educators to inform parents or the school principal about switched-off cameras, if only in order to mitigate the stressful effects associated with their inability to control students' attendance and behavioural engagement.

Susan, a 34-year-old Greek cram-school teacher, argues that '[a]s I have to deal with older students, especially over the age of 15, it is extremely hard to persuade someone who is not interested in a class to actually get involved'. Importantly, the majority of the participating educators consider the issue of class engagement, or lack thereof, as incumbent upon the students and argue that getting involved in a class is a rather individual, psychological process directly relating to the students' personal traits and character.

Christine, a 48-year-old chemistry cram-school teacher, is explicit on this: 'I believe [student engagement] is a matter of personal will, perspectives and goals'. And she continues: 'Every student has to realise why s/he is attending [a cram school]. I will challenge a student but only up to a certain point. I cannot work miracles'. Ben makes a similar point: 'Eventually, experience shows that your audience has to be receptive [in order for the message to get through]. This was a great realisation for me'.

In this sense, the educators distinguish between 'learning- and performance-oriented students, who either intrinsically value learning highly or have a high sense of responsibility, and unmotivated students who lack either the willingness or the ability to engage in a class. Digital learning seems to emphasise and exacerbate similar differences between students. Susan vents this: 'There are children who are interested, who like these [online] classes, and there are children who are not interested but are coerced into going to school and end up engaging because of their strong sense of duty. The children without this sense of duty or interest were completely detached in the online setting'.

In this sense, most educators conceived a hierarchy between 'good' and 'bad' students, and approached online education as a continuation of the physical class in terms of student performance. Ben notes: 'Good students remained good students [online], and bad students remained bad'.

Interestingly, though, and despite this 'continued contrast between physical and virtual classrooms, the above negative effects of online teaching allowing students to switch their cameras and microphones off at will, were often reversed, if only to the extent that they partly explained changes in the behaviour of offline poorly engaging students. Marion sums this point nicely: 'During the second quarantine we [me and a number of my colleagues] observed that some children who were feeling insecure [to participate in class actively], fearing that they would make mistakes, and so forth [...] once online became more courageous and took the floor very often. This is in direct contrast with their performance in the physical classroom where they would never raise their hands and would hardly participate, even when prompted to do so. Online teaching allowed these children to build their confidence and speak in front of the class'.

Despite having both negative and positive effects on different aspects of teaching, maintaining the right to switch off cameras compromises both feedback reception and clarity of the educators' goals, while it hinders various flow qualities.

Question for discussion
To what extent may the lack of flow crossover from students to teachers?

Losing presence: Online teaching as an inferior substitute to face-to-face teaching

All of the participating educators expressed a strong preference for face-to-face teaching, valuing the physical proximity between teachers and students as an indispensable precondition for learning. Most educators argue that the online environment does not allow for an effective degree of 'teacher immediacy', described as a unique combination of verbal and nonverbal cues as well as personalised strategies for supporting weaker students. Significant learning occurs when students are instructed directly and are guided through the learning process.

Susan notes: 'I was not able to monitor the students' progress, their writings [...]. On a face-to-face level, I can intervene when a child, for instance, makes a spelling mistake. Online I have no instant access to his/her writings'. Thus, the interaction that takes place in a virtual classroom is of a significantly lower quality when compared to a face-to-face encounter.

In a similar vein, Ben assumes that physical proximity between students and the instructor enables the enforcement of punishment, which works as a strategy for getting students engaged. He notes: 'Offline I would shout a bit more, because online you can be muted and thus shouting more makes no sense. Offline I would choose to inform the school principal that the student has not done his/her homework'.

In this sense, most teachers doubt whether an appropriate learning setting can be created online from the comfort of the student's domestic environment. Home is thus described as an educationally inappropriate setting crammed with various distractions, making for poor concentration conditions and leading students to detach themselves from the class. Susan remembers: 'There were instances when a student told me that he had to leave class in order to help his sister get online for her own class'.

In light of the above, the issue of lacking feedback from the environment and subjects participating in the task seems omnipresent in online teaching, and thus systematically hinders flow. Given the role and mission of educators, not being in a position to provide the appropriate, targeted, and tailored to the needs of different students' feedback hinders flow further by compromising the educator's goals, as well as by increasing the challenges posed by the task exponentially, in comparison to traditional offline teaching.

Losing time offline and gaining time online

A majority of the interviewed educators report that designing online courses and evaluating students required more time and effort when compared to teaching in a traditional setting. As Marion indicates, 'I was forced to work in three ways; it was not compulsory but in order to substitute face-to-face teaching I needed all these tools, the email, the e-me and the WebEx platforms [...] students would send me their answers either in the form of photos, a word document or [a file] on google drive. Every file needed additional technical work for corrections. So, I would end up starting work at 9 am and would not stop before 9 pm without having really completed my tasks. I would just stop'. Sara, a 61-year-old preschool teacher, similarly argues that '[y]ou had to be continuously occupied with searching for every subject; for festive seasons we were searching for fairy tales, songs, crafts, videos; we had to find funny things, something to enrich our material in order to attract the children's attention'. Thus, many teachers faced a cognitive overload while trying to adjust and enrich existing material for online teaching.

Marion mentions, '[a]ll my teaching material was hand-written, so I had to convert it to an electronic format. [This meant that I suddenly had a] huge workload [for my online classes]'.

A number of educators report significantly decreased levels of cognitive effort on their behalf as online courses progressed. This was mainly caused by two factors: (1) gradual withdrawal as an attempt to reduce stress caused by the challenge of engaging the disengaged and absent students, and (2) relaxation due to the fact that either the engaged students were performing reasonably well on exams, or that parts of the teaching material that were particularly hard, was kept for a time when face-to-face teaching would resume. This suggests that many educators construed the current phase of online teaching as a temporary suboptimal substitute for the 'real thing' that traditional teaching is.

As Rachel, a 27-year-old elementary school teacher, argues: 'When the online education started I was very organised. However, as courses progressed, I stopped being so organised. I might have gotten tired or switched to an auto mode. This happened either because I saw that I had already covered certain parts of the teaching material or because I waited for schools to re-open in order to teach certain other bits of the material that could only be taught on a face-to-face basis'.

In the same vein, Susan points out that '[a]t one point I got tired with all this situation with the cameras and the microphones. At the beginning, I was much stricter and I would continuously ask students to turn their cameras on. To be honest, I got tired of the children who were indifferent and constantly absent; this situation wore me out [...] I also realised that my students understood parts of the material (through written exams and exercises I received from them) and I got a bit more relaxed'.

For the majority of the participating educators, collaborating with their faculty peers and sharing their experiences was the greatest facilitator for dealing with the challenges of cognitive overload. To others, it was the available Internet technology that allowed them to save time as they were able to share teaching material in diverse online formats (slideshows, videos, pdfs) more easily. Christine puts it this way: 'I could forward more material to my students as I had it ready and was not forced to write on the physical board. I use a digital pen, so everything I write appears on a virtual whiteboard, and was able to also forward videos with experiments. I could thus avoid all this delay [associated with teaching] in an actual classroom'.

Moreover, teachers report that it was easier and quicker to establish and maintain an orderly environment. In a sense, classroom management became redundant once in a virtual setting. As Rachel argues, '[i]n the online setting I could be more focused on transmitting the information as I did not have to deal with monitoring what was happening in the classroom, whether students were getting noisy or playing during class'. It is worth noting at this point that the decreased need for online discipline and classroom management is inherently linked to 'bad' students being disengaged from the class.

In short, online teaching often poses overwhelming challenges and workload for the educators, reducing flow to a distant possibility. That said, certain tools and technologies associated with online teaching reduce the workload of educators and allow them more time to effectively organise and design their courses, and in this way, facilitate flow.

Conclusion

The new digital educational setting imposed by the emergent preventive measures against COVID-19 presented new social dynamics between students and educators, as well as significant challenges in adjusting certain offline practices for online teaching. However, it also provided teaching opportunities that were previously unavailable and helped identify novel aspects of teaching that might not have otherwise been discovered.

This qualitative analysis reveals that teachers' feelings while experiencing offline flow in class centred on being connected with students, understanding their level of comprehension and being able to closely monitor their degree of engagement or involvement. Thus, a very important area of consideration concerns the educators' lack of control regarding online engagement.

Students resisting the new learning setting suggests an active detachment from the online class. Older students often opt to unplug from the pressure of the classroom by switching their cameras and microphones off. The proverbial excuse of connectivity problems provides them with an ever-so-easy way to escape potential criticism, in the sense that it is much easier to momentarily escape class by clicking a button rather than stepping out of a crowded physical classroom where certain attendance rules apply.

In other cases, having the option to 'switch off' can alleviate stressed underperforming students, granting them a more controlled way to engage with their class. While in offline settings, students are compelled to follow the directives of the teacher and be silenced during teaching delivery, it seems that the affordances of the digital video camera and microphone overturn some of the traditional hierarchical power dynamics between teachers and students, leaving educators with a feeling of anxiety, incompetence and ineffectiveness. To the extent that the goal of teaching is to promote learning, teaching flow is not simply a measure of how involved students are in their learning. It is also an indication of how involving educators are for their students.

Structure and discipline are known to be important for the traditional educational settings, but it seems necessary to reassess the traditional types of interaction between educators and students, from a perspective that can serve the purposes of a non-hierarchical structure, prompts intrinsic motivation and in turn equally enhances teaching and learning flow.

> **Question for discussion**
> What seems to be the biggest challenge facing teaching flow in an online setting?

Summary points

- Factors blocking teaching flow:
    - technical problems, which hindered communication;
    - difficulties in accessing and assessing students' comprehension levels;
    - difficulties in controlling students' social presence and engagement;
    - difficulties in simulating the face-to-face particularities of offline teaching for guiding and helping students;
    - spending additional time and cognitive resources in evaluating students.
- Sharing and presenting materials more easily by leveraging online resources facilitates teaching flow.
- Receiving non-ambiguous feedback turns out to be a major facilitator for flow in the educational process, for learners and educators alike.
- The imposed online setting highlighted various aspects of forced learning and its effects for both offline and online educational practices.

Recommended reading

Csikszentmihalyi, M. (2014) *Applications of Flow in Human Development and Education. The collected works of Mihaly Csikszentmihalyi.* New York: Springer.

Csikszentmihalyi, M. and Rathunde, K. (1993) The Measurement of Flow in Everyday Life: Toward a theory of emergent motivation. In J.J. Jacobs (Ed.) *Nebraska Symposium on Motivation (40). Developmental perspectives on motivation.* Lincoln, NE: University of Nebraska Press.

Plummer, L., Belgen Kaygısız, B., Pessoa Kuehner, C., Gore, S., Mercuro, R., Chatiwala, N. and Naidoo, K. (2021) Teaching Online during the COVID-19 Pandemic: A phenomenological study of physical therapist faculty in Brazil, Cyprus, and the United States. *Education Sciences*, **11**(3), pp. 1–16.

References

Bakker, A.B. (2005) Flow among Music Teachers and their Students: The crossover of peak experiences. *Journal of Vocational Behavior*, **66**, pp. 26–44.

Basom, M.R. and Frase, L. (2004) Creating Optimal Work Environments: Exploring teacher flow experiences. *Mentoring and Tutoring*, **12** (2), pp. 241–258.

Biernacki, P. and Waldorf, D. (1981) Snowball Sampling: Problems and techniques of chain referral sampling. *Sociological Methods and Research*, **10**(2), pp. 141–163.

Braun, V. and Clarke, V. (2006) Using Thematic Analysis in Psychology. *Qualitative Research in Psychology*, **3**(2), pp. 77–101.

Csikszentmihalyi, M. (2014) *Applications of Flow in Human Development and Education. The collected works of Mihaly Csikszentmihalyi.* New York: Springer.

Decuypere, M., Grimaldi, E. and Landri, P. (2021) Introduction: Critical studies of digital education platforms. *Critical Studies in Education*, **62** (1), pp. 1–16.

Decuypere, M. and van den Broeck, P. (2020) Time and Educational (Re)forms: Inquiring the temporal dimension of education. *Educational Philosophy and Theory*, **52**(6), pp. 602–612.

Flores, M.A. and Swennen, A. (2020) The COVID-19 Pandemic and its Effects on Teacher Education. *European Journal of Teacher Education*, **43**(4), pp. 453–456.

Habe, K., Biasutti, M. and Kajtna, T. (2021) Wellbeing and Flow in Sports and Music Students during the COVID-19 Pandemic. *Thinking Skills and Creativity*, **39**, pp. 1–9.

Han, T., Öksüz, A., Sarman, G. and Nakar, A.M. (2020) Flow Experiences of Tertiary Level Turkish EFL Students in Online Language Classes during COVID-19 Outbreak. *MİLLÎ EĞİTİM*, **49**(1), pp. 1059–1078.

Hebebci, M.T., Bertiz, Y. and Alan, S. (2020) Investigation of Views of Students and Teachers on Distance Education Practices during the Coronavirus (COVID-19) Pandemic. *International Journal of Technology in Education and Science*, **4**(4), pp. 267–282.

Hodges, C., Moore, S., Lockee, B., Trust, T. and Bond, A. (2020) The Difference between Emergency Remote Teaching and Online Learning. *Educause Review*, **27**, pp. 1–12.

König, J., Jäger-Biela, D.J. and Glutsch, N. (2020) Adapting to Online Teaching during COVID-19 School Closure: Teacher education and teacher competence effects among early career teachers in Germany. *European Journal of Teacher Education*, **43**(4), pp. 608–622.

Moller, A.C., Meier, B.P. and Wall, R.D. (2010) Developing an Experimental Induction of Flow: Effortless action in the lab. In B. Bruya (Ed.) *Effortless Attention: A New Perspective in the Cognitive Science of Attention and Action*. Cambridge, MA: MIT Press.

Noah, O.O and Gbemisola, K.O. (2020) Impact of Google Classroom as an Online Learning delivery during COVID-19 Pandemic: The case of a secondary school in Nigeria. *Journal of Education, Society and Behavioural Science*, **33**(9), pp. 53–61.

Schaefer, M.B., Abrams, S.S., Kurpis, M., Abrams, M. and Abrams, C. (2020) 'Making the Unusual Usual': Students' perspectives and experiences of learning at home during the COVID-19 pandemic. *Middle Grades Review*, **6**(2), pp. 1–18.

Schiffman, S., Vignare, K. and Geith, C. (2007) Why do Higher Education Institutions pursue Online Education? *Journal of Asynchronous Learning Networks*, **11**(2), pp. 61–71.

Vagle, M.D. (2018) *Crafting Phenomenological Research*. Abingdon: Routledge.

Wong, M.M. and Csikszentmihalyi, M. (1991) Motivation and Academic Achievement: The effects of personality traits and the duality of experience. *Journal of Personality*, **59**(3), pp. 539–574.

Zhou, L., Wu, S., Zhou, M. and Li, F. (2020) 'School's out, but Class's on', the Largest Online Education in the World Today: Taking China's practical exploration during the COVID-19 epidemic prevention and control as an example. *Best Evidence of Chinese Education*, **4**(2), pp. 501–519.

11 Vignette research
An Austrian phenomenological approach to empirical research

Evi Agostini and Hans Karl Peterlini

Introduction

In 2008, the New Secondary School Reform (*Neue Mittelschule* – NMS) was launched throughout Austria as a pilot project aiming to avoid early streaming at the age of ten, and initially intending to integrate the NMS and the *Akademische Hochschule* (AHS) – grammar schools in Austria). Alongside this educational policy, *Der Wissenschaftsfonds* (FWF – the Austrian Science Fund) financed two studies to look at pupils' learning in all nine provinces of Austria. An innovative research instrument had to be developed to enable the investigation of learning in heterogeneous groups, so the data were condensed into concise descriptions of scenes of school experience, known as 'phenomenologically oriented vignettes'. In contrast with studies of learning that focus on results rather than processes and origins, a phenomenological approach such as vignettes focuses on *how* learning takes place, i.e. which stimuli learners are exposed to throughout their learning experience. Thus, learning is conceived of as experience and always occurs when there is a mismatch between one's expectations and accomplishments and new meanings are generated for previous and future experiences.

This chapter explains the theoretical and empirical foundations of vignette research in education within the Austrian political and educational framework. To illustrate the vignette methodology, it starts with a sample vignette and a vignette reading and then moves on to clarify the epistemological premises and the details of the approach. Finally, it describes broader applications for the approach. (All German quotations and the vignette have been translated into English by the authors.)

Sample vignette: 'Sanela and the first snow'

In order to let fresh air into the overheated classroom, two windows are slightly open. Loud, enthusiastic cries and amused squeals can be heard from outside. The class look curiously at the window, but the closed blinds obscure the view. Mrs Gersthuber, sitting at the teacher's desk, declares, 'Yes, it's snowing'. On the other side of the table, Mrs Kranzer shrugs and raises her arms, 'It's spitting'. 'And I'm on my bike', Mrs Gersthuber notes. The lesson continues. Looking at the teacher and from her spot next to the window, Sanela hesitantly reaches for the handle of the blind, but immediately pulls her hand back. Mrs Gersthuber is talking about history. Shortly later, Sanela gets up quietly, opens the blinds, and watches the snowflakes floating past the window. (Author: Alexander Hörmann.)

(Interpretative) vignette reading as a form of analysis

The vignette written by a student describes a scene as it might be perceived in the classroom on any day in winter and is therefore very recognisable. Is learning happening here? How and in what form does it manifest itself? An unforeseen (natural) event intervenes, attracting the attention of those present and giving rise to different responses. Reading the short scene, it becomes clear that the previous experiences and prior knowledge of those present leads them to see the same thing in different ways. The screams and squeals can be understood as an expression of joy at the newly falling snow, while one teacher's reference to the bike can be read more as a concern. Sanela is attracted to the snow. She cannot escape it and has to open the blinds to observe the passing flakes more closely.

The understanding of responses to different individual experiences is gained from the joint readings of vignettes: discursive (Agostini, 2016) or scenic (Peterlini, 2017). These start with specific actions or moments that are perceived and experienced inter-subjectively: how are they described, how can they be understood? In the process, the pedagogical actions of the teachers also come into focus. The two teachers have decided – consciously or unconsciously – to continue working on the topic and not to pay any further attention to the snowfall. What would the alternatives have been? With what consequences? Sanela turns away from the lesson and watches the falling snow. What does this mean for Sanela's learning? The readings of vignettes raise questions that cannot be answered conclusively but allow for a diversity of perspectives and thus for reflection and expansion. Vignettes do not ask what is – or would have been – 'better', but rather what different experiences reveal and how this can be dealt with from a pedagogical, experiential, and, not least, practical point of view.

Reflection on the vignette enables it to be read in all its potential ambiguity. In this context, it reveals and 'points to' (Finlay, 2009: 11) the different meanings that can be ascribed to what is perceived. In order to *point to* a possible interpretation, something is singled out in the vignette by means of phenomenological 'reduction': *what* shows up is traced back to the *way* it shows up (Waldenfels, 1992: 30). No interpretations are 'pointed out' here, i.e. no definitive answers or explanations are given that lie 'behind' or 'beyond' what is happening. Instead, there is an attempt to understand the potential for learning and teaching *at* the event, *as it is experienced* by the individual. In order to gain a broader viewpoint, experiences and actions in the learning and teaching process can also be considered from a theoretical perspective. Vignette readings look at practical situations (e.g. a teaching environment or a pedagogical action) in retrospect, i.e. from a distance, differently, or 'anew' in order to derive learning from them. At this point, despite a different understanding of experience, the phenomenological approach can be linked to John Dewey's theory that learning requires reflection on the experience itself, and a connection to be made with the conditions that necessitated or forced such experience (Dewey, 1916/2009).

> **Questions for discussion**
>
> What do you notice about the vignette? What appeals to you? What irritates you?
>
> What parallels can you draw with your own experiences?
>
> How would you read the vignette?

Premises of phenomenologically-oriented vignettes

Vignettes can draw our attention to the fact that humans, as *animals of experience* (Foucault, 1996), are always doing more than merely taking a neutral view of an immobile and well-ordered reality. As corporeal beings, we are by no means mere subjects facing a supposedly objective world head-on. Rather, we find ourselves in a world that we hear, smell, touch, see and taste; in short, we have experiences from which we emerge changed (Foucault, 1996). We always perceive experience as a specific event in our interaction with the world; the object we perceive (*facts*) and our perception of it (*mode of access*) cannot be separated from each other (Waldenfels, 1992). In the vignette at the beginning of this chapter, this is illustrated by the phenomenon of snow: While Sanela perceives snow as fascinating and worth observing, Mrs Gersthuber sees snow as disturbing, as it will most likely make it difficult for her to cycle home. Depending on the situation and on individuals' previous experiences or current interests, something can also be perceived as something else.

'To perceive otherwise is to perceive differently', remarks Emmanuel Lévinas (1983: 156). By being perceived in a particular way, an object appears in our experience *as a particular* object. That an object appears as a determinate object does not mean that it *is* a determinate object, but that it *becomes* a determinate object by acquiring meaning and thus is able to *reveal* itself *as* a determinate object in the first place. Perspectivity is a fundamental characteristic of the object, because 'only God's conception is free of shadows' (Fink, 1976: 203). Precisely because we are embodied perceivers, we can never take an absolutely objective standpoint, but can only conceive of the objects we experience within the limits of our embodied perception and understanding, i.e. against a specific (theoretical) background, in a specific context, and with a specific meaning. We have a constitutive meaning for the mode in which the object we perceive appears, and we must tolerate the knowledge that such objects also exist without our involvement.

In writing vignettes, researchers do not look at the world from the outside. They do not give things a meaning that is independent of them. What they write bears witness to their engagement with and involvement in the world. As such, vignettes have the potential to provide insights into the sensory contexts of specific pedagogical circumstances that would not be visible from the objective perspective. That is, vignettes enable researchers to visualise what is revealed to them and *how* it is revealed. They thus provide a concise but rich representation within which the so-called neutral observer's perspective is only one among many. Vignettes represent an aesthetic experience of the world. This does not replace the cognitive apprehension of the world, but it does relativise the claim of this perspective to sole authority and thus validates other modes of approaching the world (Agostini, 2017). Vignettes are a medium of sensual and aesthetic visualisation, and thus open up new spaces of cognition and interrelationship.

Fundamental to this approach, therefore, are

- the corporeality of the perceiver, i.e. the body, as distinct from a mere 'object';
- the questioning of the separation of mind and object (the subject-object dichotomy);
- inter-subjectivity.

These points are discussed in more detail below.

What is a vignette?

The word 'vignette' derives from the French terms *vigne* and *vignette*: the first means wine or grape variety; the second has a variety of meanings from the magnificently ornamented lettering in letterpress printing on wine bottles labels (Meyer-Drawe, 2012a; Schratz et al., 2012). In vignette research (e.g. Schratz et al., 2012; Baur and Peterlini, 2016), vignettes borrow from the phenomenological method of *exemplary description* (e.g. Lippitz, 1984; Brinkmann, 2011). As such, they are 'short, concise narratives that capture moments of experience (in school)' (Schratz et al., 2012: 34) and thus provide the experience of learning (Meyer-Drawe, 2010).

Language often does not provide sufficient imagery or differentiation to express the scope or depth of experienced reality. The world of experience belongs to those spheres of our existence that are so close to us that verbalisation hardly seems possible. We thus usually respond to bodily experiences with tears, laughter, nervousness, pallor, palpitations, sweat or blushing. Those who focus solely on conventional standards of scientific knowledge such as verifiability and repeatability run the risk of underestimating many non-conceptual or non-propositional forms of experience, such as are articulated in systems of artistic engagement with the world, including literature, music and images, or direct experiences such as perception and feeling. In this context, the non-conceptual is the precondition for science in the first place (Bromand and Kreis, 2010). Vignettes attempt to grasp (learning) experiences and, above all, the non-conceptual.

Based on the phenomenological understanding of learning as an experience in which expectations are thwarted, and new meanings are generated, vignettes can be created in different educational experiences, for example, within or outside of lessons at a school, or when learning about art in a museum, but also as snapshots of social interactions, for example in a train station. A vignette is thus a condensed, concise description of a selected scene of experience. It is illustrative in nature and can shed light on the general meaning of specific situations so as to enable learning to take place that will also be of benefit in other experiential situations. Vignettes, therefore, serve as examples, and enable us to draw general conclusions from a single specific situation. This means that they can also be used to prompt discussion of (further) implications for practice and theory.

In addition to the differentiated perception of and reflection on pedagogical experience that vignettes enable, they also highlight the need for pedagogical action. Therefore, as will be explained in more detail, they can also serve as a training tool.

Vignettes emerge from the co-experiential experience of vignette writers. Following Ton Beekman (1987), who coined the term *participatory experience,* vignette research traces *co-experiential* experience. Such a research stance assumes that, unlike behaviour, we cannot observe experience, but we can co-experience others as experiencers (Laing, 1977). In this sense, experiences can be shared, with researchers sharing experiences about the experiences of those involved in an experiential situation. Thus, vignettes capture *inter-subjective* moments of perception and experience by which researchers in the field are affected, or 'hit'. One can be hit when habitual courses of action and categories of understanding are thwarted, and a new meaning emerges. Vignettes are an attempt to fix this co-experienced sense of experience in writing. Memorable moments are thus transformed into narrative text and, in the course of writing, the vignette writers themselves will have had experiences and also undergone learning.

> **Questions for discussion**
>
> What makes a vignette a vignette?
>
> What are the characteristics of vignettes?
>
> How is it possible to 'experience' the experiences of others?

The phenomenological approach

Edmund Husserl, the founder of phenomenology in the twentieth century, has already highlighted that experience is inconceivable without prior anticipatory experience. Therefore, a new experience must always already be made against the background of the previous horizon of experience for something to be perceived or understood at all. Thus, every experience is actually *experiential* (Buck, 1989). Learning in vignettes or by vignette writers in the field never starts from scratch *per se*, but is based on what is already there. In this sense, prior knowledge and prior experience are the conditions for perceiving and experiencing anything at all. At the same time, prior knowledge is inevitably accompanied by a perspective. Thus, the bodily situated-ness of perceiver and perceived are a condition of cognition and this is of central significance for phenomenological research.

The phenomenological method, therefore, requires a change of attitude on the part of the perceiver. The basic phenomenological attitude of '*epoché*' initially requires the suspension or bracketing of hasty judgement or any final decision. In the phenomenological 'reduction', researchers reflect sceptically on the relationship between the object of perception and its perceivers, and *what* shows itself is traced back to the *way* it shows itself (Waldenfels, 1992).

On the one hand, researchers try to understand the experiences they encounter in their life-world: their exploratory, pre-scientific experience of the world that acts as a self-evident, unquestioned basis for their everyday thinking and acting. However, on the other hand, they must not be wholly absorbed in these worlds of experience; otherwise, they will no longer be able to reflect on them adequately. In concrete terms, this means a suspension of the unreflected knowledge and opinions of the life-world so that vague pre-conceptions and pre-understandings that affect certain phenomena, for example, based on one's own experiences, come to light, but are also suspended. This approach breaks with experience-based bias and allows researchers to distance themselves, taking the first step towards becoming more aware of their entanglement with phenomena as they then take the second step and reflect (Agostini, 2016).

Vignettes do not claim to reconstruct or provide a full contextualisation of situations, instead translating into language the actions, bodily expressions, atmospheres, and moods that are significant aspects of experience in an aesthetically concise (*pregnant*) way. Moments of condensed experience are selected for vignettes, attempting to preserve ambivalences and ambiguities in the description as far as possible. Vignettes thus describe what is stimulating, attractive or repulsive, what pre-empts preconceived expectations. They show how the learner's experience can lead them to understand the self, the world and others differently from the way they did before. Accordingly, vignette writers seek to be open in the attention they give to unexpected events that give rise to meaning by virtue of their ambiguity and, in response, make learning possible.

Inter-subjectivity of research

The vignette aims to explore *inter-subjective* experience. In line with the work of Käte Meyer-Drawe (2001: 11), vignette writers assume that this includes the world of the in-between (*inter*) and that thus experiences *between* researchers and participants are *also* inter-subjective. It is only through these that subjectivity or objectivity can subsequently be distinguished in the first place. The reference point for intersubjective perceptions and experiences is the body as the situation and reality of all experience. Thus, as with Maurice Merleau-Ponty (1966) and his concept of *intercorporéité* or *inter-corporeality*, it becomes clear that we need the alien 'other' to provide us with access to ourselves and thus to our own (bodily) experiences. The lived experiences of others elude us as perceivers, but their bodily articulations do not. As perceivers, we are always also affected by the bodily expressions of others. This means that, in shared experience, others reveal something that we can also experience in our own body. Based on the body schema developed by Merleau-Ponty (1966) in the context of inter-corporeality, pre-reflexive correspondence with the other is possible; and in this inter-corporeal encounter, meaning can emerge. In a shared experiential situation, potentially intersubjective social meaning arises and can be attributed neither to us alone nor to the other alone, but for the expression of which the other is necessary.

Phenomenological research is thus based on the intersubjective character of experience. For example, by reproducing the actions depicted in a vignette, readers can verify the plausibility of the concrete example for themselves. It is only this comprehensibility that gives validity to a vignette.

How is a vignette written?

In order to write vignettes, researchers allow themselves to be struck by what takes place in the field and what they perceive through their senses and experience inter-subjectively. The particular challenge of writing vignettes is to take into account the mood of the situation and the influences that cannot be expressed in words, i.e. to take a linguistic approach to something that cannot easily be expressed in language. Attention is, therefore, paid in particular to bodily expression, and the focus is not solely on verbal expression and cognitive performance. Researchers attempt to be open to non-propositional forms of expression such as movements, gestures, glances, interactions, moods and atmospheres that become apparent in facial expressions, gestures, tonality, rhythm and posture. In addition to *what* is said, the *how* of a speech gesture must also be noted: which verbs reflect the tone in which something was said or the sound it made? The same applies to tracing the eye movements back and forth between a thing and a person, or the verbalisation of their nuances of movement: for example, when a pupil leaves the class, do they prance, trip, glide or stumble? The focus is on experiences in which there is an impediment to or even a thwarting of learners' expectations. The art of writing vignettes is to make experiences linguistically present so that they can be re-experienced by readers (Agostini, 2017) while at the same time maintaining the ambiguity of the vignette, i.e. avoiding interpretation.

Researchers record signs of experiences in the field which they condense narratively into raw vignettes as soon as possible after data collection. In the subsequent process, the raw vignettes are discussed in the research group and/or with the participants in the field and – as with intersubjective or communicative validation – enriched and condensed. In this process, questions can also be dealt with, for instance, how the vignette presented at the beginning of this chapter could have been written in order to tie the experiences in the classroom even more closely to the bodily expressions of the participants and, for example, to use adjectives as thoughtfully as possible. However, in contrast with a behaviouristic approach, no meaning is attached to the experiences by describing them; meaning is revealed solely by the vignette reading. Likewise, the point of the co-experienced situation at which the vignette begins and ends is often also important, as both influence the meaning of the narrative.

> **Questions for discussion**
>
> How would you describe the attitude of vignette writers?
>
> What should you look for when writing vignettes?
>
> What challenges do you see in writing vignettes?

Possible uses of vignettes

Research

The development of the phenomenologically oriented vignette as a research tool is closely related to learning in heterogeneous groups in schools. The pioneering project at the University of Innsbruck mentioned above, funded by the *Austrian Science Fund*, was followed by a project at schools in South Tyrol, Italy. In the meantime, this research tool has been further refined and introduced into a broader discourse, in terms both of territory and disciplines. Vignette research is being conducted in several German-speaking countries (Germany, Switzerland and Liechtenstein as well as Austria) and in Italy, Greece, South Africa and, on a case-by-case basis, in the Asian region. It is also used in a variety of pedagogical fields going beyond the school context. Moreover, in a current project, the vignette is being used as a methodology for professionalisation. (University) teaching materials are being developed with the primary goal of learning to perceive and reflect on the teaching and learning process and pedagogical activities in a professional manner.

The new EU-funded Erasmus Plus cooperation project 'Professionalization of educators and educational leaders through learning research with vignettes' ('ProLernen': Project runtime 01/11/2020–31/11/2022) at seven European locations using vignette research ties in with the projects mentioned above and aims to develop a handbook for future educators and educational leaders based on the vignette methodology, and to develop training modules for target groups for the purpose of professionalisation.

The project focuses on the need for quality assurance, which has been considered a central challenge of educational work for decades. In this context, the focus is often on performance; however, in recent years, it has increasingly been on the professionalisation of educators and educational leaders. The ProLernen project takes up this discourse, expands it by considering approaches to learning, i.e. learners' differentiated perceptions and learning processes, and aims to make vignettes a fruitful tool for professionalising educators and educational institutions, for instance, in the context of school development processes. In this context, using vignettes as a training medium enables trainers to focus on alternative ways of perceiving situations, and of thinking and acting in such situations.

Teaching

Learning groups are heterogeneous, and in this context the question of which research instruments are most suitable arises, as does the professionalisation of educators; both can require a change of perspective. Methodological approaches that focus on teaching and student performance can reach their limits in the context of student diversity, and the requirement that schools should address the issues and needs of all users. Prior experiences and assumptions that affect perceptions in the context of schools are manifold. Particularly with regard to inclusion, it is essential to be aware that perceptions are influenced by group and category, and an understanding of what constitutes normality. Prior experiences thus have an exclusionary and limiting character which, for example, leads to an understanding of differences that arise in supposedly homogeneous groups, and affects the perception of students and their learning. Bracketing and refraining from judgement can offer a way of engaging with diversity and understanding that learning does not start from *the result* but from learning as experience; learning can thus be understood as an accomplishment or a process. For this, it is essential that an open attitude is maintained towards perception (Peterlini, 2019).

In this sense, vignettes as a 'medium of education' aim to ensure that the reading of vignettes and the writing of such texts are detached from the familiar, making the familiar unfamiliar. In the context of teacher education, professionalisation often means making something predictable (Engel and Böhme, 2015) instead of becoming aware of indeterminacy as a constitutive element of educational processes (Dörpinghaus, 2009). Certainty occurs when reality is constructed according to general rules, and expectations are fulfilled. This gives rise to habits of perception and the limitation that views of the world can only be changed with difficulty. The way vignettes deviate from expectations can be productive because they allow teachers to see what they no longer know. This is where the specific subversive power of vignettes as examples is located; they should be taken seriously as forming a relationship to and providing knowledge of the world, not as aiming to provide 'absolute truth' or to 'reconstruct reality', seeking the general rather than presupposing it. In this respect, learning from vignettes means an 'entanglement with the world in which we always risk having to restructure ourselves, the thing as well as our relation to the other' (Meyer-Drawe, 2012b: 214).

In reading, readers also encounter themselves, their prior knowledge, and their prior experiences. The irritating potency of vignettes and their dispensing with contextual information going beyond the situation described means they invite readers to bring in their own experiences and contextual knowledge. Readers' relation to the world is thus also modelled and shaped. Against this backdrop, professional teachers are shown to allow themselves to be productively unsettled. Vignettes show alternatives. Perceiving is not an act of necessity in which things and others dictate to us what they are to be taken as (Meyer-Drawe, 2008). Awareness of the sometimes inconspicuous possibilities inherent in perception, however, is something that has to be learned. A student (KD, 2020) in a seminar on vignette research came to a similar conclusion: 'From this seminar, I take with me the idea that one can and of course should also look at situations or teaching situations from a different perspective. Because often it is not the obvious things, but the little inconspicuous things that move you and make you wonder'.

> **Questions for discussion**
>
> What are the fields of application for vignettes?
>
> What are the purposes of vignettes?
>
> What other areas of application do you see?

Conclusion

The vignette research outlined in this chapter shifts the focus from evaluation and measurement of the outputs of pedagogical interventions – whether these are grades or other forms of quantification and track records – to more sensitive awareness of the processes in pedagogical relationships. In doing so, vignettes give access to the meaning-making processes that are an inherent part of the learning experience for learners. The process of vignette research is characterised by a small number of steps. The first is an attitude in the field that is open to the unexpected, where the researcher is prepared to be surprised when his/her expectations are not realised. Thus, the vignette approach is first and foremost a school of perception for researchers but also for educators; they must learn to free themselves as much as possible from their expectations, which are always present, and be open to being affected by what happens in the field. In this context, bodily expressions are of particular importance: paying attention to how children, young people, or other pedagogical subjects move, the postures they adopt, what they do with their hands, what expressions are on their faces, what gestures accompany their words, all help the observer to perceive phenomena that would escape the gaze in the course of output-oriented observation. The next step is the writing down and linguistic condensation of these experiences into vignettes. The condensation process itself, first by the vignette writers themselves, then through intersubjective validation in the group, is part of the initial review and discussion of the co-experience. This is the only way of checking whether the perceived experience has been adequately expressed in language. Hence, a concise exemplary story emerges that can be given different readings. Through subsequent reading, the vignette becomes a stimulus for reflection on pedagogical events, for understanding the possible meanings of such events, considering other readings and generating options for pedagogical practice. The vignette is suitable for different teaching and learning environments, for reflecting on one's actions in practice, for sharpening and sensitising perception to promote learning and its resistances, digressions, detours, creative leaps and fault lines, and in further education for professionalisation in different fields. At a meta-level, vignettes and vignette readings bring new perspectives to educational discussions and discourses and, at best, also disrupt established routines and habitual perspectives.

In this way, vignette research represents a response to the three desiderata that Paolo Flores D'Arcais (1995) has set out for educational research: the perception of concrete situations and critical reflection on them in order to derive normative orientations for future educational action and to influence educational discourses and structures.

Summary points

- Vignettes were developed in 2008 as a phenomenologically oriented approach to research in Austria. In recent years, they have gained international recognition and sparked interest from a wide range of institutions, environments and individuals. Vignettes are used as tools not only for research but also for professional development.
- The vignette methodology is a qualitative, narrative and phenomenologically oriented approach to learning that attempts to access learning experiences as they occur by investigating life-worlds in everyday settings.
- It enables researchers or pedagogical professionals to 'co-experience' the experience of others as they occur in the field. Hence, the writing of vignettes attempts to capture the sense-making or disruptive phenomena that learners are exposed to as part of the learning experience.
- Vignettes consist of short, concise narratives in which something surprising, unique, or peculiar is revealed, and their condensed, experiential narratives aim to exemplify learning experiences and make them physically perceptible.
- Vignettes are subjected to phenomenological analysis, a process which is referred to as 'vignette reading'. In reading a vignette, readers engage with the vignette, holding back from categorising and explaining to uncover, peel off and add layers of understanding.

Recommended reading

Agostini, E. and Symeonidis, V. (2022) 'Beyond the Reach of Teaching' – Differentiating the role of phenomenologically oriented vignettes in learning and teaching from phenomenon-based learning. In J.G. Wissema and M.A. Yülek (Eds) *Towards Third Generation Learning and Teaching. Contours of the New Learning.* London: Anthem Press.

Meyer-Drawe, K. (2017) Phenomenology as a Philosophy of Experience – Implications for pedagogy. In M. Ammann, T. Westfall-Greiter and M. Schratz (Eds) *Erfahrungen deuten – Deutungen erfahren. Vignettes and Anecdotes as Research, Evaluation and Mentoring Tool. Erfahrungsorientierte Bildungsforschung.* Innsbruck, Wien: StudienVerlag.

Peterlini, H.K. (2022) The Split School: From selective normality concepts to a phenomenology of diversity. In H.K. Peterlini (Ed.) *Learning Diversity.* Berlin: Springer Research VS.

Schratz, M. and Westfall-Greiter, T. (2015) Learning as Experience: A Continental European perspective on the nature of learning. Engl. Translation of Lernen als Erfahrung: Ein pädagogischer Blick auf Phänomene des Lernens. In H. Dumont, D. Istance and F. Benavides (Eds) *The Nature of Learning – Die Natur des Lernens. Forschungsergebnisse für die Praxis.* Weinheim und Basel: Beltz.

References

Agostini, E. (2016) Lektüre von Vignetten: Reflexive Zugriffe auf Erfahrungsvollzüge des Lernens. In S. Baur and H.K. Peterlini (Eds) *An der Seite des Lernens. Erfahrungsprotokolle aus dem Unterricht an Südtiroler Schulen – ein Forschungsbericht. Mit einem Vorwort von Käte Meyer-Drawe und einem Nachwort von Michael Schratz. Gastbeiträge von Dietmar Larcher und Stefanie Risse. Erfahrungsorientierte Bildungsforschung Vol. 2.* Innsbruck, Wien, Bozen: StudienVerlag.

Agostini, E. (2017) Lernen, neu und anders wahrzunehmen. Vignetten und Lektüren – Formen professionsbezogener (ästhetischer) Bildung? In M. Ammann, T. Westfall-Greiter and M. Schratz (Eds) *Erfahrungen deuten. Deutungen erfahren: Experiential Vignettes and Anecdotes as Research, Evaluation and Mentoring Tool. Erfahrungsorientierte Bildungsforschung Vol. 3.* Innsbruck, Wien, Bozen: StudienVerlag.

Baur, S. and Peterlini, H.K. (2016) *An der Seite des Lernens. Ein Erfahrungsbericht an Südtiroler Schulen. Mit einem Vorwort von Käte Meyer-Drawe und einem Nachwort von Michael Schratz. Gastbeiträge von Dietmar Larcher und Stefanie Risse. Erfahrungsorientierte Bildungsforschung Vol. 2.* Wien, Innsbruck, Bozen: StudienVerlag.

Beekman, T. (1987) Hand in Hand mit Sascha: Über Glühwürmchen, Grandma Millie und andere Raumgeschichten. Im Anhang: teilnehmende Erfahrung. In W. Lippitz and K. Meyer-Drawe (Eds) *Kind und Welt. Phänomenologische Studien zur Pädagogik*. Frankfurt am Main: Athenäum.

Brinkmann, M. (2011) Pädagogische Erfahrung: Phänomenologische und ethnographische Forschungsperspektiven. In I.M. Breinbauer and G. Weiß (Eds) *Orte des empirischen in der Bildungstheorie*. Würzburg: Königshausen & Neumann.

Bromand, J. and Kreis, G. (2010) (Eds) *Was sich nicht Sagen Lässt. Das Nicht-Begriffliche in Wissenschaft, Kunst und Religion*. Berlin: Akademie.

Buck, G. (1989) *Lernen und Erfahrung – Epagogik: Zum Begriff der didaktischen Induktion* (3rd expanded edition). Darmstadt: Wissenschaftliche Buchgesellschaft.

D'Arcais, P.F. (1995) Pädagogik – warum und für wen? In W. Böhm (Ed.) *Pädagogik – wozu und für wen?* Stuttgart: Klett-Cotta.

Dewey, J. (1916/2009) *Democracy and Education: An introduction to the philosophy of education*. Waiheke Island: Floating Press.

Dörpinghaus, A. (2009) Bildung. Plädoyer wider die Verdummung. *Forschung und Lehre*, **9**, pp. 1–14.

Engel, B. and Böhme, K. (Eds) (2015) *Didaktische Logiken des Unbestimmten. Immanente Qualitäten in erfahrungsoffenen Bildungsprozessen*. München: Kopaed.

Fink, E. (1976) Operative Begriffe in Husserls Phänomenologie. In F.-A. Schwarz (Ed.) *Nähe und Distanz. Phänomenologische Vorträge und Aufsätze*. Freiburg/München: Alber.

Finlay, L. (2009) Debating Phenomenological Research. *Phenomenology & Practice*, **3**(1), pp. 6–25.

Foucault, M. (1996) *Der Mensch ist ein Erfahrungstier – Gespräch mit Ducio Trombadori. Übersetzt von Horst Brühmann. Mit einem Vorwort von Wilhelm Schmid. Mit einer Bibliographie von Andrea Hemminger*. Frankfurt a. M: Suhrkamp.

Laing, R.D. (1977) *The Politics of Experience and the Bird of Paradise*. Harmondsworth: Penguin.

Lévinas, E. (1983) *Die Spur des Anderen*. Freiburg/München: Karl Alber.

Lippitz, W. (1984) Exemplarische Deskription – die Bedeutung der Phänomenologie für die erziehungswissenschaftliche Forschung. *PR Sankt Augustin*, **38**, pp. 3–22.

Merleau-Ponty, M. (1966) [1945] *Phänomenologie der Wahrnehmung. Aus dem Französischen übersetzt und eingeleitet durch eine Vorrede von Rudolf Boehm. Herausgegeben von Carl Friedrich Graumann und Johannes Lindschoten*. Berlin, New York: Walter de Gruyter & Co.

Meyer-Drawe, K. (2001) [1984] *Leiblichkeit und Sozialität: Phänomenologische Beiträge zu einer pädagogischen Theorie der Inter-Subjektivität* (3rd edition). München: Wilhelm Fink.

Meyer-Drawe, K. (2008) Aisthesis. In W. Böhm, U. Frost, V. Ladenthin and G. Mertens (Eds) *Handbuch der Erziehungswissenschaft Vol. 1. Grundlagen Allgemeine Erziehungswissenschaft*. Paderborn: Ferdinand Schöningh.

Meyer-Drawe, K. (2010) Zur Erfahrung des Lernens. Eine phänomenologische Skizze. *Filosofija*, **18**(3), pp. 6–17.

Meyer-Drawe, K. (2012a) *Diskurse des Lernens* (2nd edition). München: Fink.

Meyer-Drawe, K. (2012b) Sich vorausgaben. Ein Beitrag zu einer Theorie der ästhetischen Bildung. In B. Engel, T. Loemke, K. Böhme, E. Agostini and A. Bube (Eds) *Im Wahrnehmen Beziehungs- und Erkenntnisräume eröffnen. Ästhetische Wahrnehmung in Kunst, Bildung und Forschung. Didaktische Logiken des Unbestimmten Vol. 4*. München: Kopaed.

Peterlini, H.K. (2017) Die Geburt des Pathos. Performative Anstöße zu pädagogischen Verstehens- und Handlungsmöglichkeiten durch Vignetten, Zeichnungen und szenische Darbietung. In M. Ammann, T. Westfall-Greiter and M. Schratz (Eds) *Erfahrungen deuten – Deutungen erfahren. Experiential Vignettes and Anecdotes as Research Evaluation and Mentoring Tool. Erfahrungsorientierte Bildungsforschung Vol. 3*. Innsbruck, Wien, Bozen: StudienVerlag.

Peterlini, H.K. (2019) Falsche Kinder in der richtigen Schule – oder umgekehrt? Auslotungen eines Perspektivenwechsels von selektiven Normalitätsvorstellungen hin zu einer Phänomenologie des 'So-Seins'. In J. Donlic, E. Jaksche-Hoffman and H.K. Peterlini (Eds) *Ist inklusive Schule möglich? Nationale und internationale Perspektiven*. Bielefeld: Transcript Verlag.

Schratz, M., Schwarz, J.F. and Westfall-Greiter, T. (2012) *Lernen als (bildende) Erfahrung. Vignetten in der Praxisforschung*. Innsbruck, Wien, Bozen: StudienVerlag.

Waldenfels, B. (1992) *Einführung in die Phänomenologie*. Weinheim und Basel: Beltz.

12 Summing it all up
A concluding attempt

Tom Feldges

Introduction

Editing a book like this one, where authors from various European countries offer their views upon educational issues, problems and potential solutions as they emerge in the context of their own national context, brings with it the rewarding task of providing a sense of coherence in all of the contributions. Of course, each of the European countries of the various chapters leads to a very wide field of topics, making it almost impossible to forge them into something of a single coherent conclusion. Putting such a disclaimer right at the beginning of the attempt may incite some readers to think that it seems impossible and so should not be attempted. However, that would be too hasty an assumption. As suggested in the Preface to Section III, one always has to remember that it might not be helpful to keep running head-on into that metaphorical brick wall. A different approach may be a better solution, one that avoids doing the same thing repeatedly just to be left with nothing but the same (insufficient) result. That is of course easier said than done: how would one go about categorising a chapter on educational poverty together with one that focuses upon the reflective gains that general practitioners yield and another about students' aversion to learning a foreign language. Of course, chapters on educationally relevant topics are to be expected in a book about education. But when moving 'education' in the background for a moment, is there anything that could hold these chapters together. As already mentioned in the introduction in Chapter 1, one feature that appears in almost all the chapters is at least a partial focus upon the experience of teaching or being taught. However, as also discussed in the introduction, any interpretation of human experiences is dependent upon the *situated-ness* of the person undergoing the experiencing. In order to make sense of the experiences the experiencing subject utilises a culturally dependent frame of reference. And, although there is something of a common cultural heritage in Europe, every nation still has its own peculiarities (see Chapter 2). So these concluding remarks will assume the importance of the subject making sense and finding meaning within a cultural sense-giving frame of reference. In order to achieve this all the chapters will be 're-read' with this focus, and issues that are relevant within this chosen context will be made explicit.

The Introduction

The first chapter provided the groundwork by defining the relevant concepts of 'Europe' and 'Education' and laying out what the book is intended to cover. Three issues are of key-importance in this re-reading with a subject-centred focus. The first concerns the cultural situated-ness of any human being. A second topic was the geographical and cultural concept of Europe, while a third introduced the educational sub-concept known as *Bildung* in the German language. These issues will be briefly discussed in that order.

First, situated-ness allows a member of a society to acquire the store of inherited beliefs, customs and values of its cultural tradition and which serves as a framework of meaning and sense for life's encounters. Such a framework of meaning is always tacitly applied to any experience. Chapter 2 exemplifies this in relation to a difference in the value that is applied to punctuality within two distinct national cultures. Chapter 3 exemplifies it in relation to learning a foreign language where such a compulsion is seen as a hostile incursion, although most UK citizens would find no hostile intention there. In that respect we encounter a 'horizon of meaning', a background against which every aspect of conscious sensing is perceived. It's a horizon that always influences what one becomes aware of with that store of culturally shared beliefs, customs and values. This framework works silently along, and sometimes against, individual likes, dislikes and inclinations.

The second issue concerned the concept of Europe. With the discussion about the difficulty to put a finger on what Europe is supposed *to be,* the idea was introduced that the essence of Europe could be captured as a continuous process of discussing what it *ought to be.* Rather than *being something,* Europe was characterised as a constant process, an on-going struggle *to become* (a better?) Europe. Europe's characteristic feature, i.e. a constant process of discussion of what Europe ought to be, is thus also subject to constant reflective engagement within the public sphere to discuss *where Europe is* and to continuously negotiate what it ought to develop towards.

A third and final issue to be picked up here was a specific sub-concept of the overall concept of education, namely in *Bildung*. This is no longer an exclusively German concept (cf. Mezirow, 2018, Taylor and Cranton, 2012). But German Education Studies has developed this concept away from a cognitively mediated transformation towards one that is initiated by the experience of a crisis moment (cf. Meyer-Drawe, 2012). Hence, the transformation of perspective is the result of a reflective process that is sparked off by the uncomfortable experience that previously held beliefs no longer fit the encountered situation. Despite a far-ranging debate about *Bildung*, it is important to recognise the break away from a merely cognitively mediated transformation. This is achieved by putting the emphasis upon individual experiences regarding the uncomfortable misfit of what one thought something would be and the realisation that actual reality turned out to be quite different. This move brings exactly this individual experience to the centre of interest. More could be said, but this topic will be picked up again in the first section to be discussed below.

However, one further remark might be in order. There is a strange similarity between the idea of Europe – capturing itself within the continuous reflective and discursive process of becoming what it ought to be – and the human being, undergoing transformative learning experiences, engaging in a reflective and discursive process of transforming him/herself. In that respect it appears that, much as we Europeans shaped the Enlightenment and Modernity, the European accomplishment of an enlightened Modernity shaped us Europeans as well.

Section I – The 'pains' of learning

The Preface to this Section takes aim at the experiential quality of learning. It is pointed out that the current emphasis regarding these experiences is one mostly directed at enjoyable ones with the aim of enhancing the motivation to engage with learning. Negative affective states are often ignored, or advice is provided on how to avoid them. The negative affective side of human life is not made an explicit topic for teaching practice and theory. However, affective states come into play where an elated, happy mood at the beginning of a lesson turns sour and into anxiety, anger and even hate as the demands on the pupils are raised beyond their current capabilities. It was therefore argued that educational practice should acknowledge the spectral nature of human affection and seek ways to incorporate all of these affective states into research, practice and the development of theory.

Chapter 2 from the space 'between two countries', namely the UK and Germany, discusses the German concept of *Bildung* while putting it into the educational debate in the UK. It thereby highlights not only the effects of the differences in the cultural situated-ness between two national contexts but also a remarkable difference in existing educational theory. The example case provided serves to get the subsequent theoretical discussions about normative and situational justifications started. However, most important in the current context are the explanations provided that focus upon the experience of a crisis, necessary as the initiating precursor of the desired reflective process of *Bildung*, or transformative learning. The word 'crisis' denotes a situation in which the necessity to discern, to judge or to distinguish emerges. Put like this, one may think that such a crisis could fit with Piaget's concept of the disequilibrium, i.e. a situation that could be solved by cognitive capabilities only. However, if the mere application of reason to reach a decision within a clear decisive matrix would be all, then it must remain questionable as to whether such a crisis deserves to still be called a crisis! So it looks as if 'a crisis' requires the uncomfortable feeling of having to decide in a situation where one experiences uncertainty about potential outcomes and where these outcomes and the decision matter. The uncomfortable and uncertain feeling, probably sprinkled with some fear of failure, is what makes such a critical moment a crisis for the one facing it. The experiences of these affective moments in a moment of crisis resist their complete capture by cognitive-psychological approaches (Feldges, 2017). Therefore, researching these important and uncomfortable affective episodes needs a clear focus upon the experiencing subject to be able to bind the relevant states appropriately into educational theories and practice. Highlighting the importance of these aversive and/or negative experiences, and justifying their educational usage (the affective states of the young man were deliberately induced by the teacher), this chapter makes a strong case for a subject-centred approach in teaching and learning. Nevertheless, the chapter also lends gravity to the importance of the cultural frame of sense-making by pointing clearly to the perceptive differences that educators from various national backgrounds might have towards the same incident (sending a student out to re-enter).

Chapter 3 from France focuses upon the learning of a foreign language, English in this case. The author discusses the theoretical aspects of why and how the *other*, *otherness* and *othering* emerges in the context of the nation-state and via national curricula that ponder on the binary oppositions of correct-incorrect, pure-impure and normal-abnormal. These kinds of *either–or* dichotomies, when applied to the correct, pure and normal use of one's own (or a foreign) language, come with a set of very specific problems. Douglas (2002) already discussed this in 1966 in her book *Purity and Danger*. While the 'pure' is fine, the 'impure' signifies danger, a danger to the integrity of a nation, that at least partially rests upon a shared 'normal' and codified language spoken by all its citizens. But danger is also assigned to those who speak in an 'impure', 'incorrect' manner: i.e. the *other*. These underlying assumptions have found their way into the relevant educational policies and provide the sense-making framework according to which policy-makers, educational managers, educators and students, but also the wider society, perceive issues and demands around the compulsory learning of a foreign language. But this also holds for the ascription of sense to the ones not being able to use the nation's language in a formal manner, who speak 'impurely' or 'incorrectly' (Mecheril, 2010), and who therefore are made the *other*. On accepting such a national situated-ness in terms of language-use and -learning, it is not too surprising that students show a reluctance to engage with the 'inpure', be it another language (that of the enemy), or be it to their fellow citizens who are not able to speak in a 'correct' and 'normal' manner. It is here that the need for a re-contextualisation of language and foreign language learning needs strong theoretical challenges. However, it appears necessary to build at least some of these challenges upon a basis that includes the experiential reality regarding the aversion of those who refuse. This is all the more important as the nation state is not merely a political entity. It is also a very important focal point for citizens to satisfy their urge to belong, to be part of something, and with that to create a sense of self.

Chapter 4 from Germany offers a comparison between German *Pädagogik* and the (New) Education Studies in the UK. The comparison makes visible the underlying philosophical differences that drive and enable the respective theorising in both national contexts. It reveals substantial differences in the attitudes, expectations and theories about educational theory and practice. It thus becomes evident that a simple theory-transfer from one national context to another cannot be achieved. The German idea of *Bildung*, developed and informed by an idealistic philosophical assumption of an *ideal citizen* towards which the self-perfecting subject should strive, cannot be grafted onto UK discourses that are predominantly based upon pragmatic philosophical assumptions (see also Preface to Section II). However, it is still possible to try to develop a similar concept within the UK context as Mezirow (2018) and Taylor and Cranton (2012) have done with their theory of 'transformative learning'. In that respect it appears that the borders between national theory traditions remain permeable to some extent. But it is important to bear in mind that such a sense-making frame of reference, the store of beliefs, values, customs and values, cannot be changed quickly. This is also evident in this chapter where a status-reduction of the (German) theoretical groundwork is detected. It is of course possible to decry this status-reduction. But it could equally be perceived as the German academic educational discourse with its strong philosophical grounding, as a unique development within Europe, being slowly permeated by an overarching sense-making frame, i.e. that of a truly European space for academia (*europäischer Hochschulraum*) as Liessmann (2009) called it. This unified space, brought about not at least by the Bologna process (Preglau, 2009), buys – so to say – the mutual recognition of academic qualifications for mobile citizens by paying for it with a requirement to level the achievement requirements to gain academic qualifications of equal standing and value. Viewed from this perspective there is, of course, reason to criticise some European influences upon national educational discourses and traditions (cf. Kellermann *et al.*, 2009). Indeed, in relation to the earlier discussion about a meaning-providing horizon, such critique must arise as new developments stand against established traditions. However, any such critique would also have to cast an eye on the benefits brought about by these European harmonisation efforts for the qualified and for the studying citizen. Nevertheless, what seems clear is that the introduction of the 'pains of learning' as discussed here, or even the comprehensive utilisation of affective states, including averse and negative ones, will not find a quick application in cultural contexts that have a different theoretical tradition themselves.

Section II – Learning to become a 'whole' human being

The preface to this section develops the difference between a mere human being as opposed to the person, as an acting subject, one that has its own view on its surroundings and one that devises its own plans for its own future. Undoubtedly, it is a pre-condition for becoming such a subject that a human being is born with the enabling biological layout. However, being born and having this layout is simply not enough. This is the point at which education unfolds its shaping influences on the human to turn her/him into a 'whole' human being. Of particular interest is Benner's (2001) conception of the duty to not only form a reasoned and logical coherent opinion but also to submit this to the public discourse to truly participate as a citizen.

Chapter 5 from Norway discusses the values-education for Norwegian children. Whereas the approach to *Fundamental British Values* in the UK is one that is conceived as being nationalistic and aiming to secure the status quo by a politically conservative move (McDonnell, 2020), the Norwegian approach derives its normative basis from the United Nations. Although a reference is made to Christian and Humanist traditions and to the Norwegian cultural heritage, this does not constitute a nationalistic move. Indeed, the Norwegian intention is one that strives explicitly to prepare the pupils to connect with a wider international community. Rather than merely teaching these values, the Norwegian approach aims to enable the pupils to experience these universal values and the impact they yield on their (school-)life. At the same time this approach allows a sense of belonging to emerge: a belonging to a nation with its own past and traditions, a nation firmly rooted within a community of other countries that share the same values, be it within the continent of Europe (European Convention on Human Rights) or globally (UN Universal Declaration of Human Rights). This places the innate human need to belong into a modern sense-giving horizon, one where it is possible to be the proud citizen of a nation while also sharing in the positive experience of a strong connection that reaches beyond national borders. Hence, an emerging 'whole' human being would not need to endure the tension between 'them' and 'us', but could – if everything works out fine – be living a free existence where borders still matter, but where borders do not pose an insurmountable obstacle.

Chapter 6 from Italy introduces the novel concept of 'educational poverty' which, although not explicitly mentioned, revolves around the issue of social participation. It is the expressed aim of education to educate the young that they can, once old enough, take their place in society, a society in which they are hoped to participate, not only in economic terms but also by taking part in its social and cultural life and participate in the relevant public debates. This is where the problem of educational poverty arises. If a child is deprived of the chance to visit a theatre, a museum or a concert, has no opportunity to practise sport or has never read a book, it is safe to assume that such a child's cultural horizon will be narrow. The child will be constantly burdened with the feeling of not being equal to the others who can easily utilise those experiences and will experience their world as being much smaller and less interesting than that of their fellow pupils.

Chapter 7 from Germany was a late and controversial addition to the collection because of its unusual academic style. However, as already mentioned in the Introduction (see Chapter 1), the topic and the gripping writing style was just too interesting to be missed. Two issues need to be explicitly mentioned here. First is the importance of the body. In the opening section the warming-up, loosening-up game of the sculptor and the statue is introduced. This is picked up at the end of the chapter again and shows how important the body is as a means to experience emotions oneself and equally to express these states to others. Any successful emotional moderation only becomes possible with clarity about one's own affective states. The second point is on the concept of *Bildung* (or transformative learning). Here the creation of reflective space is not happening solely in the mind of the reflecting individual. It is rather facilitated via writing, where feelings, moods and emotions are put into words and conceptualised (see on this issue: Feldges, 2014). In that way these affective states can become subject to rational thought and lead to the transformation of individual perspectives upon the self, others or the world. Both aspects are arguably important skills that – when sufficiently developed – facilitate the ability for social participation.

Chapter 8 from Belarus/Lithuania takes the view that a child raised by an authoritarian approach to education will replicate the experienced hierarchical dynamics in its own life. This means that such a child may also suffer the inability to 'be itself' because it is made 'to be' within the limiting parameters of an authoritarian society. The chapter offers a cunning way of overcoming such a situation: to alter the culturally approved frame according to which sense-making is supposed to happen. By drawing on existential-philosophical texts, and with the support of educational-phenomenological literature, differences are clearly laid bare, differences between the child's and an adult's ways of experiencing their world and themselves. With such a difference revealed a remedy to address this difference is suggested. In this respect the chapter demonstrates how existing (international) philosophical literature can be used to elaborate on fundamental issues in order to introduce a new concept (anti-authoritarian education). With this enrichment of the culturally situated educational discourse, it becomes possible to speak about these issues and (hopefully) to bring about a paradigm change, resisting the currently authoritarian approach to education.

Section III – The problem of research

So far the chapters from a wide range of European countries have shown an explicit, or sometimes more implicit, focus upon the experiencing subject as well as upon the sense-giving horizon of a culture. These frames of reference provide the tool to sort individual experiences into a cultural context and thereby to sort experiences under concepts. However, such cultural and individual influences upon what one sees and how it is subjectively rated when having a certain set of experiences complicate research in the psychological processes or, to put it more bluntly, in the process of learning, rather than merely testing and quantifying the results of learning. At the end of the discussion it was suggested that utilising the experiences that a learning individual has as a means to gain – at least some – increased clarity about the processes within a learning subject.

Chapter 9 from the Netherlands introduced a Dutch training scheme for medical doctors. The Learning from Experiences programme has experiences as its core. Although the chapter places its emphasis upon the training scheme, it is nevertheless relevant to research. It shows that, while leaving goals and results out of the focus, the programme is about how and in what ways environments or situations in which something was learned were experienced. Based on these results the chapter makes a strong case for the importance of the subject and for the individually (pre-consciously) employed processes of learning. Hence, emergent, individual processes in relation to others' or one's own environment while trying to make sense of them.

Chapter 10 from Greece employs a qualitative research approach. However, there is a marked difference in the way the questions are employed. These are not only trying to yield insight into the participants' value-judgements, i.e. how they may feel about having to teach a certain subject. Here importance is put upon the specific concept of 'flow'. By reading the answers for the phenomenological markers of experienced – or absent – characteristics of such a flow experience, it is possible to reveal whether online teaching facilitates an environment whereby teachers and students can reach this specific state of being absorbed in a specific task. The chapter lends support to the idea that even 'normal' qualitative research methods can yield insight into the processes of learning, if only the questions focus upon these processes rather than on individually held beliefs and value judgements.

Chapter 11 from Austria introduces a genuinely new approach to capture the experiences of a learning and/or teaching individual, and to develop questions regarding the relevant processes that these experiences may spark off. Together with phenomenologically inspired techniques, it becomes possible to lift the results of these interpretations above the level of mere idiosyncrasies. In that respect this novel approach yields results that have their clear focus directed towards the processes of learning, but also possible distractions to these processes, rather than quantifying learning simply by the results it has produced.

Where are we now?

At the end of this book – or rather at the end of this journey through a number of European states and a bit of 'educational sight-seeing' – it is time to take stock of what we were exposed to. That is, what was it that perhaps stirred some uncomfortable feelings once we stopped reading, feelings that may persist and keep lingering in the reader's mind. Feelings that may even force the reader to engage in some occasional cognitive revisiting. Perhaps a focused reflection now and then upon these lingering problems that have so far resisted being sorted into a pre-existing frame of making sense of educational issues? 'Nonsense!' someone might say, and thereby hope to have dissolved this nagging thought and/or doubt. But, in fact, this solution would only resemble the child covering his/her ears when being told off. By not standing up to the affective demand that such lingering issues exert upon us, one gambles away his/her chance to profit from such moments. This is so because these moments resemble exactly the sort of crisis that was repeatedly discussed here. Crisis-moments cause problems when trying to reconcile the resulting uncertainty with what one previously took to be safe and sound in educational theory and practice. The problem occurs when trying to dissolve these feelings of ambiguity and uncertainty into well-known and practised approaches and theories of learning. It is quite easy to ascertain that these experiential approaches do not make a good fit with cognitive learning theories (Feldges, 2017) and that the issue therefore should not be followed up any further. But the problem with these theories is that they cannot capture exactly that important moment of the affective quality of having a nagging doubt. These theories do not allow the contextualising of the tension that wants to be resolved. Rating these challenging ideas as nonsensical is nothing but a rather easy move to avoid the 'pains' of having to alter one's perception of oneself, of others and the world. That is, avoiding learning something new and growing from what one has been before towards what one *could* be by having made the transition evoked by the crisis moment.

Another way of engaging with the problems of lingering uncertainty in relation to an experienced misfit between what one thought and what one experienced would be to engage with novel and unfamiliar theories and approaches. This way one would broaden one's own horizon and thereby – probably – find out that if another way to think about a problem has been found, the problem may be solved quite easily or may even no longer exist. One just has to think about the infamous developmental psychology question that pitches nature against nurture: human development being inborn versus human development as a result of individual adaptation to environmental demands. Putting nature and nurture in binary opposition creates the question of having to decide which one does the job. However, as discussed in the Preface to Section II, human beings, as a biological species, have the ability to learn. In short, humans become what they are because they belong to a biological species with certain capabilities (nature-component), one of which is to add new experiences (nurture-component) to their coping strategies to safeguard survival.

In relying on these general thoughts on the pains of learning and the becoming of a 'whole' person, it is quite easy to spot the importance of the experiences at play. One only has to be willing to overcome the often discussed mind-body dichotomy: our supposedly base and animalistic nature against the presumed beauty of our rational capacity to seek and find the truth. But as discussed in the Preface to Section II, the person – or subject – not only has to devise plans (rational thought) for her/himself. To be a person one also has to have the capability to see these plans through and to enact them through the body. In that respect body and feelings mediated through the body belong to our very existence, and it looks like a grave failing to not acknowledge this in educational theorising. So, if someone had been enticed to consider the ideas presented here, someone who had been lured into thinking about these ideas in quiet moments, that someone would have to admit that this kind of (low-level) worry could only happen because these ideas somehow mattered. However, if they do matter one would experience exactly this: i.e. that they mattered! But if some ideas do matter so much that a nagging doubt persists until the issue can be resolved, then the argument is made for the importance of experiencing these affective episodes in learning. Therefore, it is now safe to argue that exactly the processes that matter are of key importance and need to be considered when talking about teaching, learning and education in general.

The introduction (Chapter 1, but also Chapter 2) portrayed the European idea as it is currently understood as a partial achievement of the reason-guided manner of thinking that emerged during the Enlightenment and Modernity. Quantifying attempts to determine the laws of nature, to tame nature and predict events are a characteristic feature of Modernity. So the question may arise as to whether the promotion of affective states and their importance is the right agenda to pursue for humans in modern and post-modern times. Or, alternatively, would such a shift of focus not simply constitute a counterproductive move? Would it not be something akin to retreating from what was already achieved? Now to answer such a question one finds at least two broad avenues to take. One would concern the fact that Modernity has turned itself into what is now widely acknowledged to be 'Post-Modernity'. This is not the space to develop the concept of Post-Modernity in any greater detail, but the fact that core-beliefs of Modernity are already cast into doubt by post-modern thought weakens the 'grand-narrative' that was once promised by Modernity (Lyotard, 1984).

But there is another obvious avenue to refute the accusation of moving backwards, and it is the more important one in this context. It concerns the 'object' of educational concern, the 'object' that is to be studied, researched and theorised about. Only the 'object' of education is not a stone or a garden bench, neither a car nor a computer. The 'object' of educational concern is the living human being, i.e. a subject with its own outlook upon its world. These subjects resist being pressed into causal stimulus-response chains, they resist being predictable and they resist being reduced to mere biological or (hypothetical) cognitive data or processes. Considering how far humankind came in taming nature, how far it came in turning unanimated objects into instruments for its use and how far it came in creating the most sophisticated objects itself, it remains very surprising how little is known about human consciousness (Chalmers, 1996). The universe is measured and explained, while the universe of our mental life remains a mystery. In a philosophy seminar someone once said: 'If the human mind would be so simple that we would be able to understand it, we would be so simple that we couldn't!' This sort of fatalistic statement indicates nothing less than that another metaphorical brick wall had been hit. So, it's time to consider a different question. If the true nature of a subject cannot be explained with the methods of the natural-scientific toolset for enquiry, it is probably time to think about a different toolset to be put to use. Indeed, a growing body of academics from all over Europe and beyond have begun to incorporate the body and bodily/affective feelings into their educational theorising (cf. Brinkmann et al., 2019). These approaches have already yielded results that could not have been produced by an exclusive natural-scientific method. In that respect it is safe to make the claim that any incorporation of affective states and their role in a learning subject's existence is not at all a step backwards as mentioned above. It is rather an enrichment of the available research options and theoretical frameworks to understand how learning in institutionalised settings is best understood. Remaining ignorant of such a broadening of the available tools would probably be just that: ignorant.

This book is about education in Europe – the title said as much. Therefore, it might be worth spending the final words of this conclusive chapter on an issue pertaining exclusively to Europe. In some quarters of Europe much is nowadays made of the notion of 'sovereignty'. This concept is often used as a (false) justification to reject anything not home-grown, not native, i.e. anything alien, foreign or *impure*. However, quite often it seems poorly understood, or not sufficiently appreciated, that closeness always entails a certain limit to one's own autonomy and freedom – or sovereignty. One just has to think about a meaningful partnership; if the partners live together as if they were not in such a partnership, their partnership is not likely to stand the test of time. Therefore, the close proximity, and the wish to establish such a meaningful partnership with one's neighbours was the founding idea of the supranational entities of Europe. And there are a few. The Council of Europe for instance is an international organisation that promotes human rights, democracy and the rule of law. The European Union, on the other hand, is a congregation of twenty-seven sovereign nation states that have decided to cease some of their sovereignty to cooperate closer in an attempt to better their respective peoples' lives. Of course, it is legitimate to consider not wanting to belong to any of these organisations and – even more so – it is equally legitimate to cancel a membership that had once been obtained. But whatever the membership-status of any European nation-state may be (remember Norway is not a member of the EU and Belarus is neither a member of the EU nor of the Council of Europe), the proximity to other European states and its shared cultural heritage will not make it possible to simply ignore the other European nations or to prosper without any meaningful ties being maintained. If – as this book is about education – looking at the educational implications of a nation distancing itself from the community of European states, one finds a good number of European programmes of great educational importance. One of these is the Erasmus and the Erasmus+ scheme. Erasmus facilitates and funds students wanting to study for some time at a foreign university, while Erasmus+ funds vocational training and sports at foreign schools and other educational institutions. Both of these schemes are supposed to promote young people's ability to participate in democratic societies. Another European initiative is the academic research-funding programme Horizon Europe, the key funding agent for academic research to be conducted at the universities of participating nation states. That means that non-participating states will not be able to apply for the approximately £80 billion of available funds. Neither will young vocational or academic students be able to widen their horizon as a result of spending some time abroad, experiencing how other societies function and getting an inside view into those communities that goes deeper than the shallow promises of a glossy tourist brochure. Here is not the space to consider in any greater depth what sort of long-term effects the cessation of a participation in those schemes will yield. When young roofers cannot go abroad to learn the ancient technique of thatching, students cannot study for a year abroad while their professors are cut off from research funding and doctoral and post-doctoral researchers will not find positions because research has moved elsewhere then the educational impact of cutting ties with these supranational schemes is not to be underestimated. But if education is, as discussed in Section II, about widening the intellectual horizon of pupils and students, then a cessation of close ties to the European neighbours appears counter-productive, to say the least. Of course, reasons for wanting to distance a country from these European supranational entities may be many, but one should always take a focused perspective upon what is close to one's heart. In the case of an educationalist that – hopefully – would be the topic of education. And that issue must be assessed in terms of a realistic cost-benefit analysis. And any such analysis must be made beyond just the current impact upon young people but also in terms of the generations of learners to come – those who never had a democratic chance to have their say about these issues while still having to suffer the consequences. Education in Europe is a multifaceted compound of opposing views, different traditions, varied theoretical approaches and diverse social expectations about what it should aim for. But despite all these differences, education in Europe's nations unfolds in close proximity to each other and is based upon a shared cultural heritage. In dividing that, what could ever be the gain of such a division?

Recommended reading

Brinkmann, M., Trusting, J. and Weber-Spannknebel, M. (2019) *Leib – Leiblichkeit – Embodiment*. Wiesbaden: Springer VS. (*Partially written in English.*)
Taylor, E.W. and Cranton, P. (2012) *The Handbook of Transformative Learning: Theory, research and practice*. San Francisco, CA: John Wiley and Son.

References

Benner, D. (2001) Bildung und Demokratie. *Zeitschrift für Pädagogik*, **43**, pp. 49–65.
Brinkmann, M., Türstig, J. and Weber-Spannknebel, M. (2019) *Leib – Leiblichkeit – Embodiment*. Wiesbaden: Springer VS.
Chalmers, D. (1996) *The Conscious Mind*. Oxford: Oxford University Press.
Douglas, M. (2002) *Purity and Danger*. Abingdon: Routledge.
Feldges, T. (2014) Understanding Pain and Neuroscientific Approaches to Pain. In T. Feldges, J.N.W. Gray and S. Burwood (Eds) *Subjectivity and the Social World*. Newcastle upon Tyne: Cambridge Scholars Publishing.
Feldges, T. (2017) Motivation and Experience versus Cognitive Psychological Explanation. *Humana Mente*, **33**, pp. 1–18.
Kellermann, P., Boni, M. and Meyer-Reschhausen, E. (2009) *Zur Kritik europäischer Hochschulpolitik*. Wiesbaden: GWV Fachverlage GmbH.
Liessmann, K.P. (2009) Bologna-Prozess und die aktuelle Hochschulentwicklung. In P. Kellermann, M. Boni and E. Meyer-Reschhausen (Eds) *Zur Kritik europäischer Hochschulpolitik*. Wiesbaden: GWV Fachverlage GmbH.
Lyotard, J.F. (1984) *The Postmodern Condition: A Report on Knowledge*. Manchester: Manchester University Press.
McDonnell, J. (2020) How Do You Promote 'British Values' When Values Education Is Your Profession? *Cambridge Journal of Education*, **51**, DOI: 10.1080/0305764X.2020.1844149.
Mecheril, P. (2010) *Migrationspädagogik*. Weinheim: Beltz Verlag.
Meyer-Drawe, K. (2012) *Diskurse des Lernens*. München: Wilhelm Fink.
Mezirow, J. (2018) Transformative Learning Theory. In K. Illeris (Ed.) *Contemporary Theories of Learning*. Abingdon: Routledge.
Preglau, M. (2009) 'Bologna' in Theorie und Praxis – Ein europäisches Projekt im Lichte lokaler Erfahrungan an der LFU Innsbruck. In P. Kellermann, M. Boni and E. Meyer-Reschhausen (Eds) *Zur Kritik europäischer Hochschulpolitik*. Wiesbaden: GWV Fachverlage GmbH.
Taylor, E.W. and Cranton, P. (2012). *The Handbook of Transformative Learning: Theory, research and practice*. San Francisco, CA: John Wiley and Son.

Index

Åberg, I. 63
affective states 142–149
agency 46, 94, 117
Agostini, E. 131, 135
Ainely, M. 11, 12
Ainley, P. 47
Altfelix, T. 38, 46
anti-authoritarian pedagogy 93, 94, 96, 99, 100, 146
Appiah, K.A. 64
appraisal 12, 13
Arendt, H. 60, 65
Atkinson, R.C. 104
attention 11, 12, 14, 78–80, 88, 104, 108, 111, 113, 114, 116–118, 126, 131, 132–135, 138
authoritarian pedagogy 8, 55, 93–96, 99, 100, 146
Avants, B.B. 78

Baer, M.F. 104
Bakker, A.B. 121
Barnett, R. 19
Barrow, R. 40, 43
Bartlett, S. 37, 44, 47, 104
Basom, M.R. 121
Bauman, Z. 69
Baur, S. 133
Bayly, C.A. 2, 5
Becker, N. 105–107
Beekman, T. 133
Bengtsson, J. 65
Benner, D. 4, 45, 52–55, 145
Bhabha, H.K. 34
Biernacki, P. 122
Biesta, G. 37, 41–44, 47, 60, 113–115, 118
Bildung 4, 17–25, 38, 42, 46–47, 51–55, 83, 142–144, 146
Binder, U. 46
Böhm, W. 42
Böhme, K. 137
Brague, R. 66

Braun, V. 122
Brinkmann, H.U. 25
Brinkmann, M. 95, 133, 149
Bromand, J. 133
Bruner, J.S. 101
Bruzzone, D. 79
Buber, M. 65
Buck, G. 43, 134
Burgess, A. 113
Burm, S. 112
Burton, D. 37, 44, 47, 104
Byram, M. 28, 33–34

Casale, R. 38
Casartelli, A. 78
Chalmers, D. 148
Cheli, E. 69, 78
citizenship 8, 35, 55, 57–58, 61, 64
Clarke, V. 122
Coffey, S. 30, 33
cognitive neuroscience 14
Corsaro, A.W. 95
Cranton, P. 11, 142, 144
Crawford, M. 116–117
crisis 4, 7, 9, 11, 19, 20, 22–26, 110, 142–143, 147
Crook, D. 13
Csikszentmihalyi, M. 121
cultural: heritage 15, 58, 63, 64, 66, 141, 145, 149, 150; learning 27, 32, 35; positioning 34, 35; situated-ness 9, 23, 49, 61; techniques 84

D'Arcais, P.F. 138
Dasen, P.R. 105
Davies, N. 5, 6
de la Croix, A. 112
Decuypere, M. 120
Delors, J. 72, 73
deprivation 68–71, 77, 80
depth grammar 23, 25
Dervin, F. 31

Dirim, I. 24
Dodi, E. 78
Dörpinghaus, A. 137
Douglas, M. 143

educational poverty 8, 55, 68, 70–80, 141, 145
Egan, K. 99
embodied education 109
embodiment 83, 96, 132
empiricism 42
Engel, B. 137
enlightenment 1, 21, 51, 94, 142, 148
epistemological 38, 39, 42, 46, 94, 130
epoché 134
existence 14, 29, 39, 52, 54, 60, 62–65, 87, 93–98, 114, 133, 145, 148, 149

Fairtlough, A. 113
Faulstich, P. 46
Faure, E. 73
Feldges, T. 4, 14, 20, 23, 53, 83, 103–105, 143, 146, 147
Fink, E. 56, 95, 100, 132
Finlay, L. 131
Fischer, F. 47
Flores, M.A. 120
flow 9, 107, 120–128, 146
folk-psychology 103
Foucault, M. 132
Frankl, V.E. 79
Frase, L. 121
Freud, S. 52
Friesen, N. 40, 43, 95

Galtung, J. 42
Gardner, H. 78
Gbemisola, K.O. 120
Gennep, A. 83
Gingell, J. 42
Giradi, F. 70
Giussani, L. 65
Giustini, C. 69
Goffman, E. 86
Goldszmidt, M. 112
Grimes, J. 47
Gross, R. 105

Habe, K. 121
Habermas, J. 54
Han, T. 121
Hebb, D.O. 106
Hebebci, M.T. 120
Heidegger, M. 56, 95–97, 99, 100
Heimes, S. 85
Helsper, W. 18
Hildebrand, D.v. 64

Hodges, C. 120
Horgan, T. 130
Holzkamp, K. 6, 19
Honderich, T. 3
Hopmann, S. 43
Horizon (of experience) 131, 142, 144–150
Hörster, R. 18
Humboldt, W.v. 2, 18, 19, 22–26

Iavarone, M.L. 70
Idealism 41, 42, 43, 52, 144
Imperialism 27
Indoctrination 4, 54
Inequality 20, 72, 75, 123
Intercultural 27, 30, 31, 34, 36

Jagusch, B. 84
Joas, H. 64
Johanessen, M. 59

Kant, E. 20, 21, 25, 43, 51, 64, 94
Kautz, T. 71
Keiner, E. 47
Kellermann, P. 144
Kierkegaard, S. 56, 95–100
Kiper, H. 46
Kokemohr, T. 46
Koller, H.C. 18, 19, 42, 83
König, J. 120
Kraft, V. 44
Kramsch, C. 27–34
Kreis, G. 133
Krüger, H.H. 18
Kuh, G.D. 11

Laing, R.D. 133
Landwehr, A. 6
learning: context 13; digital 120, 121, 124; experiences 12, 13, 106, 107, 130, 133, 138, 139, 142, 147–149; from experience 8, 109, 111, 114, 118, 146; lifelong 69, 73, 76, 105; motivation 104; of another language 24, 25, 27, 31, 32, 34, 35, 51, 141, 142, 143, 144; outcomes (or objectives or goals) 9, 46, 110, 113, 115, 123; process 9, 109, 125, 131, 136, 137, 146, 147; success (or result) 6, 103, 107, 146; transformative 11, 142, 143, 144, 146
Leonard, J.A. 78
Lévinas, E. 64, 132
Liddicoat, A.J. 30, 31
Liebau, E. 46
Liessmann, K.P. 144
Linguistic community 7, 24, 25
Lippitz, W. 133
Lo Bianco, J. 28–30, 33
Løvaas, B.J. 113

Luhmann, N. 13, 14, 18, 21
Lyotard, J.F. 14, 62, 148

Mareschal, D. 14
Maritain, J. 64, 65
Masschelein, J. 65
Mazzeo, R. 69
McDonnell, J. 145
McGuirk, J. 81
Mecheril, P. 20, 24, 25, 144
mereological fallacy 104
Merleau-Ponty, M. 56, 94, 135
Meseth, W. 20
Meyer-Drawe, K. 19, 133, 135, 137, 142
Meyer, J.W. 14
Mezirow, J. 11, 142, 144
Milani, P. 78
mindfulness 84
Modernity 1, 2, 51, 93–95, 100, 142, 148
Moller, A.C. 121
Monrouxe, L.V. 110

Nagel, T. 2
Nairz-Wirth, E. 91
national identity 31
Neubert, H. 40
New Education Studies xiii, 7, 11, 15, 37, 44, 144
Noah, O.O. 120
Noels, K.A. 46
Normativity, problem of 7, 17, 19, 20–22, 25
Nussbaum, M.C. 71

Oelkers, J. 40, 41, 48
Othering 27, 31, 143
Otherness 27, 30–35, 94, 115, 143

Pädagogik xiii, 7, 11, 15, 18, 37, 38, 40–48, 144
Palaiologou, I. 46
pedagogical: action 131, 133, 136; experience 133; field 136; intervention 138; method(s) 100, 120; practice 18, 21, 73, 138; theory 94; tradition 40
performativity 43
Peterlini, K.H. 131, 133, 137
Petrie, P. 43
phenomenology 18, 79, 80, 93, 95–100, 109, 121, 122, 130–135, 139, 146
Piaget, J. 19, 95, 105
Pieczenko, S. 6, 19, 104
Pietropolli Charmet, G. 77
plasticity 78, 105, 106
Pongratz, L. 39
Post-Modernity 148
poverty, educational 8, 55, 68–80, 141, 145
Pragmatism 46, 52

Prange, K. 44
Pratesi, M. 77
Preglau, M. 144
Public debate 54, 55, 145

Quattrociocchi, L. 75

Radoilska, L. 52
Rees, C.E. 110
Ribolits, E. 42
Riquarts, K. 43
Ritze, R. 90
Rudrauf, D. 105

Said, E. 5
Saraceno, C. 69
Sauer, M. 25
Scaparro, F. 77
Schaefer, M.B. 120
Scherer, K. 12, 13
Schiffman, S. 120
school drop-out 51, 73–76, 83, 90, 91
Schorr, K.E. 13, 14
Schratz, M. 133
Schut, S. 110
Scott, W.R. 14
Shchyttsova, T. 8, 56, 94, 95
Shifrin, R.M. 104
Simmons, M. 65
Smith, B. 41
Snow, C.P. 39
social actor 6, 8
socialization 3, 4, 18, 52, 80, 84, 88, 95, 109, 114, 115
Sorrells, K. 33
Spence, J.T. 104
Spence, K.W. 104
Spinner, K.H. 86
Staempfli, A. 113
Standish, P. 39, 47
Stehr, N. 12
subject-centred 3, 6–9, 95, 107, 141, 143
subjectification 109, 114–118
surface grammar 23
Swennen, A. 120

Tarnas, R. 5
Tayor, E.W. 11, 142, 144
Taylor-Leech, K. 30
Technologiedefizit 14, 18
Territorialisation (of language and culture) 7, 27, 29, 32, 35
theory of (other) mind 103, 106, 107
Thoma, H. 21
Tolomelli, A. 69
Treml, A.K. 45, 105–107
Triani, P. 72

Trotmann, D. 42
Tubbs, N. 47

Uljens, M. 37

Vagle, M.D. 122
van Braak, M. 110–113, 115
van den Broeck, P. 120
Veen, M. 110–112, 116
Vico, G. 77
vignette 130–140
Vråle, G.B. 113

Waldenfels, B. 131, 132, 134
Waldorf, D. 122
Ward S. xiii
Weber, M. 5
Weiß, M. 38
Winch, P. 42
Wittgenstein, L. 23, 24, 107
Woodward, J. 103

Zarate, G. 27, 28, 31, 33, 34
Zhou, L. 120
Zudeick, P. 24

For Product Safety Concerns and Information please contact our EU
representative GPSR@taylorandfrancis.com
Taylor & Francis Verlag GmbH, Kaufingerstraße 24, 80331 München, Germany